IMAGES
of America

WEST POINT

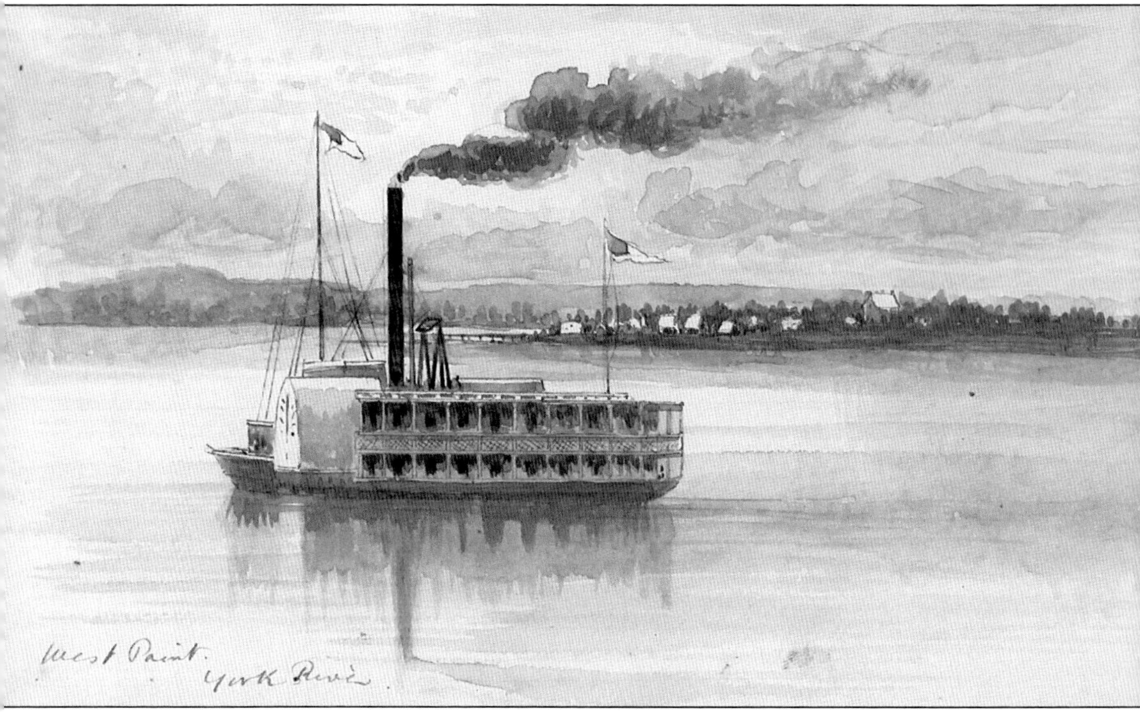

A steamboat arrives at West Point in 1860. This pen, ink, and wash sketch by the British artist Lefevre J. Cranstone shows a sleepy steamship port just before the Civil War. The Richmond & York River Railroad was in the process of completing a temporary rail line down to West Point's old wharf on the Mattaponi River, while new wharf facilities were under construction on the Pamunkey River side of the peninsula. (Courtesy of the Lilly Library, Indiana University, Bloomington, Indiana.)

ON THE COVER: Workers at the oyster farm of the Chesapeake Corporation sort oysters grown in racks in the 1940s.

IMAGES
of America

WEST POINT

William J. Addison and
Kathryn Jewett Hogenson

ARCADIA
PUBLISHING

ISBN 978-0-7385-9273-2

Published by Arcadia Publishing
Charleston, South Carolina

Printed in the United States of America

Library of Congress Control Number: 2012931258

For all general information, please contact Arcadia Publishing:
Telephone 843-853-2070
Fax 843-853-0044
E-mail sales@arcadiapublishing.com
For customer service and orders:
Toll-Free 1-888-313-2665

Visit us on the Internet at www.arcadiapublishing.com

To Virginia D. Addison
—Will

To Frederick F. Jewett
—Kathy

Contents

Acknowledgments

We wish to thank the many people who made this publication possible. Special thanks go to Pemmy Peterman and Avril Williams, the archivists of the Historical Society of West Point. Other members of the historical society who were especially helpful were Tyler Bland III, Richard Hosfield, William Palmer, James Dopp, John Lee, Donald O'Connor, and Sandra Willis. We also wish to thank James M.H. Harris Jr. and Bibb Edwards, historians of West Point and the surrounding areas, for generously sharing their own research and resources. Local photographer Theresa S. Bohannon assisted with acquiring images. Elizabeth Hogenson provided technical and editing assistance.

Many people contributed photographs, postcards, and information, including Carol Fetterolf, Dennis Roane, Charles Burnett, Richard Hosfield, Tyler Bland III, Juanita Oakley, Clarence Epps, Bill O'Connor, Pemmy Peterman, author William J. Addison, Janie Wampler, Maureen Medlin, John Lee, Vincent Hodge, Virginius Thornton, Janice McGowan, Roberta Dobbins Jarvis, the Diggs family, Ellis Olsson, Arthur Anderson, Betty Jenkins, Frederick Jewett, and James M.H. Harris Jr.

We also wish to thank C&F Bank, especially its president, Larry Dillon; thanks also goes to the West Point School District and its staff. In addition, Joshua Lawson and the West Point Volunteer Fire Department provided photographs

This book has been in the good hands of editor Brinkley Taliferro Gary. We also wish to acknowledge the assistance of Heather Beattie at the Virginia Historical Society, Heather Moon at the *Richmond Times-Dispatch*, and especially Erin Lopater, photographic archivist at the Mariners' Museum.

The Mattaponi Reservation and its chief, Carl Custalow, deserve special thanks for sharing the history of the Mattaponi people. We urge those who wish to know more to visit their museum on the reservation (1467 Mattaponi Reservation Circle, West Point, VA 23181; 804-769-4508).

Above all, this work would not have been possible without the patient support of our spouses, Virginia Addison and Gary L. Hogenson.

Unless otherwise noted, all images and photographs come from the collection of the Historical Society of West Point.

Introduction

A narrow peninsula created by the confluence of the Pamunkey and Mattaponi Rivers, where they form the York River, has been the stage upon which significant contributions to every era of American history have taken place. It is not an exaggeration to say that Pamunkey Neck Peninsula and its surrounding area boasts one of the richest legacies of any comparably sized region in the United States.

The York is a tidal river that flows along a straight course to Chesapeake Bay, 30 miles from its headwaters at West Point, on the tip of Pamunkey Neck. With channels that can accommodate oceangoing vessels, the York has long been an important highway for shipping and a center for water-based industries. The Pamunkey and Mattaponi Rivers become freshwater within a few nautical miles of the tip of the peninsula as they snake their way through marshes abundant in edible water plants that fed the area's earliest inhabitants and continue to serve as spawning grounds for numerous aquatic species and as a habitat for waterfowl and other wildlife.

This bounty naturally attracted the Native Americans who made Pamunkey Neck and its environs their homeland for thousands of years. At the time of their first contact with Europeans, the Algonquin-speaking Eastern Woodlands Indians were using it as their regional center. Not only were numerous villages scattered along its riverbanks, but the region's most significant religious shrine was located on a bluff overlooking a bend in the Pamunkey River at the edge of the present town limits of West Point. This temple, Uttamussak, was so venerated that everyone passing by it presented an offering, including those on the river, who would throw an offering into the water. Uttamussak also served as a mortuary for the remains of chiefs.

When the Spanish explored the Chesapeake region beginning about 1559, they abducted a native boy and took him back to Spain, where he was given the Christian name Don Luis de Velasco and trained to be a monk. A decade later, the Spanish returned. Don Luis and a small contingent of Spanish clergy were to establish an outpost to bring Christianity to the natives. They were deposited on the south bank of the York, possibly at what is now called Stone House, about five miles down the river from West Point. Don Luis soon escaped and returned to his own people. The natives attacked and killed all of the Spaniards except one boy. When the Spanish returned, they hanged 10 native men in retaliation. This atrocity was a catalyst for the consolidation of the eastern tribes, who collectively referred to themselves as Powhatans (meaning "governed by priests"), into a confederation under one paramount leader. This powerful man, Wahunsenaca, was known to the English by his title: Powhatan.

Little wonder, then, that when the English established their first permanent settlement in 1607 at Jamestown, situated about 25 miles from Pamunkey Neck, the Native Americans saw an opportunity to establish an alliance that would protect them from their common enemy: the Spanish. Within months of the landing at Jamestown, during the winter of 1608, Capt. John Smith was captured by the natives while exploring the region and brought to West Point to be examined by one of the most powerful subordinate chiefs of the region and brother of Powhatan, Opechancanough, whose primary village, Cinquoteck, was located on what is now called Broaddus Hill in West Point. Smith returned to Cinquoteck a number of times to trade for food.

Powhatan's favorite daughter and the most famous of Indian maidens, Mattoaka—known to history as Pocahontas—was, according to Mattaponi oral history, born to a Mattaponi mother on Pamunkey Neck. After she was weaned, she was brought to live at her father's primary residence and capital, Werowocomoco, located about 10 miles downstream from West Point at Purtan Bay on the York River. After the English took her prisoner, she was brought to Matchot (across the water from Cinquoteck) to plead with her father to redeem her.

A few years after Powhatan's passing in 1619, Opechancanough became the paramount chief of the Powhatan confederacy. It was most likely at Chinquoteck that he planned the uprisings against the English of 1622 and 1644. It was to Chinquoteck that the English came, first for revenge and later to negotiate peace, resulting in a 1646 treaty guaranteeing that the English would not settle north of the Pamunkey or York Rivers. The treaty was breached by the English within less than a decade. In the 1650s, the Virginia House of Burgesses set aside lands for the Pamunkey and Mattaponi peoples along the rivers that bear their names, several miles upstream from present-day West Point. These ancient tribal lands are the only remaining Native American reservations in Virginia.

After establishing settlements along the James River, the English turned to the York and began to dot its banks with farms known as plantations. The powerful West family, which produced three royal governors of the colony, was granted the tip of Pamunkey Neck and much of the surrounding area, thereby giving the future town of West Point its name. The first member of that family to live in West Point was probably Col. John West II, who built a home in 1655 where the Pamunkey River begins its first bend. Delaware Town, named after the first resident royal governor of the Virginia colony and brother of John West, Thomas West, Lord Delaware, was established on the peninsula by act of the Virginia House of Burgesses in 1705. Delaware Town sat on the site of an earlier small English settlement, but this second attempt to create a town on the site ultimately failed, and the peninsula remained a plantation. During this period, ships from Europe began to dock at a wharf on the banks of the Mattaponi at West Point, and crude ferries plied the mouths of the Mattaponi and Pamunkey Rivers.

In 1677, settlers (primarily from the poorer classes) from throughout the region joined in Bacon's Rebellion, an uprising that in part aimed to push the Native Americans further from their lands. The primary victims of the violence were the Pamunkey and Mattaponi tribes. The rebels established an encampment at West Point. There, the last sizable group of rebels, about 400 in number, surrendered to the forces of Gov. William Berkeley near the tip of the peninsula by the Mattaponi River. One of their leaders was tried and expeditiously hanged from a mulberry tree at that site as an example to the other colonists.

With increasing settlement by the English, grand homes rose along the banks of the rivers as plantation after plantation generated tobacco-based wealth. Waterways were the highways of Colonial Virginia, and the depth of the channels surrounding Pamunkey Neck allowed ships from Europe to dock at the plantations and take on loads of locally grown tobacco, lumber, and cotton bound for the markets of Europe in exchange for British goods. In 1731, at Chestnut Grove Plantation along the Pamunkey several miles from West Point, the Dandridge family welcomed a daughter, Martha. Years later, she would marry neighbor Daniel Parke Custis, who owned another Pamunkey plantation further upstream, White House Plantation. After her husband's early death, the young widow was wooed and won by a gentleman planter who became the nation's first president: George Washington. Their wedding took place at the bride's home, White House Plantation, in 1759. For the rest of his life, George Washington took charge of the running of the substantial Custis properties in the area. His trips to the banks of the Pamunkey brought him to West Point and its environs many times, including soon after the surrender at Yorktown when he was summoned to the deathbed of his stepson at Eltham Plantation.

The Revolutionary War came to West Point. Carter Braxton, a patriot born in nearby King and Queen County, purchased the plantation at West Point in 1776, ending the West family's more than 120 years of unbroken possession of the site. Braxton, a signer of the Declaration of Independence on behalf of Virginia, lost his fortune because of the war and died destitute. In

1781, during the last months of the Revolution, Washington and his French allies feared that the British would try to sail up the York to escape the trap laid at Yorktown. The Marquis de Lafayette had already established a headquarters at nearby Chelsea Plantation on the Mattaponi and set up artillery along the tip of the peninsula. There, the small contingent of French soldiers became a nuisance to the residents, pilfering livestock and produce prior to that decisive final battle. James Armistead Lafayette, a slave of great capacity from the New Kent County side of the Pamunkey, was recruited by Lafayette to serve as a spy. He provided such valuable intelligence to Washington and the marquis about the British that the Virginia General Assembly awarded this hero his freedom. During the months following the Yorktown victory, the Comte de Rochambeau sent even more artillery to West Point, lest Gen. Charles Cornwallis's captured army be rescued.

In the early 1800s, West Point's port began to expand. The early steamboats could not reverse and therefore needed wide areas in which to turn around. The York at West Point was perfect. Little wonder that in the 1850s, as the railroads were expanding rapidly, it was decided that the terminus for the Richmond & York Railway would be at West Point, further enhancing its importance as a transportation hub. In 1855, the West Point Land and Development Company purchased 500 acres of high ground on the point of the peninsula, and a true town was arranged on a grid. Tracks were laid to White House Plantation, and a railroad bridge was constructed to span the Pamunkey, but the start of the Civil War delayed the laying of the last span of permanent tracks into Pamunkey Neck.

When war broke out between the North and the South in 1861, it was inevitable that the port of West Point, with its proximity to Richmond, would be embroiled in the fighting. During the early months of the war, Confederate dissidents were interned at West Point. A regiment of hometown men and boys, as well as recruits from the surrounding area, trained in West Point—the very troops that would be in the center of Pickett's Charge at the Battle of Gettysburg. Their training included raising breastworks, which were inspected by Gen. Robert E. Lee. Union gunboats bombarded the town, evidently leaving a cannonball hole in the wall of a home still standing. When 11,300 Federal troops tried landing directly across the river from the town on May 7, 1862, Confederate forces challenged them in the Battle of Eltham's Landing. That same day, however, West Point fell to the Union under the command of Capt. Isaac Wistar. By April 1863, about 4,800 Union troops would be stationed in the town under the command of Gen. George Henry Gordon. In 1864, Union troops again occupied the town.

West Point's peak years as a port came after the Civil War, when the railroad was finally completed all the way to present-day Second Street. Not only was it a center for shipping, it became a hub for passenger excursions to Baltimore and New York. Trains brought people from all over the state, especially the Richmond area, to catch the steamers. The lovely river views also attracted vacationers. A number of small hotels dotted the town, dominated by an imposing grand hotel at the tip of the peninsula, the Terminal Hotel, with its riverside swimming pool, boardwalks along the York, and amusement park. In 1870, by act of the Virginia General Assembly, the town was incorporated.

In 1880 and again in 1881, fire broke out onboard a ship on the wharf, destroying the adjacent business district, which had grown up along the railway tracks near the wharfs. Many merchants rebuilt, but this time along present-day Main Street. In 1895, West Point was devastated economically by the decision to move the railway terminus to Portsmouth. Virtually overnight, about a third of the population—hundreds of families—left to follow the railroad. Businesses closed, and property values in the town plummeted. Just as the town was beginning to recover from this calamity, a second fire in 1903 destroyed much of the commercial district, but these disasters did not spell the end of the town. The oyster industry was growing; indeed, West Point had become famous as a center for oyster processing, as its products were shipped to restaurants in New York and Philadelphia. Later, a group of entrepreneurs decided to take advantage of the rivers and abundance of local pine forests to establish a mill operation, first for pulp and then for paper manufacture. The paper mill expanded and prospered when a young Swedish chemist, Ellis Olsson, assumed ownership in 1918. Christoffer Hannevig, a Norwegian shipping financier, joined Olsson as both investment backer and the company's first president. This partnership would ultimately lead to the creation of the Chesapeake Corporation, providing the town with a strong economic anchor.

In 1911, Crosby Thompson, a businessman from Ohio, bought 2,000 acres of what had been the original West family plantation on the outskirts of the town and set about establishing a deepwater port to serve the City of Richmond. He founded the Old Dominion Industrial Corporation with capital supplied by New York City backers. Over the next few years, his efforts resulted in the establishment of a small community christened Port Richmond, which attracted a few small merchants and light industries. Eastern European immigrants from the mining regions of Pennsylvania and West Virginia were recruited to work in these enterprises. The dream of a major deepwater port never became reality, however, and was replaced by the idea of an air hub. The small airfield Thompson built was used by military aircraft until the planes built for World War II required a longer runway. Port Richmond was annexed by the Town of West Point in 1963.

During World War I, a shipyard, the York River Ship Building Corporation, was established by Thompson along the Mattaponi riverbank. Polish shipbuilders were recruited to lend their expertise to the enterprise. The shipyard produced only two vessels before the war ended, and it closed shortly thereafter.

In 1926, the Terminal Hotel burned down, and with it died West Point's position as an important destination resort for vacationers.

In 1898, Lt. Gen. Lewis Burwell "Chesty" Puller was born in West Point on First Street and was raised both there and in nearby Middlesex County. Revered as "the Marine's Marine," he was an acclaimed hero of both World War II in the Pacific and the Korean War and remains the most decorated US Marine in American history.

In 1952, the national news media put a spotlight on West Point when a group of African American parents refused to send their children to a segregated school in King William County. Their lawsuit, *Dobbins v. Virginia*, was a landmark in the civil rights movement. The African American segment of the community, the descendents of slaves who had worked the local plantations, had a proud lineage of civic-minded community leaders, such as Beverly Allen and his son Beverly Allen Jr. These two men worked tirelessly to better the circumstances of African Americans during the years they were restricted from participating in much of the activities of the wider society. The area's African American community emphasized education for its children and erected the Beverly Allen School building with contributed labor from parents. This substantial segment of the population also owned and operated a number of successful small businesses and established one of the oldest congregations in West Point, Mt. Nebo Baptist Church.

In the 1990s, the Mattaponi tribe fought yet again for its ancestral rights to the bounties of the area's rivers when it led the challenge to the City of Newport News's plan to draw water from the Mattaponi River to create a reservoir. The region is at the center of a number of efforts to protect the environment. The mill at West Point, in particular, has made great strides at reducing air and water pollution.

Beginning in 1982, the annual Crab Carnival celebrates the town's connections to the sea. This two-day festival attracts thousands of visitors with all things crab and provides a charming glimpse of vintage small-town Americana.

The great steamers docking at West Point's wharfs are gone, but the proud heritage remains. Today, the rivers that surround West Point are full of fishermen and water skiers, kayakers, and those who just love to be near the water. There has been a revival of the Victorian beauties that still grace its oldest neighborhood, known locally as downtown. The town's school system has attained and maintained a statewide reputation for excellence. The population has become increasingly diverse and integrated, with neighbors of all colors and from many corners of the globe. The oystermen are gone, replaced by crabbers with their boats stacked high with crab pots. Beautiful, high bridges span the Mattaponi and Pamunkey Rivers. But on a fall evening, when deer creep out of the marshes to explore the town, one can still feel the presence of Pocahontas and know that the web of life that is Pamunkey Neck and its environs is very ancient and rich indeed.

One

Native Americans, Colonists, and the Revolution

When Capt. John Smith explored the waterways of the Chesapeake region, he mapped the native villages by name, with special markings for each "King's House." These important villages were evenly scattered throughout the region, except for the vicinity of West Point, where there wasn't one—there were four. As a primary stronghold for the Powhatan peoples, it was attacked multiple times by the English as part of the Indian wars that ebbed and flowed after the 1622 native uprising—most likely organized from the environs of West Point—until a treaty was signed in 1677. Only after the natives were driven west, up the Pamunkey and Mattaponi Rivers, could the English settle the area.

The first white man to build a home in West Point was more Virginian than English, for Col. John West II was the first white child born along the banks of the York. He was 11 during the second native uprising in 1644, and 22 when he established West Point in 1655. Growing up as a minority in an Algonquin world, this scion of the De la War family had a British wife but also an attachment to the Queen of the Powhatan Nation, Cockacoeski. He is buried in an unmarked grave in West Point near Seventh Street.

By 1700, the land along the banks of the three rivers began to take on attributes of a British landscape, with lawns flowing down to riverbanks and field after field of cash crops. The 1677 treaty gave the natives rights to their lands on either side of the peninsula a few miles inland from its tip. The fight was no longer in them; instead, they strove to maintain their heritage while adopting many of the British goods, like cotton cloth and iron tools, that made their lives easier. The area was at peace.

With its proximity to Williamsburg, the Colonial capital of Virginia, it was inevitable that the planters of the region would become embroiled in the political upheavals of the Revolutionary period. Again, West Point would know war. Not only was West Point's shipping impeded by the Revolution, the Marquis de Lafayette recognized its strategic location and placed both Continental and French troops along its shores in 1781.

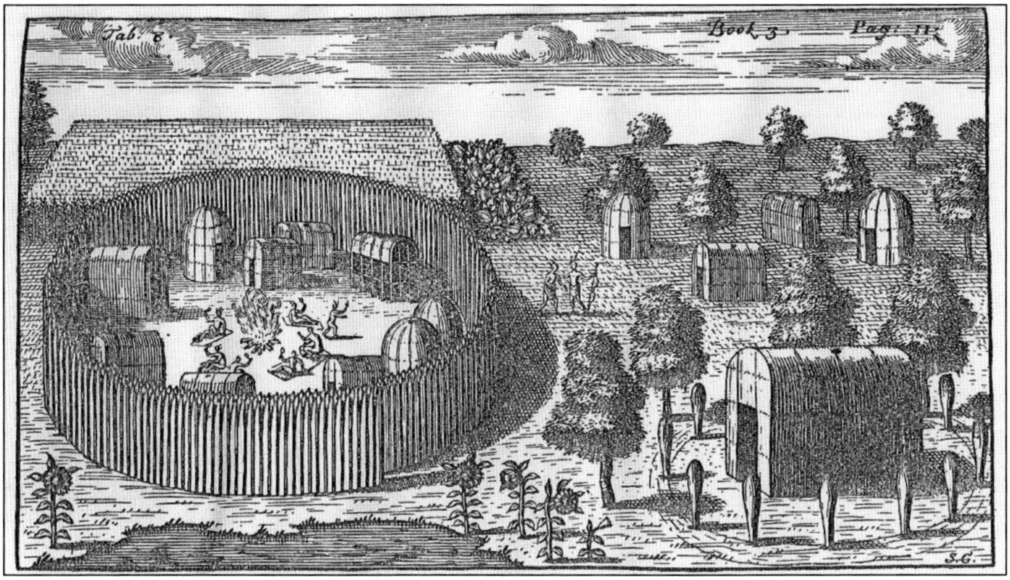

A typical Algonquian-speaking village in the mid-Atlantic region in the late 16th century is captured in this European engraving. There were a number of both large and small villages at West Point and the neighboring areas on both the peninsula and other sides of the rivers. In 1607, the primary village at West Point was Cinquoteck, whose chief was Opechancanough, Powhatan's brother and one of the paramount chief's top lieutenants. This Simon Gribelin engraving is based on a John White drawing.

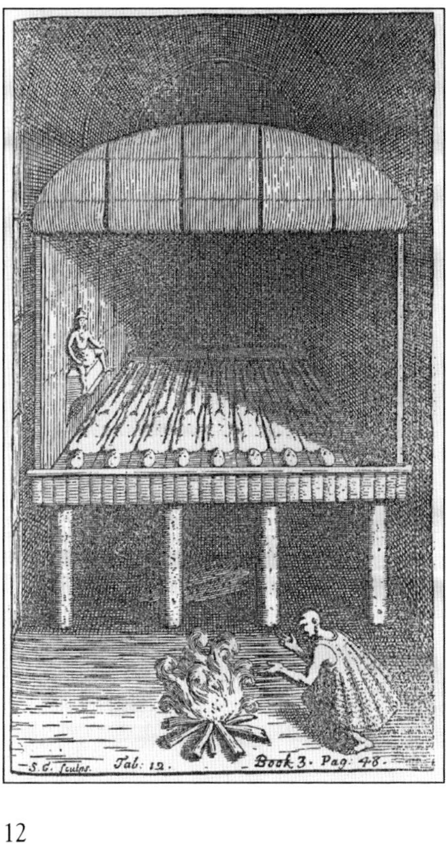

The Uttamusak temple complex was located at the edge of the present town limits of West Point on a bluff overlooking the Pamunkey. Even though most villages included a small temple, Uttamusak was the regional center for worship. Only priests and the paramount chiefs were allowed to enter the main building; trespassers could be killed. The focal point of the temple was a large clear piece of quartz, the Mussa (Mussac) Stone. The complex also included a mortuary, shown in this engraving, where the mummified remains of chiefs were kept. It was dismantled, and the remains were moved to safety, as English encroachment threatened this sacred spot. This Simon Gribelin engraving is from John Smith's *Generall Historie* (1624).

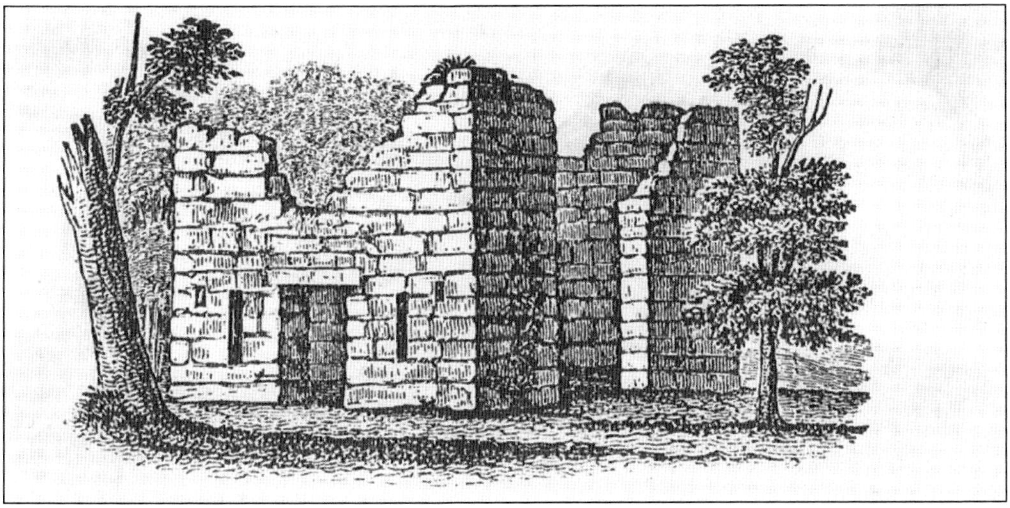

Stone House is the remnants of a building along the southern shore of the York River about five miles from West Point. Its origin and use are mysterious because its stone cannot be found in eastern Virginia. One theory suggests that it was part of a 16th-century Spanish outpost. Its walls were still visible until the 19th century, when the sketch on which this etching is based was drawn. This image was published in Henry Howe's *Historical Collections of Virginia.*

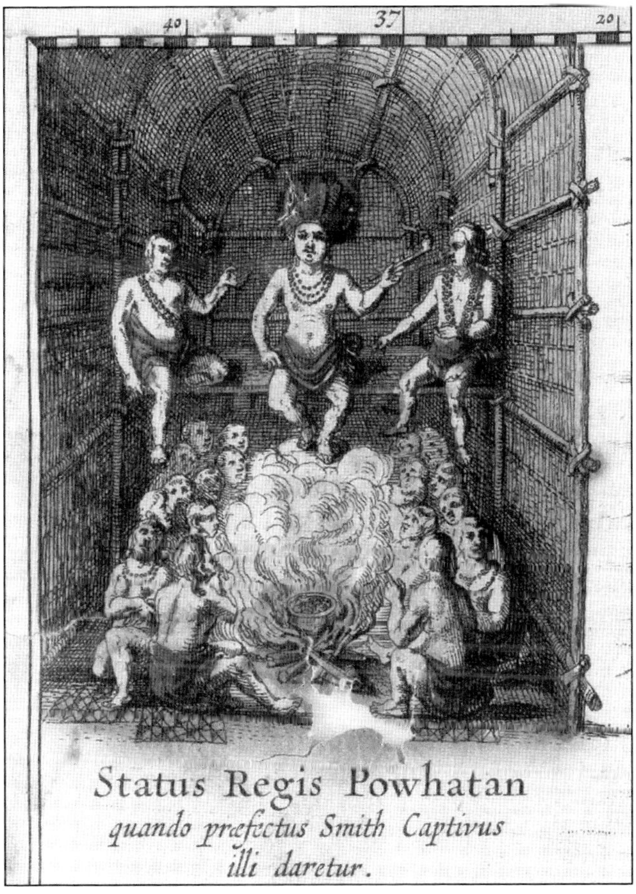

Chief Powhatan, whose true name was Wahunsunaca, was the paramount chief of eastern Virginia at the time the English arrived in 1607. He had his capital about 10 miles down the York from West Point at Werwocomoco at Purtan Bay. As relations with the English deteriorated, he moved his headquarters first to a site on the Chickahominy River and then to Machot, a village directly across the Pamunkey from West Point at what is now called Eltham. He is buried along the banks of the Pamunkey on the last remaining tribal land of his Pamunkey people. (Courtesy of the Mariners' Museum.)

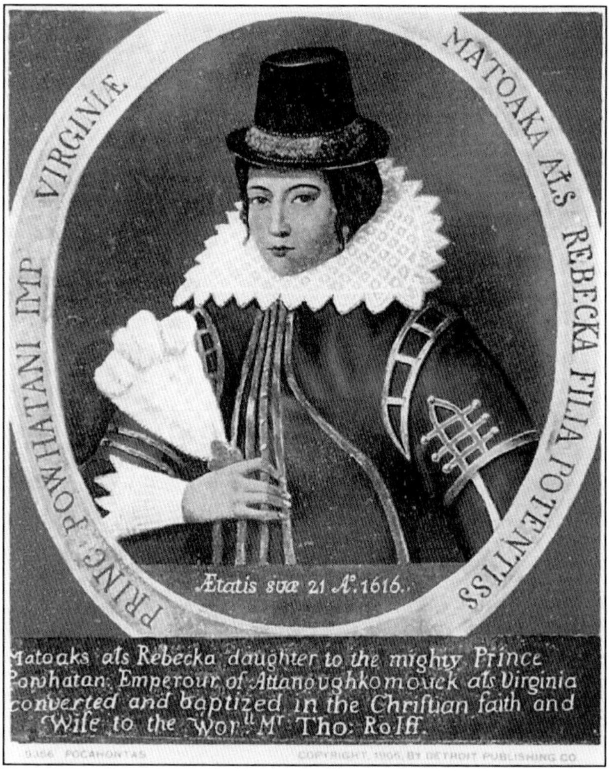

Pocahontas, the favorite daughter of Powhatan, was credited by Capt. John Smith with saving his life on several occasions. When, as a teenager, she was brought as a prisoner of the English to Machot, the village across the Pamunkey from West Point (at Eltham's Landing) for negotiations with her father, John Rolfe made public his desire to marry her. Their marriage created a brief period of peace between the two peoples. This engraving is based on a portrait done from life during her visit to London as Rebecca Rolfe. (Courtesy of William J. Addison.)

In 1899, descendants of the first peoples of West Point posed in traditional clothing at the Pamunkey Indian Reservation. (Courtesy of the National Anthropological Archives, Smithsonian Institution.)

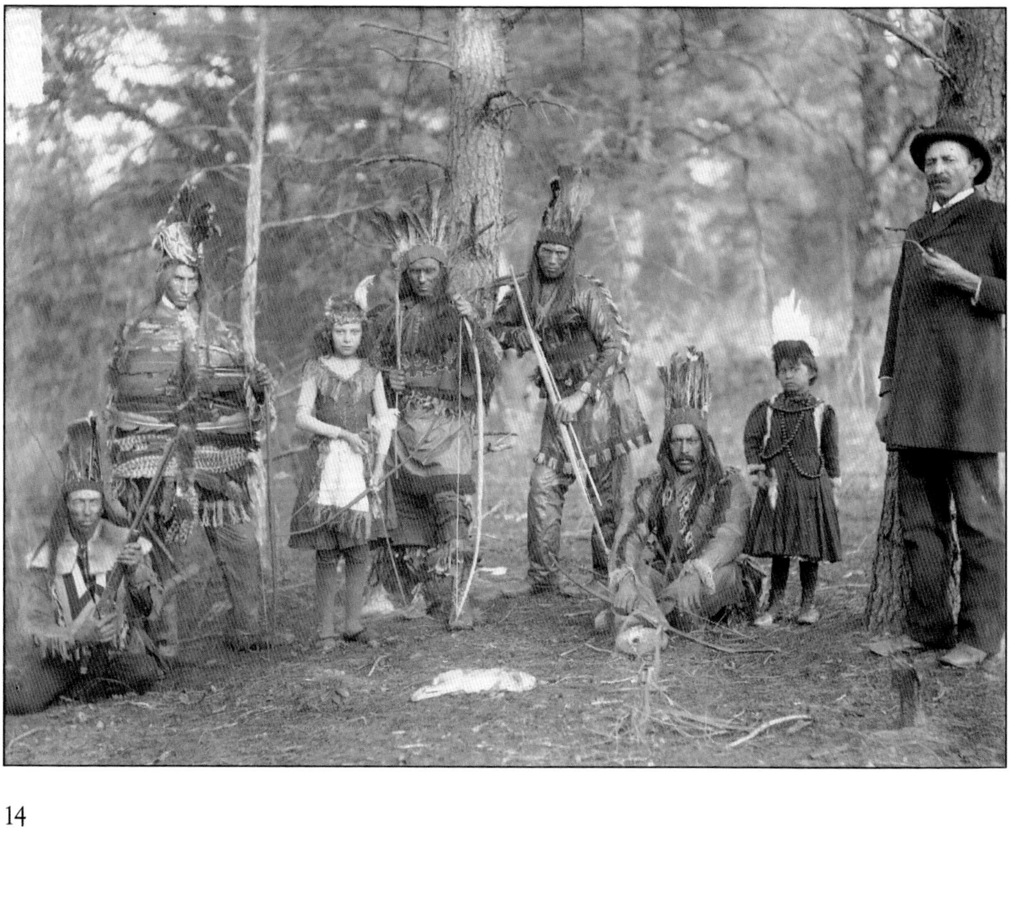

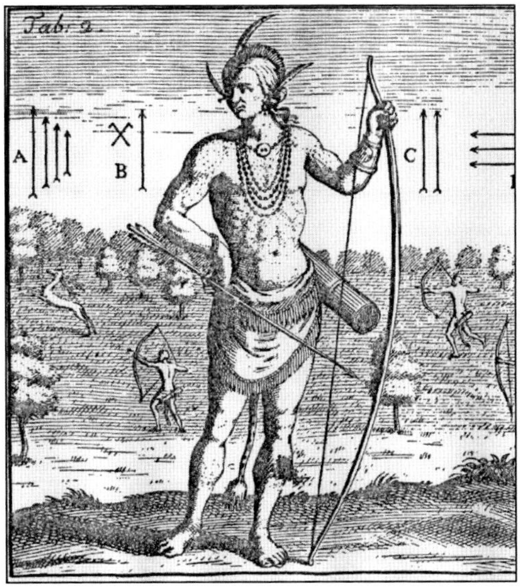

Capt. John Smith returned to West Point a number of times, primarily to trade for food. During one visit, he suspected that Chief Opechancanough was about to ambush him and his men. He grabbed the chief's hair forelock and, with a gun to the chief's breast, safely extricated himself and his men. Opechancanough became the paramount chief about 1620 and ordered and organized the uprisings of 1622 and 1644 that resulted in the deaths of hundreds of settlers and natives. His capital was based at West Point and, from time to time, farther up the Pamunkey River. This engraving of an Eastern Woodland warrior, such as Opechancanough, is by Simon Gribelin and based upon a John White drawing.

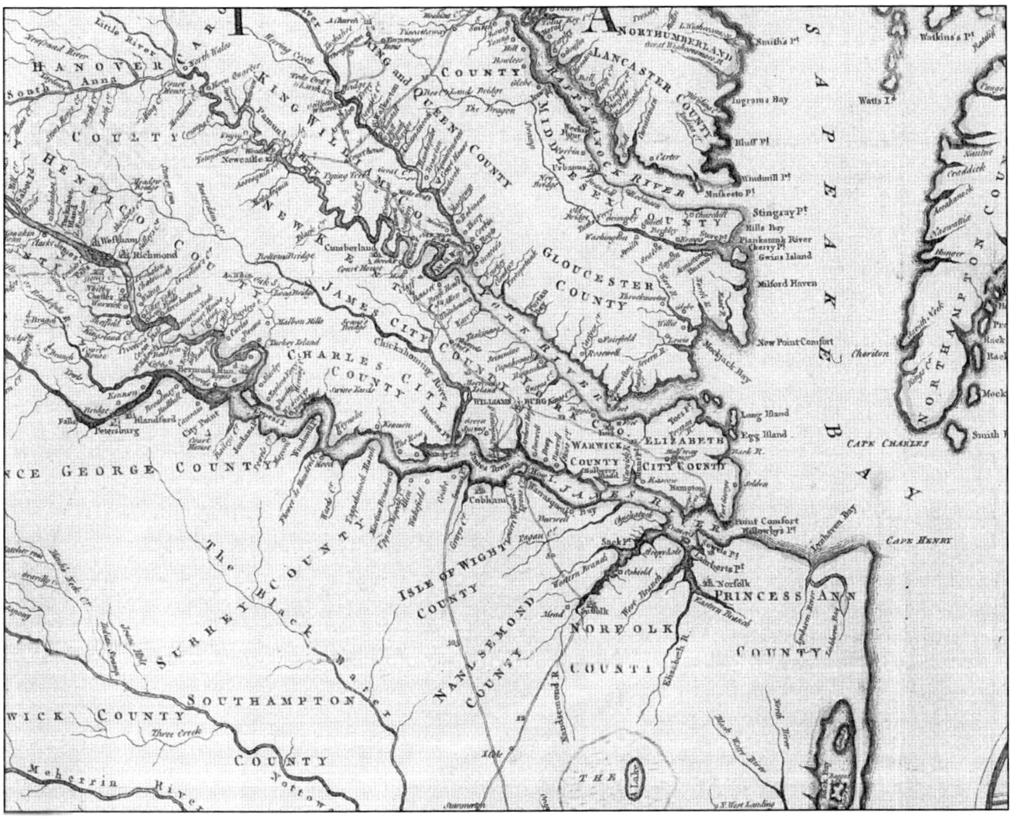

This detail from a 1659 map shows how the English had begun to settle the York River basin and reach into the remaining territory of the Powhatan people. Bacon's Rebellion was the final violent push that forced the remaining natives from the West Point environs, with the exception of their designated reservations. The queen of the Pamunkeys appealed to the King of England, complaining that her people had lost their lands, including the areas where they hunted and foraged for food. (Courtesy of the Mariners' Museum.)

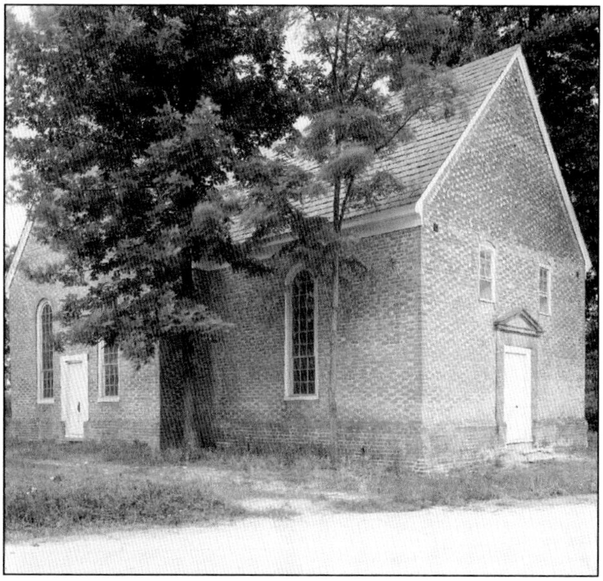

St. John's Episcopal Church in King William County was built in 1734. When the English established farms at West Point, they also tried to create a town. Delaware Town never became bigger than a small village, and its only house of worship was a small chapel near the corner of Fifth and Main Streets. This fine brick chapel about eight miles from the earlier one was built to take its place when the original chapel was deemed to be beyond repair. This photograph was taken in the 1930s by Frances Benjamin Johnston. Old St. John's was rededicated in 2010 after being fully restored. (Courtesy of the Library of Congress.)

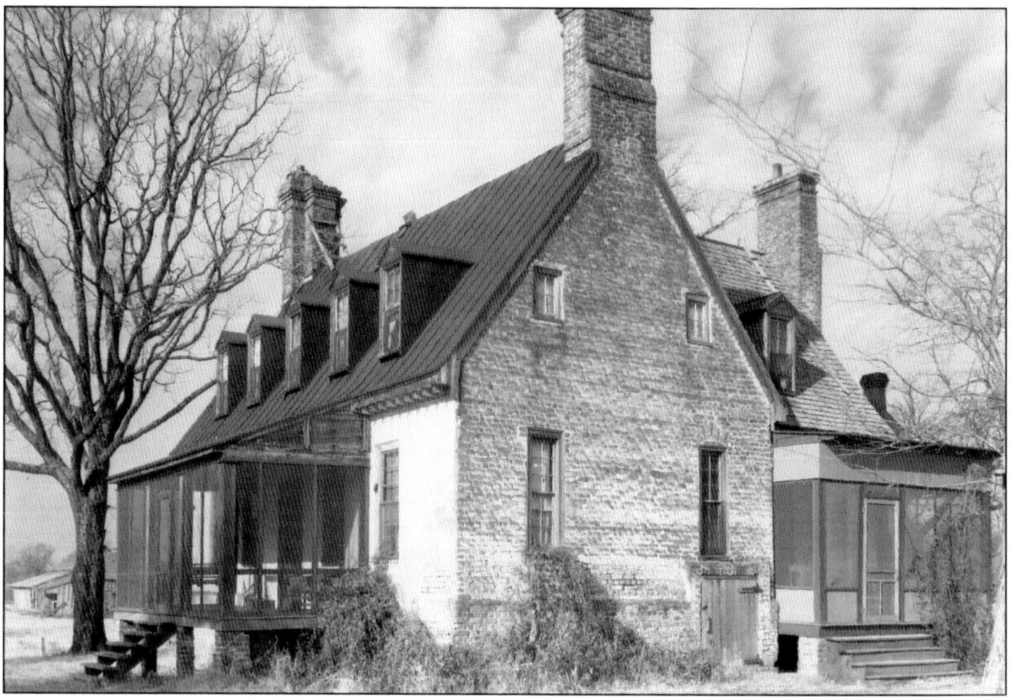

Sweet Hall Plantation along the banks of the Pamunkey, upriver from West Point, was part of the land of William Claiborne, official surveyor of the colony. Branded as a pirate for his settlement of Kent Island, Maryland, he was the second Englishman to reside at West Point. He obtained a land grant beginning at what became Romancoke Plantation, running northwest along the Pamunkey. Claiborne was the head of the militia that led raids against the native people at West Point and its vicinity during the wars of the 1620s and 1640s, finally driving the natives from the area. He and his men burned villages, destroyed crops, and killed defenders. The present residence at Sweet Hall was built by his grandson Thomas Claiborne in 1720. (Courtesy of the Library of Congress.)

Chelsea Plantation, located on the banks of the Mattaponi near West Point, was built by Augustine Moore in 1705. During his lifetime, it was reputedly the colony's most prominent plantation for tobacco cultivation. It was from Chelsea that Gov. Alexander Spotswood and his party of prominent Virginia planters, remembered as Knights of the Golden Horseshoe, left to explore the foothills of the Appalachians in 1716. In August 1781, a contingent of the Continental Army under the command of the Marquis de Lafayette was encamped at Chelsea for about two weeks.

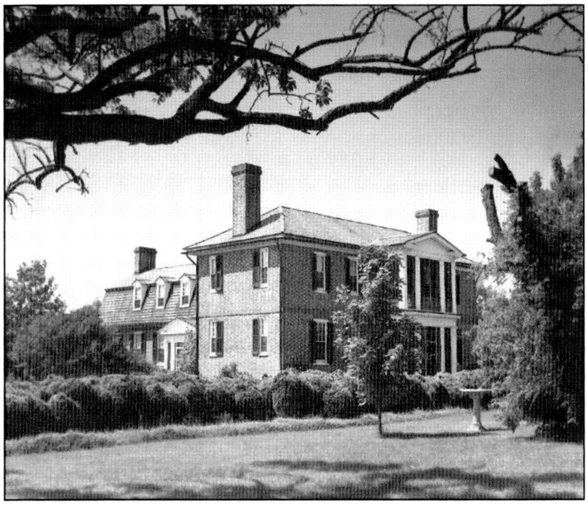

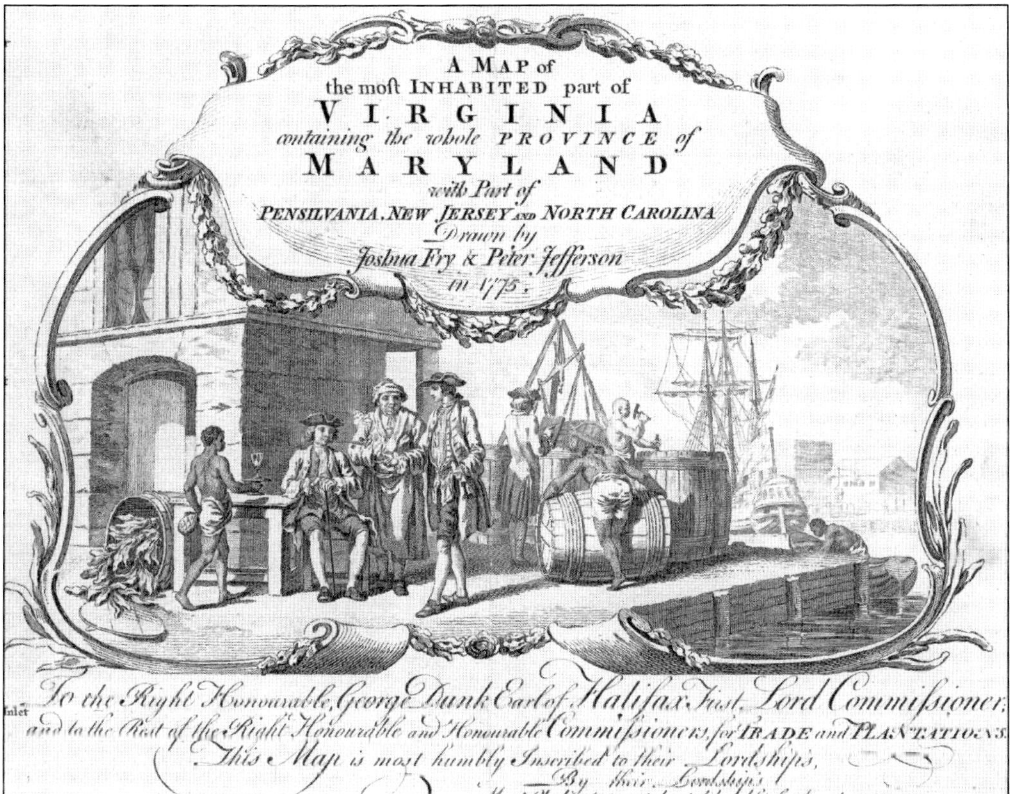

Carter Braxton was born into a prominent family whose wealth was derived from cash crops, such as tobacco. He owned several large farms in and around West Point, as well as ships. As a delegate to the Continental Congress, he was one of the signers of the Declaration of Independence. While he was in Philadelphia during the summer of 1776, his home at Chericoke along the Pamunkey River burned down. He then purchased the West Plantation at West Point and made it his home. The British blockade of the colonies cost him his wealth. The engraving shows a typical scene of Virginia planters, such as Braxton, shipping their tobacco using the labor of slaves. (Courtesy of the Mariners' Museum.)

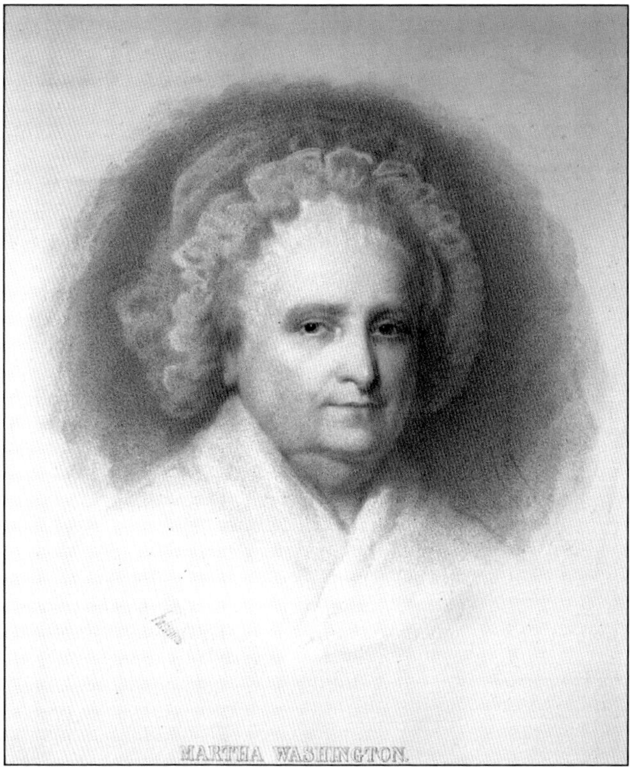

Martha Dandridge Custis Washington, wife of George Washington, was only 25 when her first husband, Daniel Parke Custis, one of the wealthiest landowners in the colony, died, leaving her with two young children and a large inheritance that included extensive tracts of land. The Custis holdings included Romancoke at West Point and her residence, White House Plantation, on the New Kent side of the Pamunkey, situated directly across the river from the Pamunkey Indian Reservation. (Courtesy of the Library of Congress.)

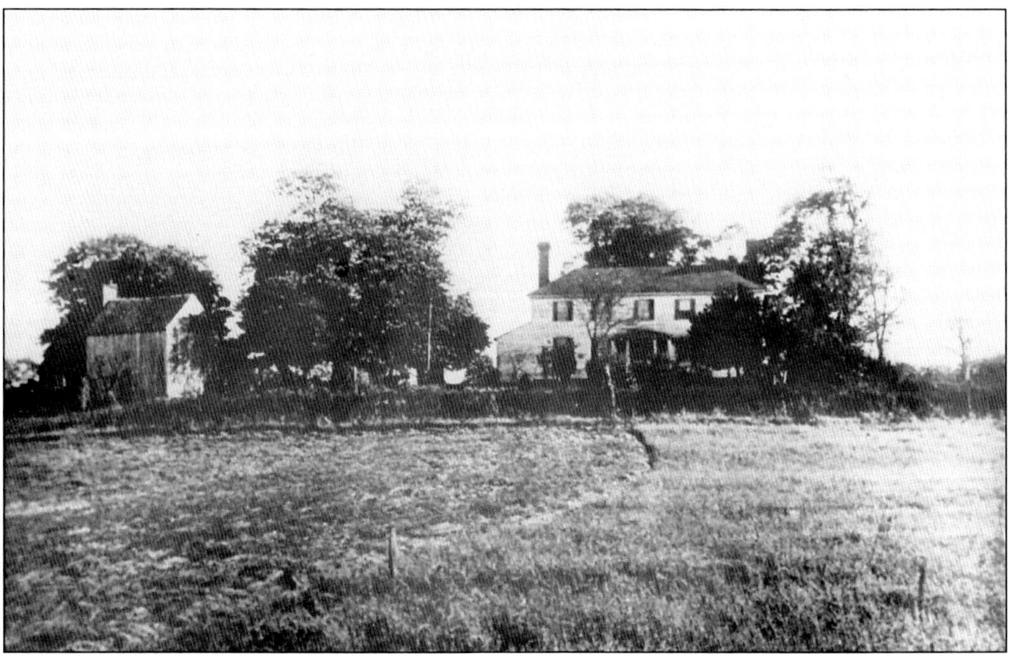

This is the only known photograph of Chestnut Grove, the birthplace of Martha Washington. The plantation was purchased around 1730 by her father, John Dandridge, and was located along the western bank of the Pamunkey near West Point. It burned to the ground in 1926. (Courtesy of James M.H. Harris Jr.)

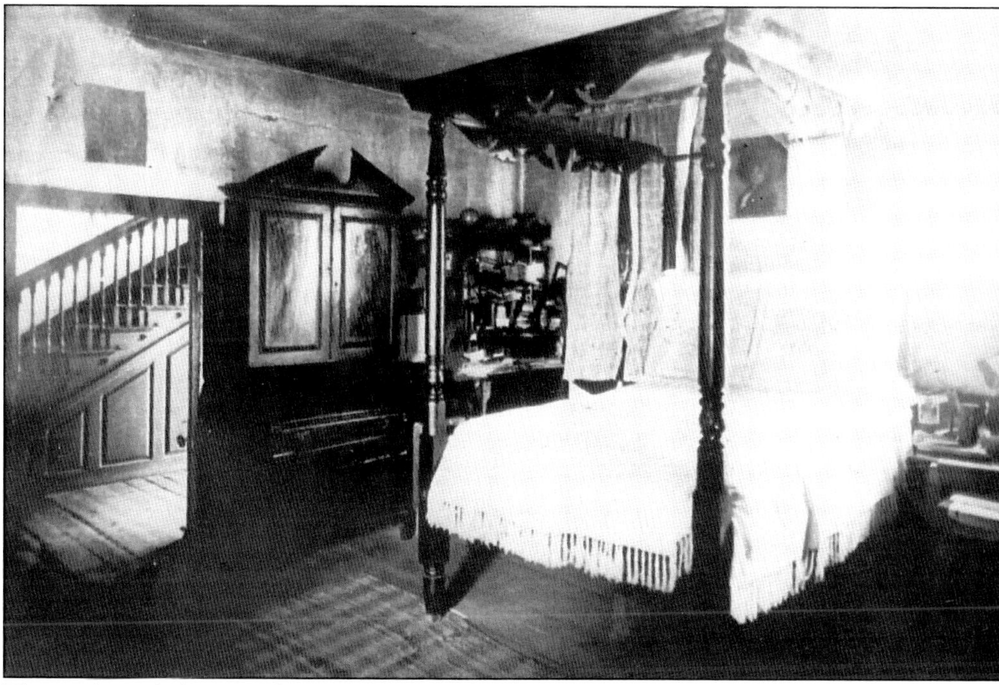

This is the only known photograph of the room where Martha Washington was born in 1731. Martha's world during the first decades of her life revolved around homes that lined the Pamunkey River between West Point and White House Plantation. She met her second husband, George Washington, at Poplar Grove Plantation on the Pamunkey River, and they married at White House Plantation in 1759. Her descendants—the wife and children of Gen. Robert E. Lee—continued to own and live at some of her holdings in the area into the 20th century. (Courtesy of James M.H. Harris Jr.)

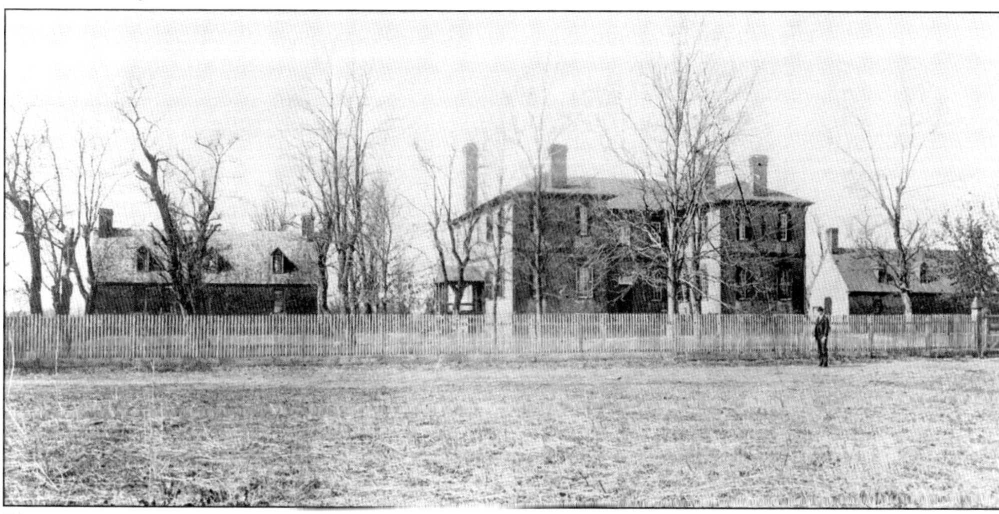

Elsing Green Plantation was built in 1717 by Martha Washington's uncle William Dandridge, on the eastern banks of the Pamunkey across from White House Plantation. Originally part of the land conveyed to John West by the Pamunkey Indians, Dandridge acquired it through his marriage to Unity West. Legend has it that Martha rode a horse into the foyer of the home during her youth. (Courtesy of the Library of Congress.)

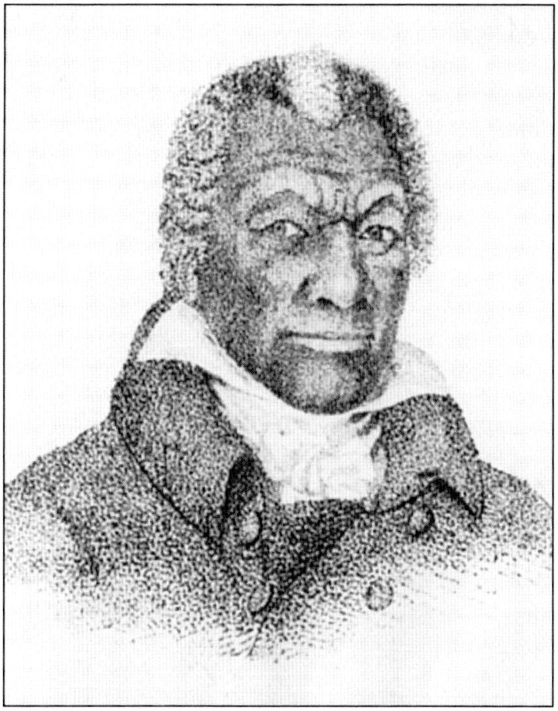

James Armistead was a slave from the Armistead Plantation in New Kent County when the Marquis de Lafayette arrived in the area. The marquis recruited him to spy on the British army encamped at Portsmouth. It was his intelligence that alerted Washington that the British army under the command of Lord Cornwallis intended to move to Yorktown to await the arrival of a British fleet. Based on his reports, Washington decided to attempt to capture Cornwallis at Yorktown. This resourceful spy continued to provide valuable information from behind the British lines during the battle. In gratitude for the services James Armistead Lafayette rendered Washington and the marquis, the Virginia General Assembly granted him his freedom, a pension, and a tract of land, and the marquis granted him permission to take the last name of Lafayette.

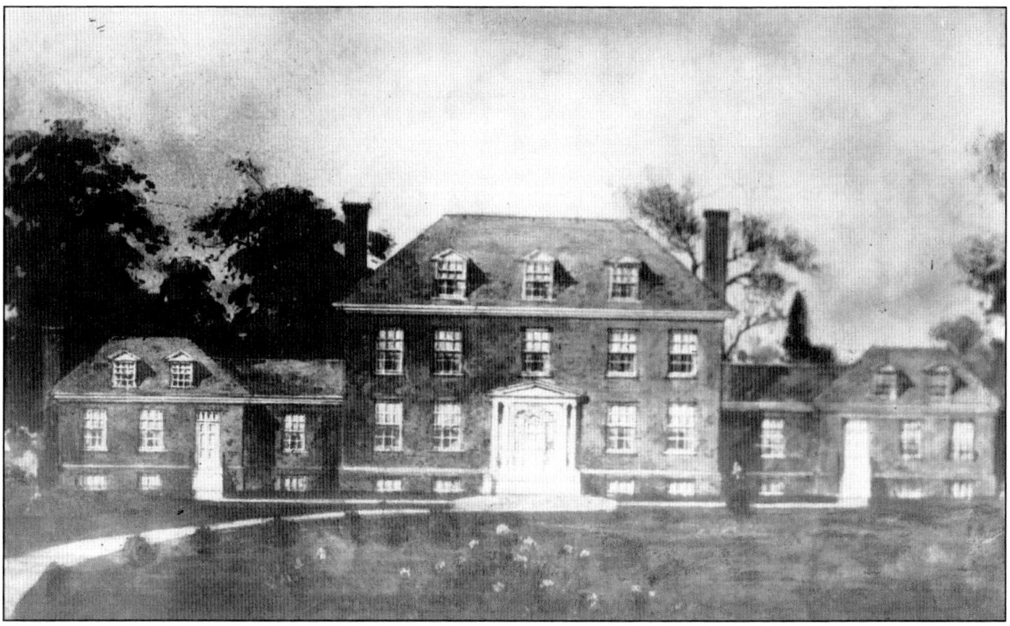

Eltham Plantation, built before 1695 by the Bassett family, was later inherited by the brother-in-law of Martha Washington. This watercolor was done from memory after the building burned down in 1875. The elegant brick mansion stood not far from the Pamunkey River near the site where the Pamunkey village of Matchot had stood. When Martha's last surviving child, John Parke Custis, took ill at the end of the Battle of Yorktown, he was brought to Eltham. General Washington was summoned and arrived just as his stepson passed away. (Courtesy of James M.H. Harris Jr. and the Virginia Historical Society.)

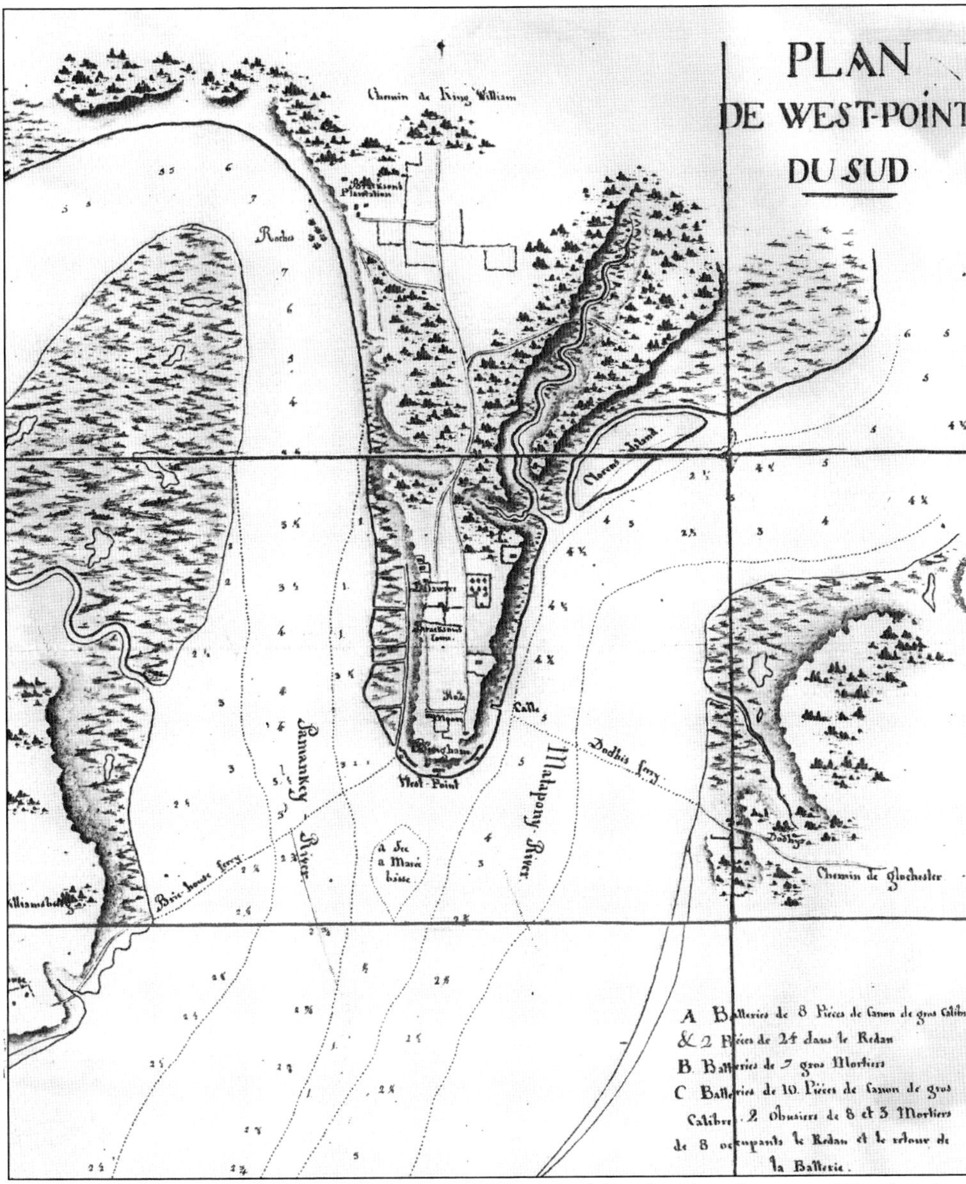

This map of West Point and its environs was produced for the French general Rochambeau in 1781 as part of the operations related to the Battle of Yorktown. French artillery was placed at either end of the tip of the peninsula. Following the surrender of Cornwallis, more artillery was placed at West Point lest the British send forces to try to rescue the captured British army. The map reveals that during the Revolution, West Point was sparsely populated and primarily the plantation of Carter Braxton, whose home is noted on the map. The map also marks the location of John West's former home, which was the first English home in West Point. (Courtesy of the Library of Congress and James M.H. Harris Jr.)

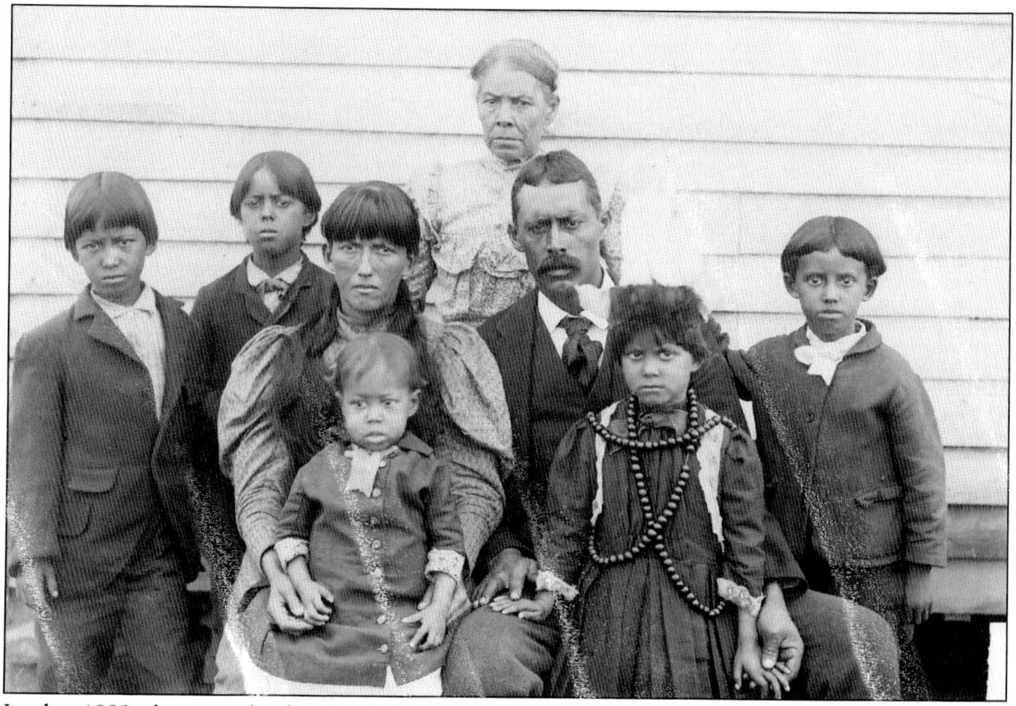

In this 1899 photograph the Cook family poses in front of a home on the Pamunkey Indian Reservation. Though most of their ancestral lands had been usurped by English settlers, they kept a world within a world on their last tribal land while participating within the wider community at the same time. (Courtesy of the National Anthropological Archives, Smithsonian Institution.)

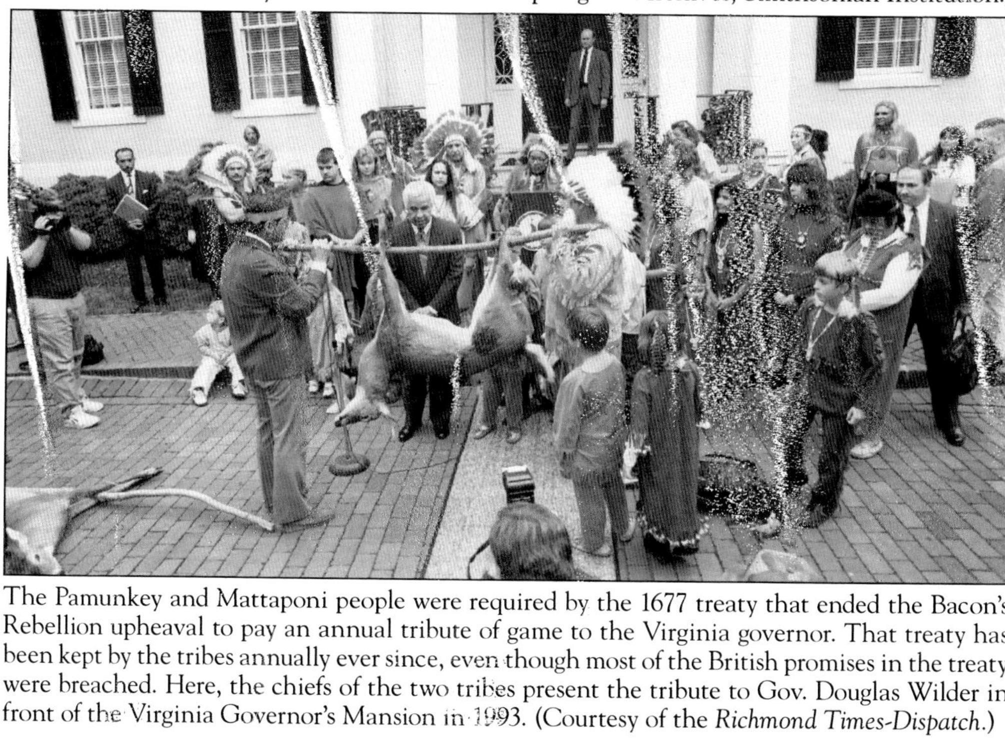

The Pamunkey and Mattaponi people were required by the 1677 treaty that ended the Bacon's Rebellion upheaval to pay an annual tribute of game to the Virginia governor. That treaty has been kept by the tribes annually ever since, even though most of the British promises in the treaty were breached. Here, the chiefs of the two tribes present the tribute to Gov. Douglas Wilder in front of the Virginia Governor's Mansion in 1993. (Courtesy of the *Richmond Times-Dispatch*.)

Two

The Railroad and the Civil War Come to West Point

During the Colonial period, West Point never fully developed into a town, only a small collection of buildings. There were a few homes, a tiny Anglican chapel, and a few warehouses and supply stores—just enough to qualify as a small village integrated into a plantation. There was a wharf at West Point on the Mattaponi River, but the large plantations of the area, with deep water near shore, primarily used their own private docks. Such farm and plantation self-sufficiency made a central shipping point or market towns unnecessary.

The Richmond & York Railway decided to make West Point its terminus and port in the 1850s. A bridge was constructed across the Pamunkey River at Martha Washington's former home, White House Plantation, and tracks were laid into West Point. Unfortunately, the project was only partially complete when the Civil War began in 1861.

Having already experienced firsthand the horrors of the Indian Wars of the 1600s and the final days of the Revolution in the 1700s, West Point would have another turn at war. Shortly after Virginia seceded from the Union, Union sympathizers from the Norfolk area were arrested and interned at West Point. Maj. Harrison Ball Tomlin of King William County successfully raised a company of 219 men called "the Mattaponi Guards." On May 9, 1861, Confederate troops began to fortify the strategic peninsula, which controlled traffic entering the Mattaponi and Pamunkey and provided a railhead, but most of the troops from the peninsula were transferred in December of that year, leaving it vulnerable.

The town was first taken by Union troops under Gen. Isaac Wistar in May 1862, but after less than a month, the Union troops departed, having first freed the interned civilians. On April 17, 1863, two Union gunboats entered into a duel with artillery on the New Kent side of the York. The town came under Union occupation again in 1863 from April through July under Gen. George H. Gordon. Once again, on May 1, 1864, General Wistar's decimated troops, the 71st Pennsylvania, returned to the town they had occupied in 1862.

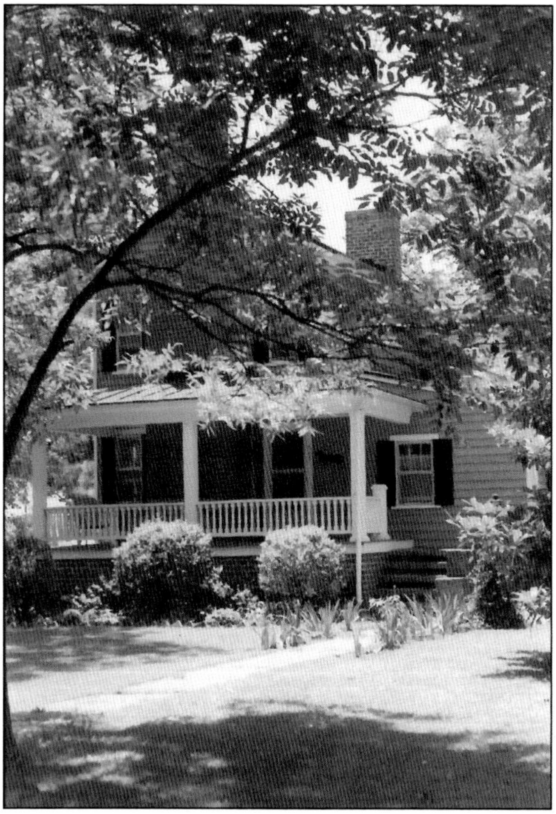

This home at the corner of Third and Main Streets is the oldest remaining home in West Point. Though records are no longer available, it was probably built in the 1840s. During the late 1850s, the village started to grow as construction began on a new wharf and railroad tracks. But most of the newcomers would abandon West Point during the Civil War, and their homes would be used to quarter troops. (Courtesy of William J. Addison.)

Steamboats such as the *Elm City* docked at the old wharf on the Mattaponi River side of the peninsula. In 1858, the Richmond & York Railway began construction of a new wharf with rail service on the Pamunkey River side. Temporary tracks were laid to the old wharf along Lee Street. This project came to a halt when the Civil War started in 1861 and retreating Confederate troops burned both the old and new wharfs and removed the rails. (Courtesy of the Mariners' Museum.)

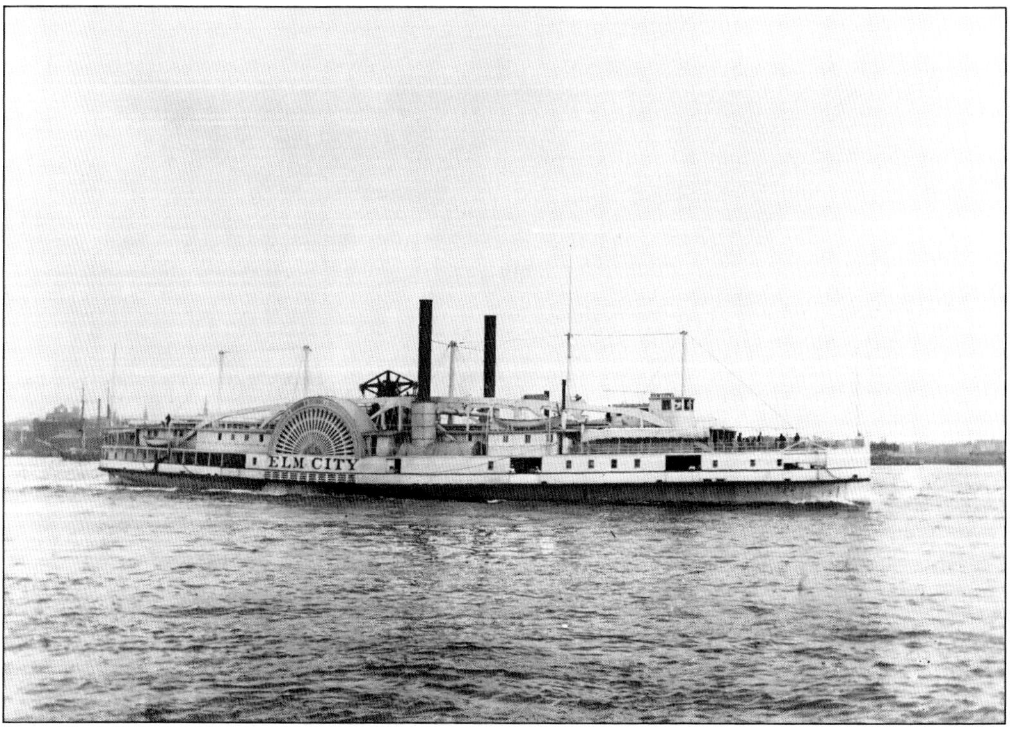

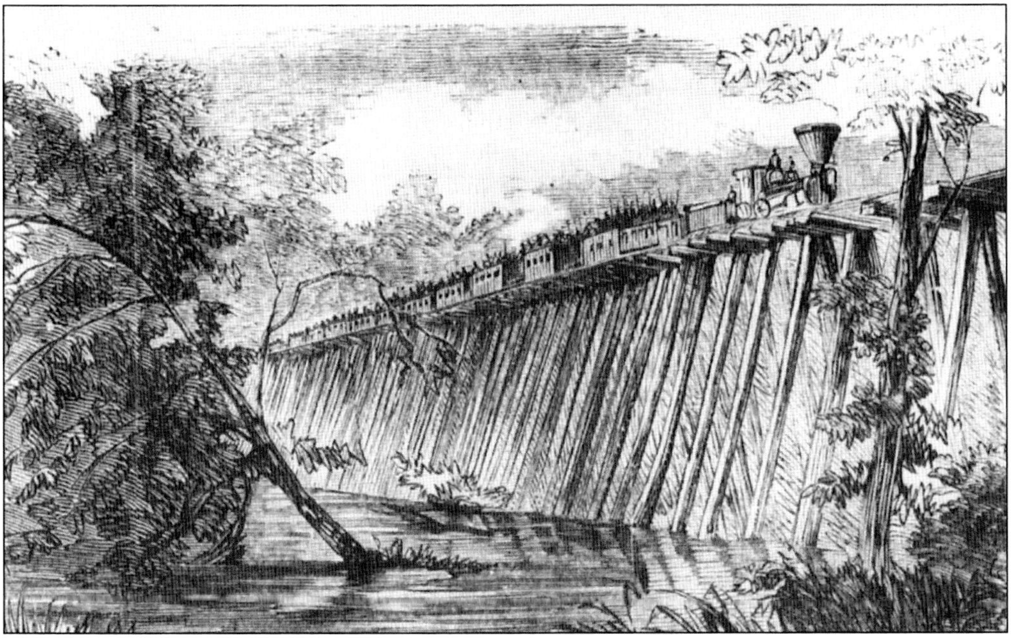

The railroad bridge crossing thc Pamunkey River was new when the Civil War began. Trains from Richmond and points south headed to the newly enhanced port at West Point, crossing the river at White House Plantation, the former home of Martha Washington, and arriving at West Point on temporary tracks that ended near the Colonial wharf at Fourth and Lee Streets. This drawing appeared in *Harper's Weekly*.

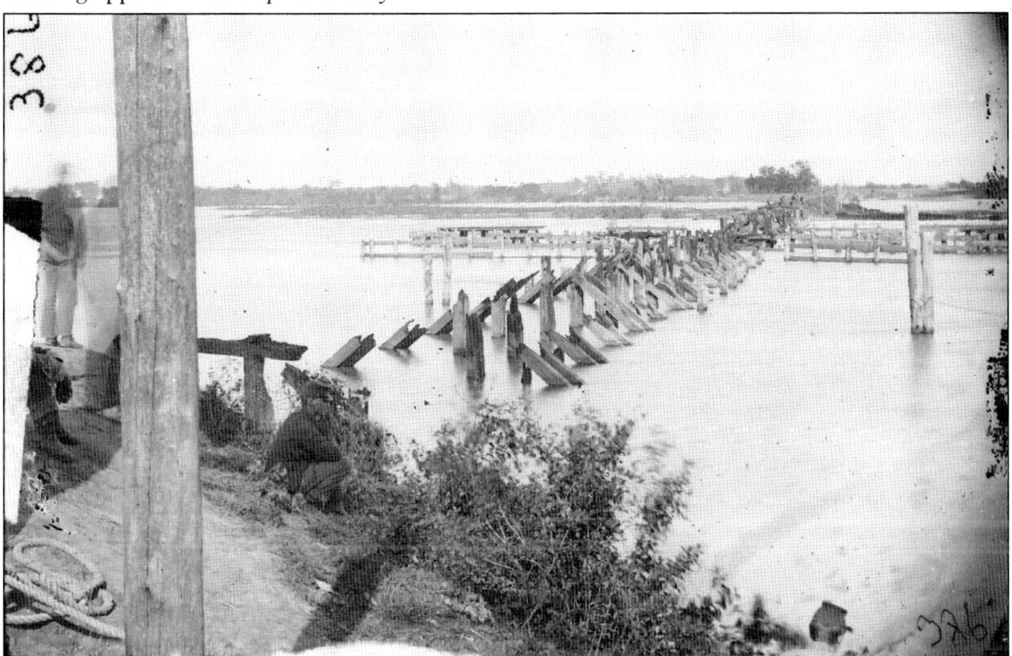

On May 17, 1862, Confederate forces burned the railroad bridge at White House Plantation, ending rail access to Pamunkey Neck and West Point. Union soldiers in the foreground of this photograph survey the ruins. (Courtesy of the Library of Congress.)

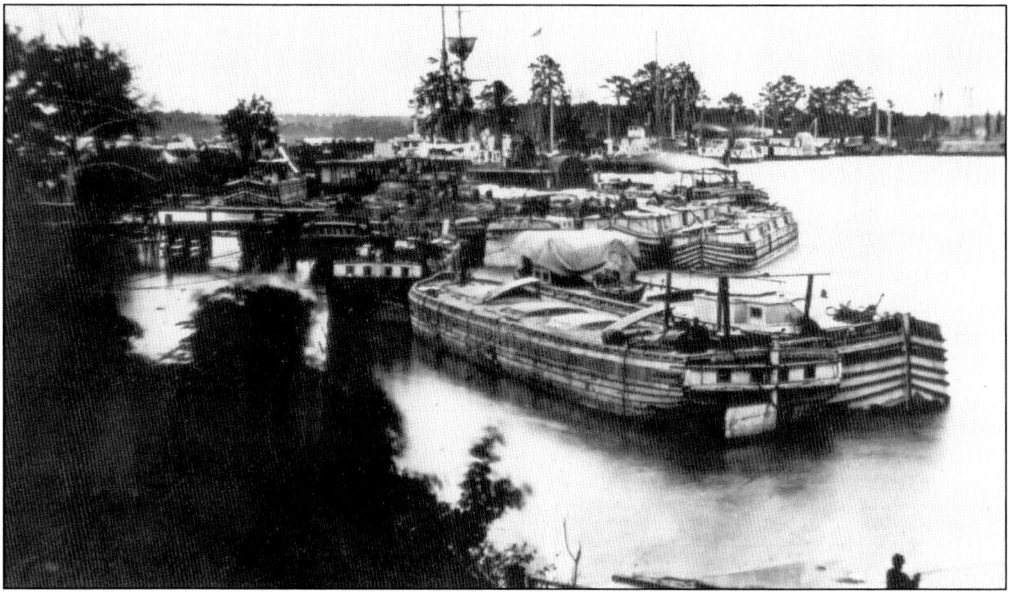

Maj. Gen. William B. Franklin was ordered by General McClellan to bring troops up the York to prevent Confederate general Joseph Johnston's army from reaching Richmond. In an attempt to flank Johnston's march up the Lower Peninsula, Federal troops came ashore on May 6, 1862, at Brick House, an old Colonial landing. The next day, Confederate general John Bell Hood's troops slowed them down in the Battle of Eltham's Landing. Also known as the Battle of Barhamsville, 56 men died in the skirmish. In this photograph, boats impressed into service by the Union forces unload troops and equipment along the western banks of the Pamunkey River. (Courtesy of the Mariners' Museum.)

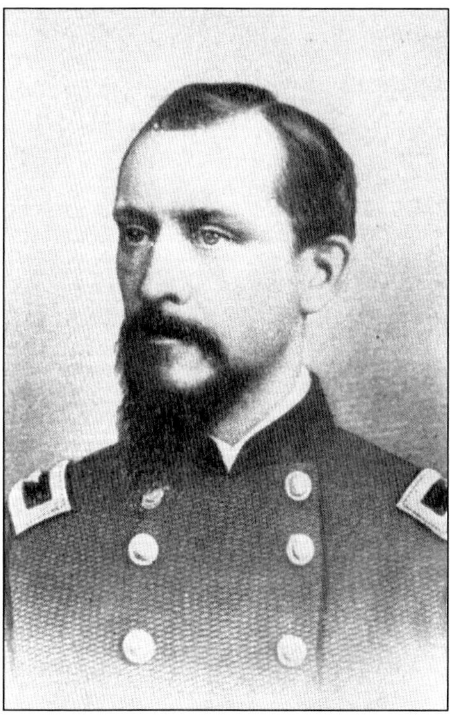

Gen. Isaac Wistar, shown right, and his Pennsylvania troops took West Point at about 1:00 a.m. on May 6, 1862, after facing light resistance from retreating Confederates. The Pennsylvanians immediately set to work rebuilding the old wharf on the Mattaponi that had been destroyed by the withdrawing Southerners. They dismantled houses and impressed slaves into service in order to quickly restore the wharf for immediate use. General Wistar and his troops spent only a short time here in 1862, but would return again in 1864. This engraving of Wistar is from Francis Trevelyan Miller and Robert S. Lanier's *The Photographic History of the Civil War*, Vol. 10. (Courtesy of James M.H. Harris Jr.)

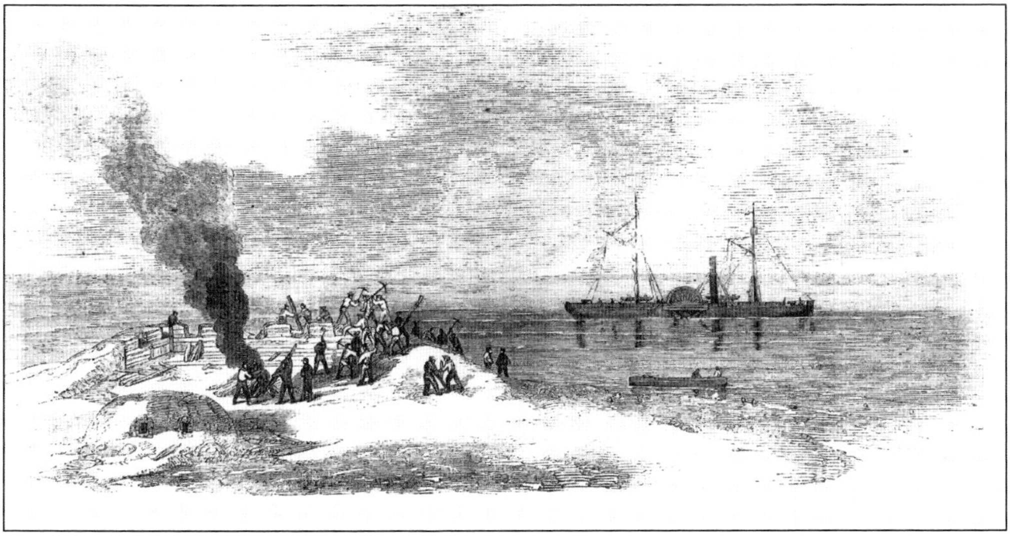

In this illustration, Union troops under the command of Brig. Gen. Isaac Wistar fortify West Point while a gunboat provides protection. The locations used to place artillery were the same as those used by the French during the Revolution. Trenches also guarded the northern limits of the town. A few remnants of the earthworks are still extant. This drawing appeared in Frank Leslie's *Illustrated Weekly*, Vol. XV from 1862.

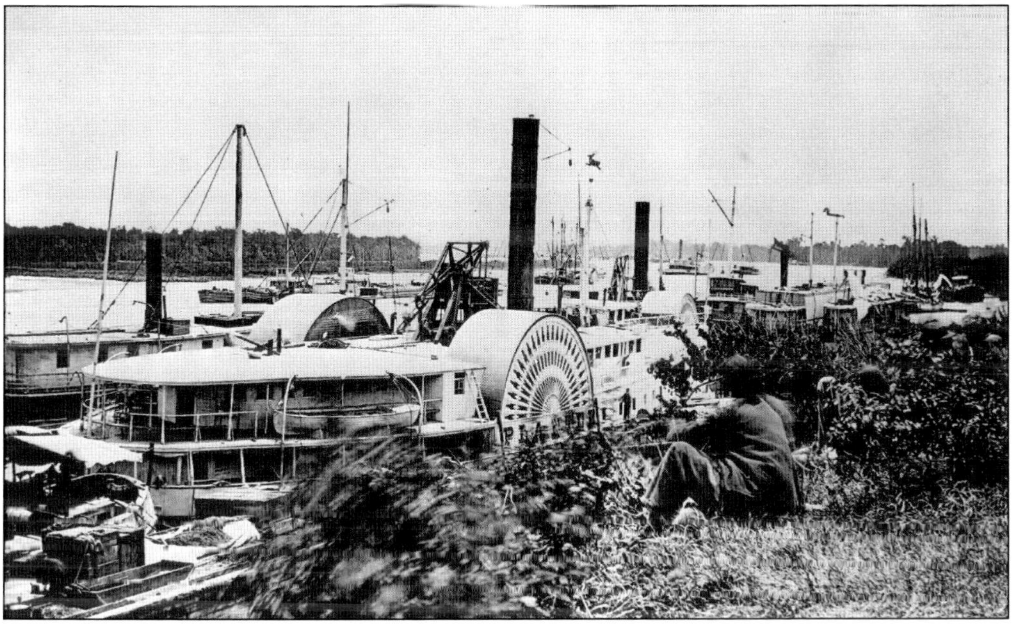

After West Point fell to Union forces in 1862, the Union army under Gen. George McClellan moved troops and supplies up the Pamunkey River to the landing at White House Plantation, where it could use the newly laid Richmond & York Railway tracks in its march to take Richmond. When the Union forces first took White House Plantation, Mary Anna Randolph Custis Lee, the great-granddaughter of Martha Washington and wife of Robert E. Lee, was there in residence. The original home of her illustrious ancestor had burned and been rebuilt. Despite her pleas to remember that the plantation had been the location of the Washingtons' marriage, Union troops torched the home as they left. (Courtesy of the Mariner's Museum.)

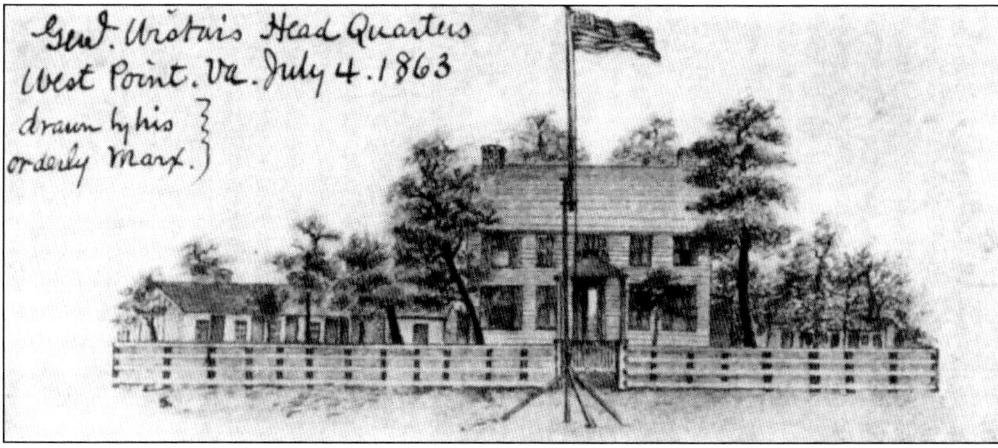

The former home of Carter Braxton was used as headquarters of Union general Isaac Wistar, who commanded the thousands of Union troops encamped at West Point. This sketch of the Braxton home was made by a Union soldier on July 4, 1863. After the war, the house became the Grove Hotel, the center of the town's social life and makeshift house of worship for local congregations. It burned down in the Great Fire of 1903. (Courtesy of James M.H. Harris Jr.)

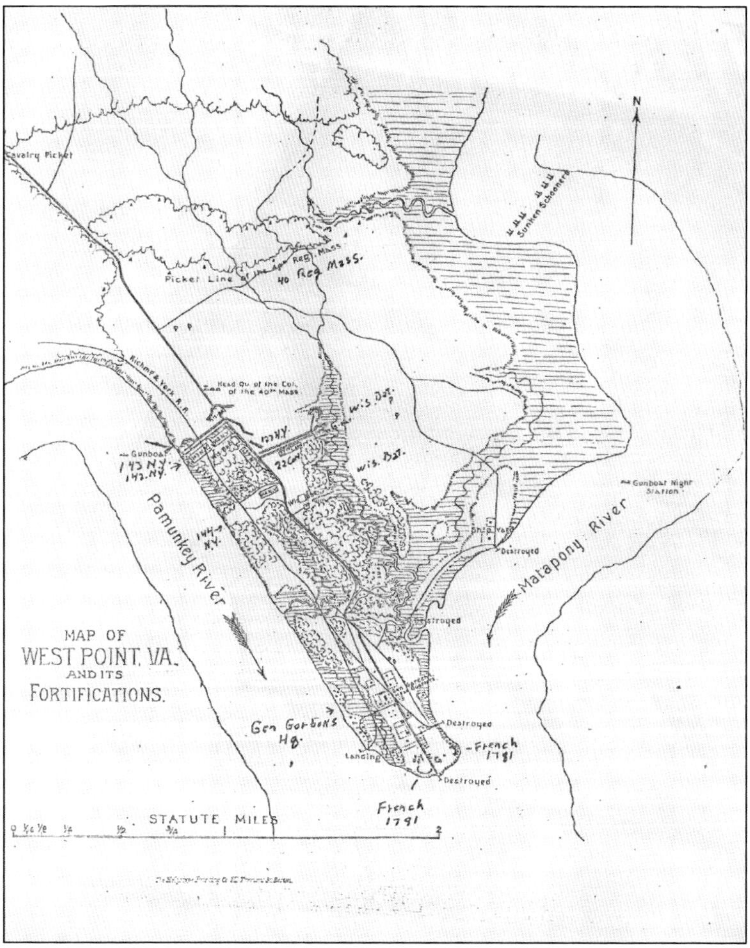

This map of West Point was made during the Civil War for the United States military. Note the sunken schooners in the Mattaponi and the markings of where the French artillery had been placed in 1781. The word "Destroyed" marks the wharfs burned by retreating Confederate troops. (Courtesy of William J. Addison.)

After the Civil War, veteran Joseph Upsher Fogg and his wife, Annie T. Fogg, took up residence at West Point, where he operated a harness shop and served as a volunteer fireman. He served in the Confederate army and was with Gen. Robert E. Lee at Appomattox. In addition to Confederate veterans, several Union veterans settled in West Point after the war because they had found Tidewater Virginia to be to their liking during their military service. (Courtesy of Marianna Chestnutt.)

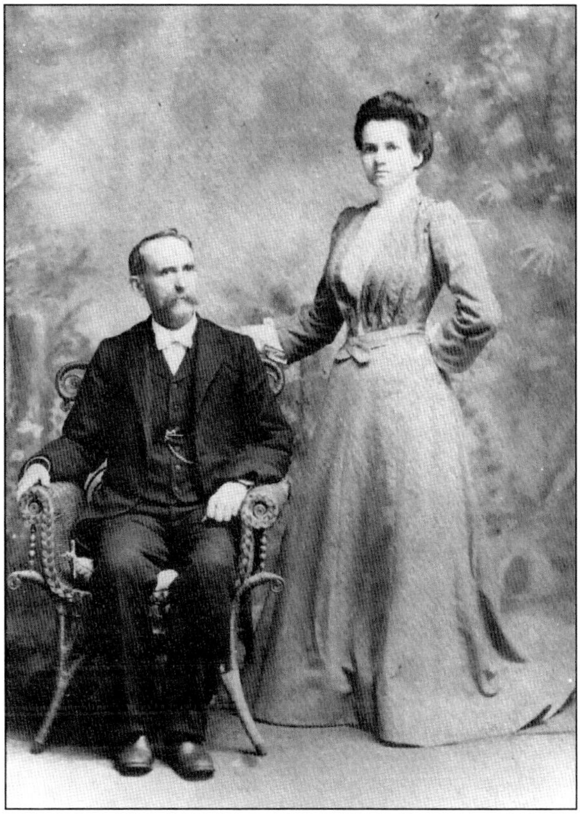

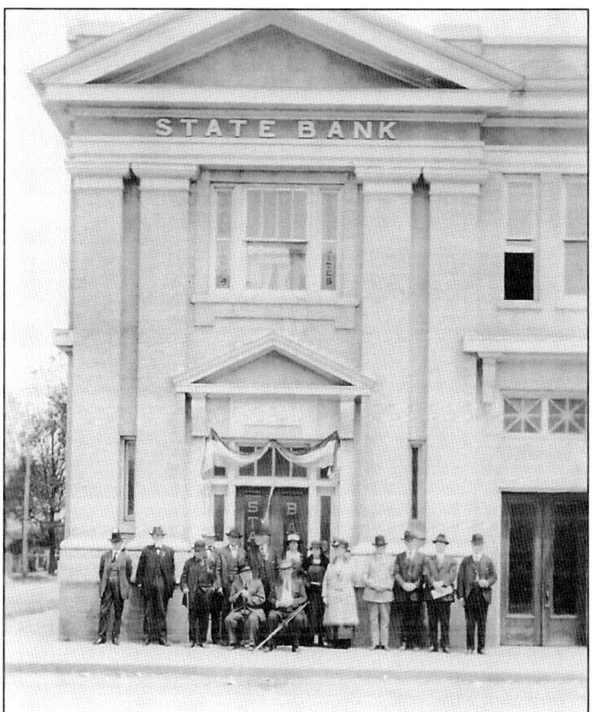

Civil War veterans from West Point and the surrounding area posed in front of the State Bank at the corner of Main and Eighth Streets during a reunion in the 1920s. The units from West Point participated in a number of important battles, including Pickett's Charge at Gettysburg, where they were troops that rushed "the Angle," the center of the Union lines where the fiercest combat took place. They had trained at West Point in the first months of the war under the command of Maj. Harrison B. Tomlin. (Courtesy of William J. Addison.)

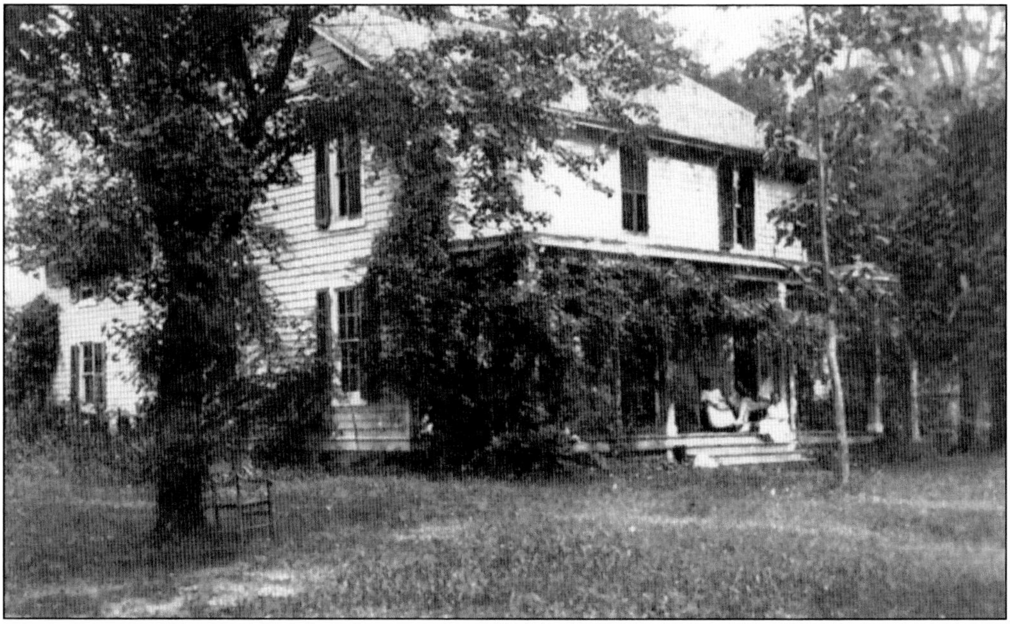

After the Civil War, Robert E. Lee Jr., a son of the Confederate general, built this home along the Pamunkey River at Romancoke, a Custis and Washington holding inherited through his mother's family located on the outskirts of West Point. The Romancoke tract has been pivotal in West Point history. It is believed to be where William Claiborne landed militia to fight the Indians following the 1622 uprising and where Claiborne's property began and the West family's ended when they became the first English to settle the area. It is now owned by the Olsson family.

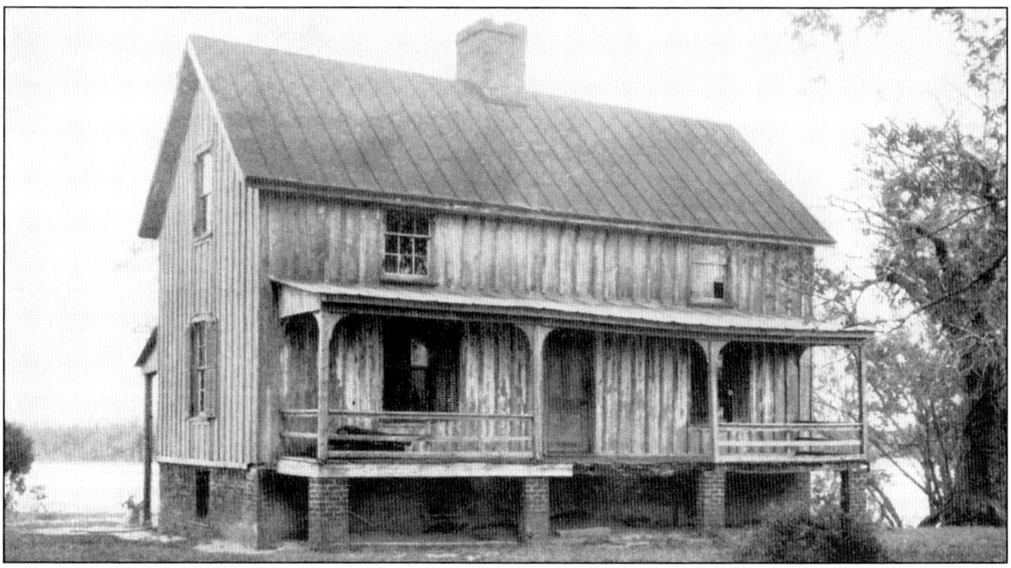

Robert E. Lee's son William Henry Fitzhugh Lee lived in this Colonial building on the grounds of his ancestral home, White House Plantation, after the war. He served in the Confederate army as a cavalry general and later in the US Congress. This building, Rockohoc, was located near the site of Fort Royal on the Pamunkey River, erected after the 1644 native uprising as one of a series of forts that marked the frontier of English settlement at the time. (Courtesy of James M.H. Harris Jr.)

Three

A Thriving Transportation Hub

The Civil War was an economic disaster for Virginia, but the end of the war ironically brought unprecedented prosperity to West Point. The railroad bridge was rebuilt, beginning in 1873, and new tracks were laid all the way to the wharfs of a new port at the mouth of the Pamunkey River, making the town a transportation hub for the region and a port of call for ships from near and far. During this time, it became the nation's sixth-busiest cotton port, as well as a regional center—"the big city"—where the rural folk of the region came to shop and conduct business.

In 1870, the Virginia General Assembly granted a charter of incorporation to West Point, giving it an independent government apart from King William County, even though less than 100 people lived there at the time. To the present day, it has had not only its own government, but its own police department, school system, and municipal services.

By 1895, the town had over 3,000 inhabitants and a thriving central business district in the middle of the peninsula surrounding the former home of Carter Braxton. That downtown sprung up following a fire among the businesses built closer to the railway tracks. But the economic basis of the town was fragile, based as it was primarily on the terminus of the Southern Railway. In 1897, the company announced that it was moving the seaport terminus to Portsmouth, with its deeper port and greater rail connections. Within weeks of the announcement, hundreds of families had left. Businesses closed. Homes stood empty with little hope of being sold. It would be many decades before West Point would regain its previous level of population and prosperity.

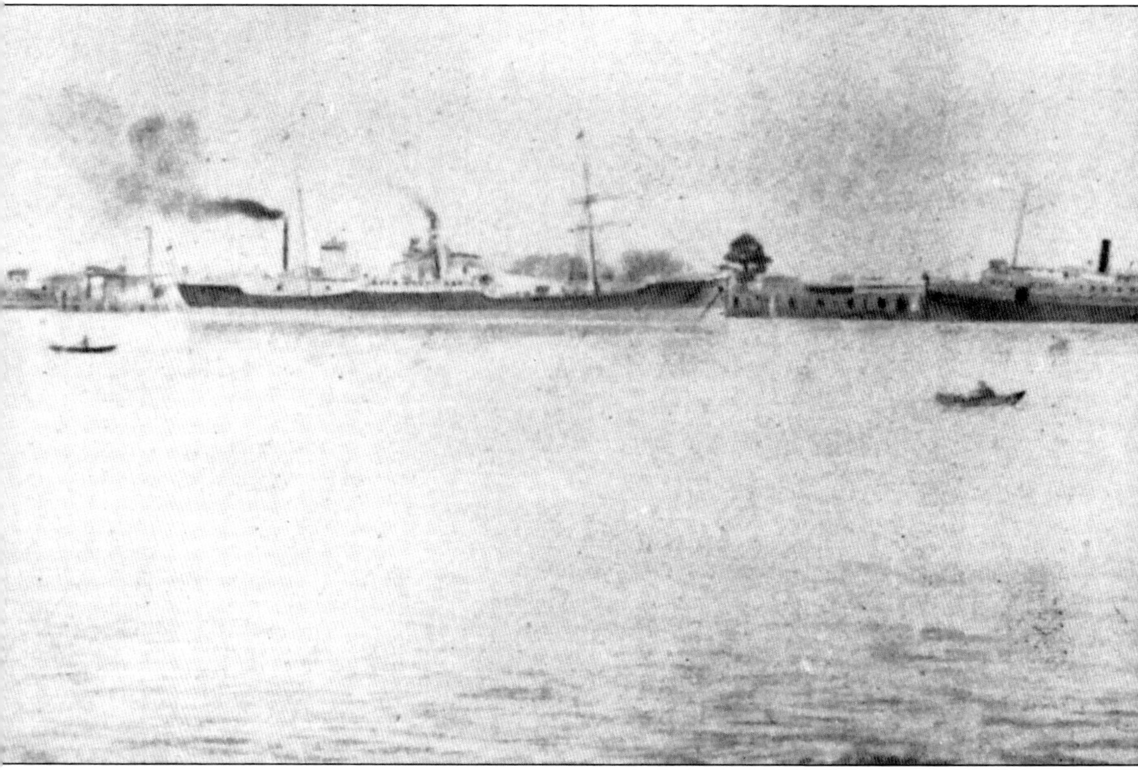

This undated drawing, printed by Bendann Company of Baltimore, depicts the bustling port of West Point after the Civil War, when the port and railway came under the ownership of the Richmond & West Point Terminal Railway & Warehouse Company, which was finally able to

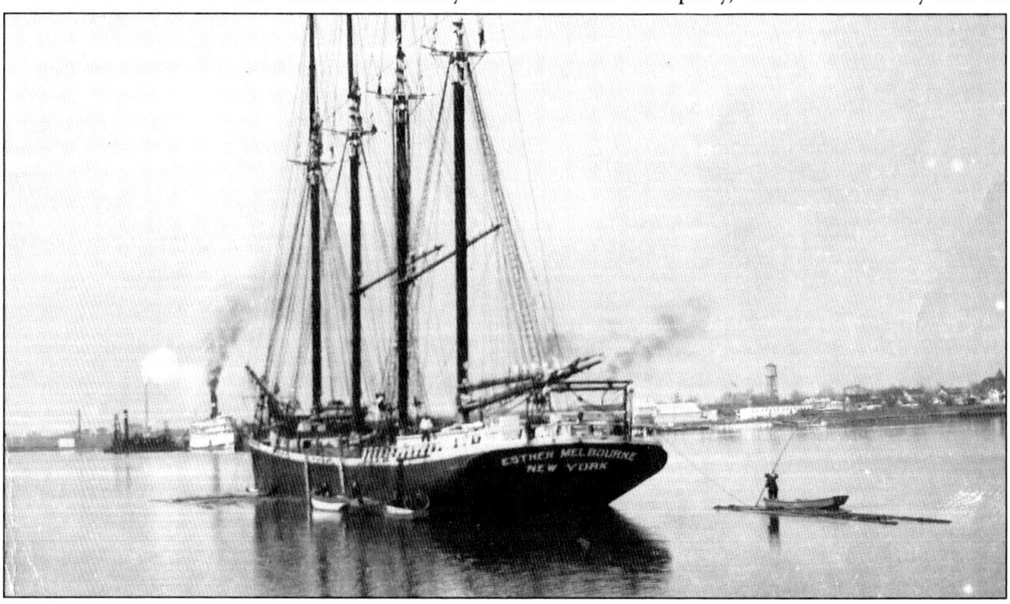

Small boats navigate logs as a schooner takes on a load of lumber at West Point around 1928. Note the dredger next to the steamboat docked at the wharf in the left background. (Courtesy of James M.H. Harris Jr.)

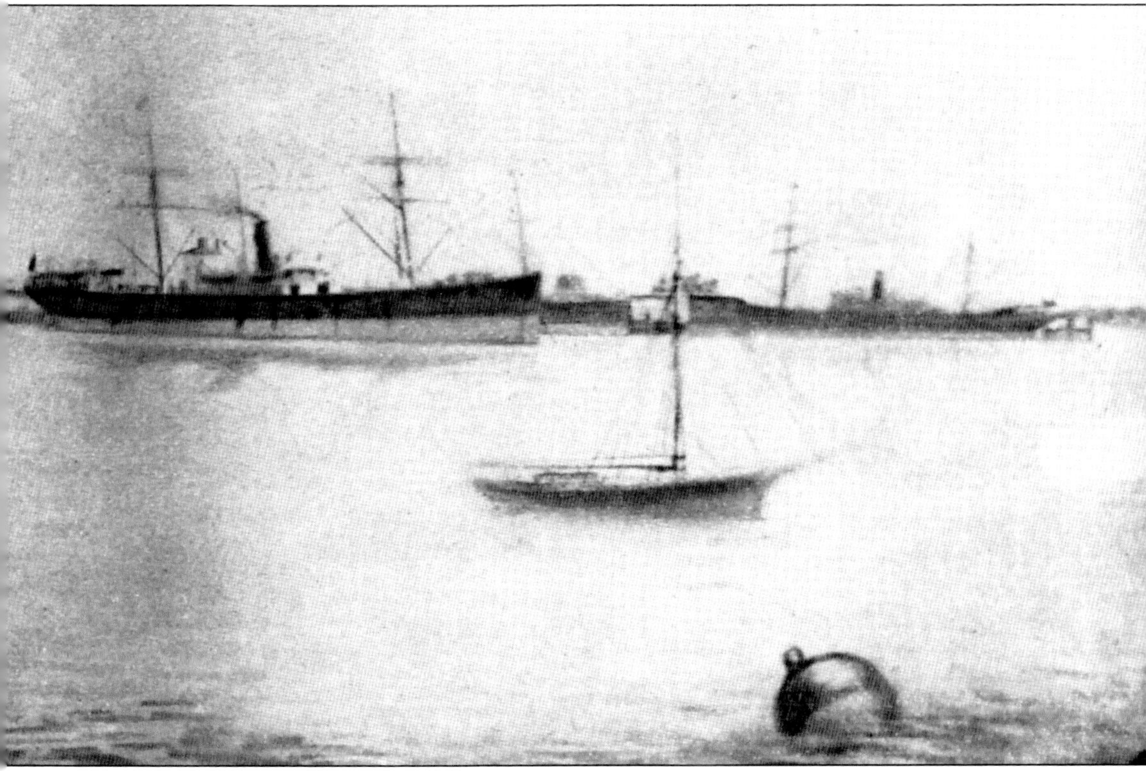

complete the terminus. At one time, the port was the sixth-busiest cotton port in the United States. (Courtesy of the Mariners' Museum.)

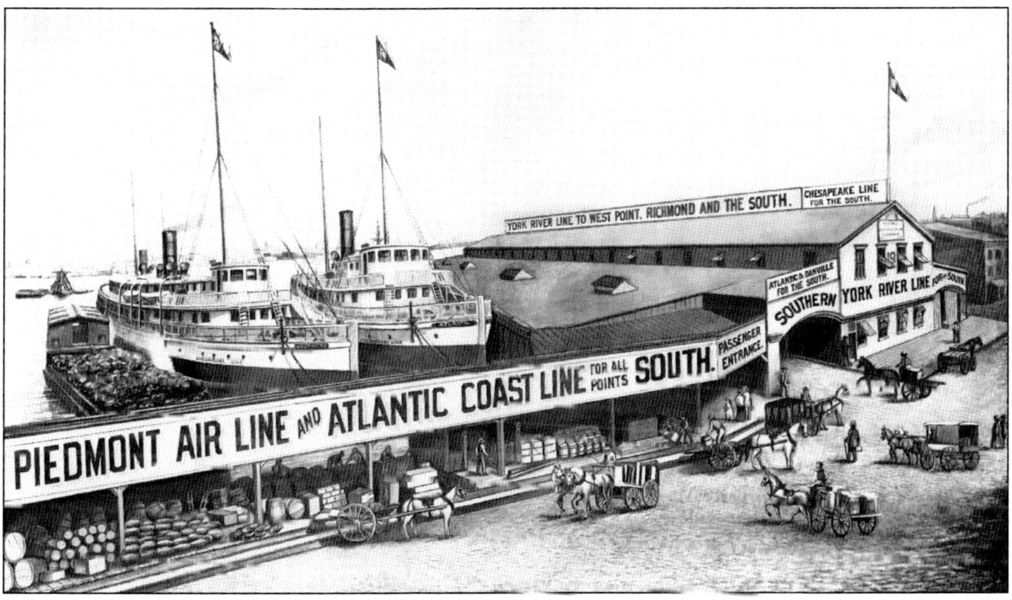

The port at West Point quickly became the region's transportation hub after its infrastructure was completed. A natural by-product was that it also became the market town of the region. Its population grew from a few hundred to thousands. This image depicts a Baltimore port with ships loading the York River Line to West Point. (Courtesy of the Mariners' Museum.)

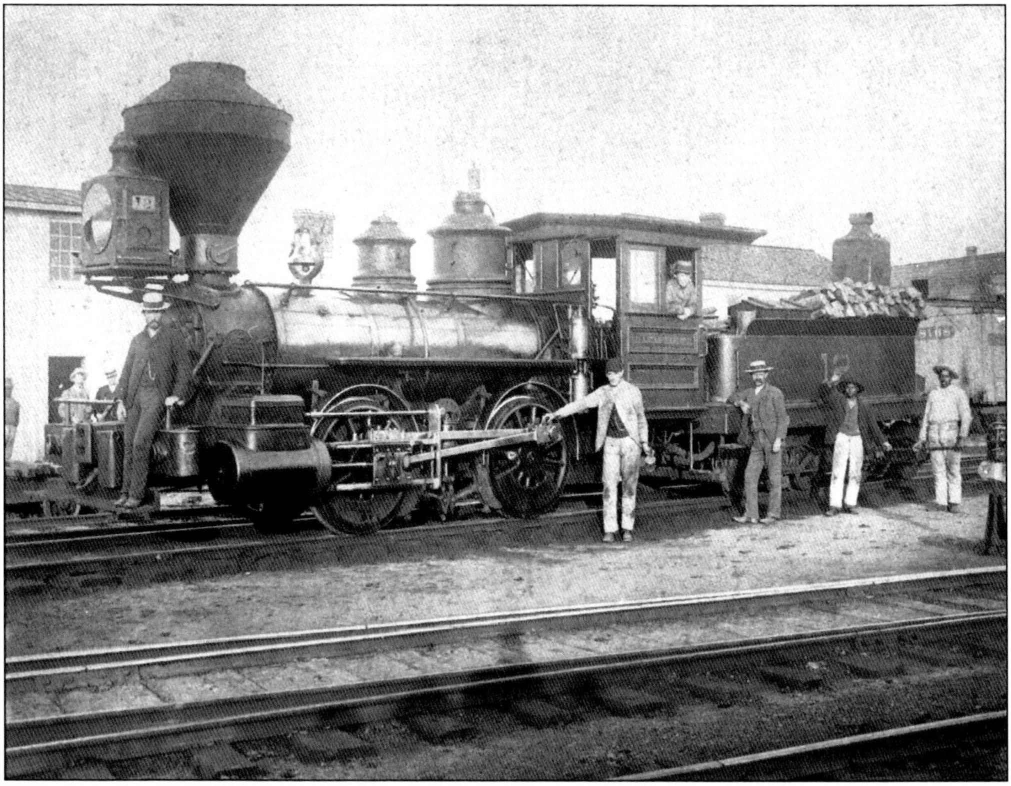

Following the Civil War, it took several years for the railroad bridge at White House Plantation to be rebuilt and the tracks to be restored after they were scavenged or burned by both armies. By 1880, West Point was filled with the sounds of trains. (Courtesy of the Mariner's Museum.)

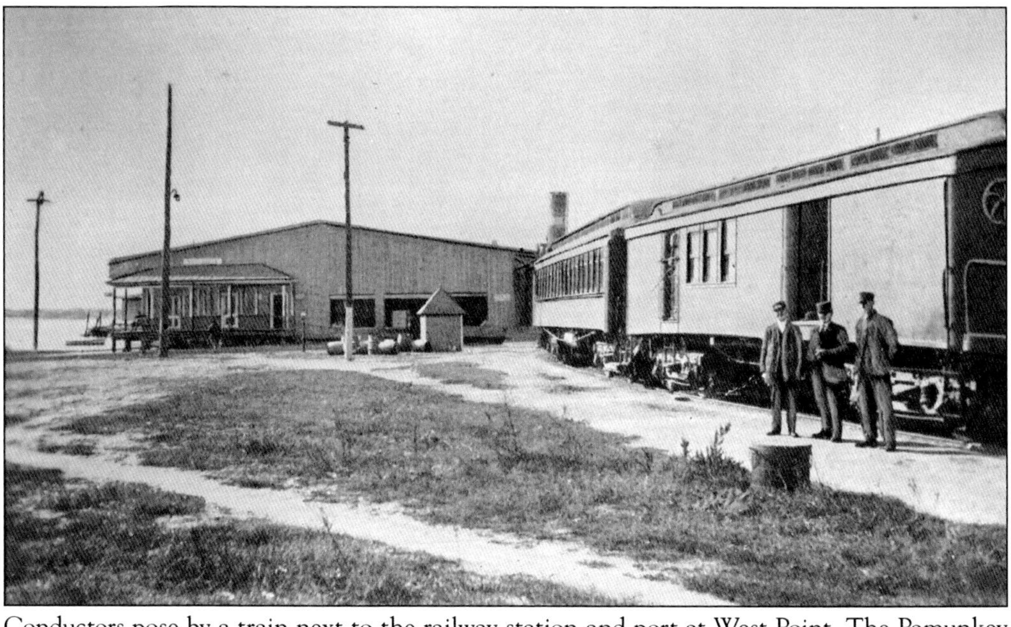

Conductors pose by a train next to the railway station and port at West Point. The Pamunkey River is to the left. (Courtesy of the Mariner's Museum.)

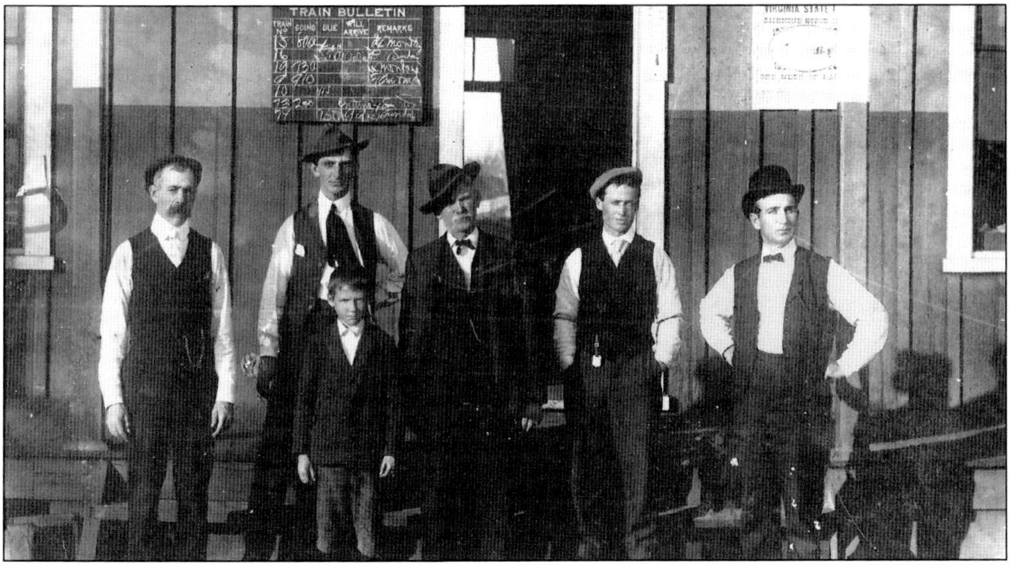

In 1893, the Richmond & York River Railway was reorganized and became the Southern Railway under the management of J.P. Morgan of New York. Here, the proud men of the West Point station pose below the train schedule around 1900. The men from left to right are Charles B. Stark and R. Bruce Ware (clerks), George Field (telegrapher) and his son Bernard, Sam Hardy (handyman), Robert C. Carden (station agent). (Courtesy of the Mariner's Museum and William J. Addison.)

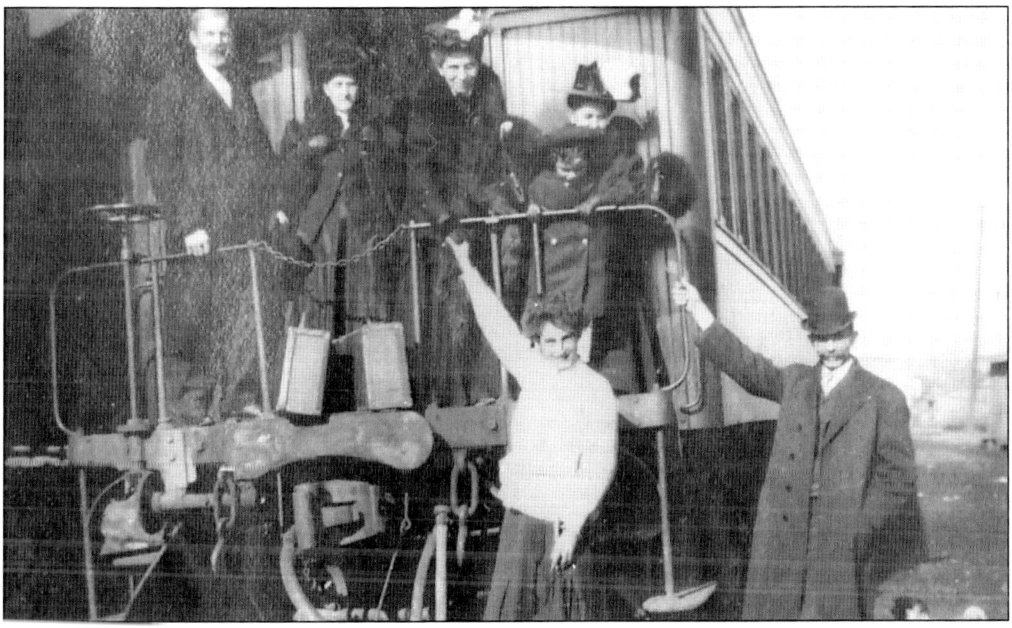

Trains brought not only cargo to and from the ships, they also brought passengers. It became fashionable for ladies in Richmond to take a train to West Point and, from there, catch a steamer for Baltimore, where they could shop for goods not available at home. Trains also brought vacationers seeking the beauty and health benefits of the rivers. Round-trip excursions by train between West Point and Richmond cost 50¢ in 1900. Many holidaymakers would come just for the day on Saturdays in the summer. (Courtesy of Dennis Roane.)

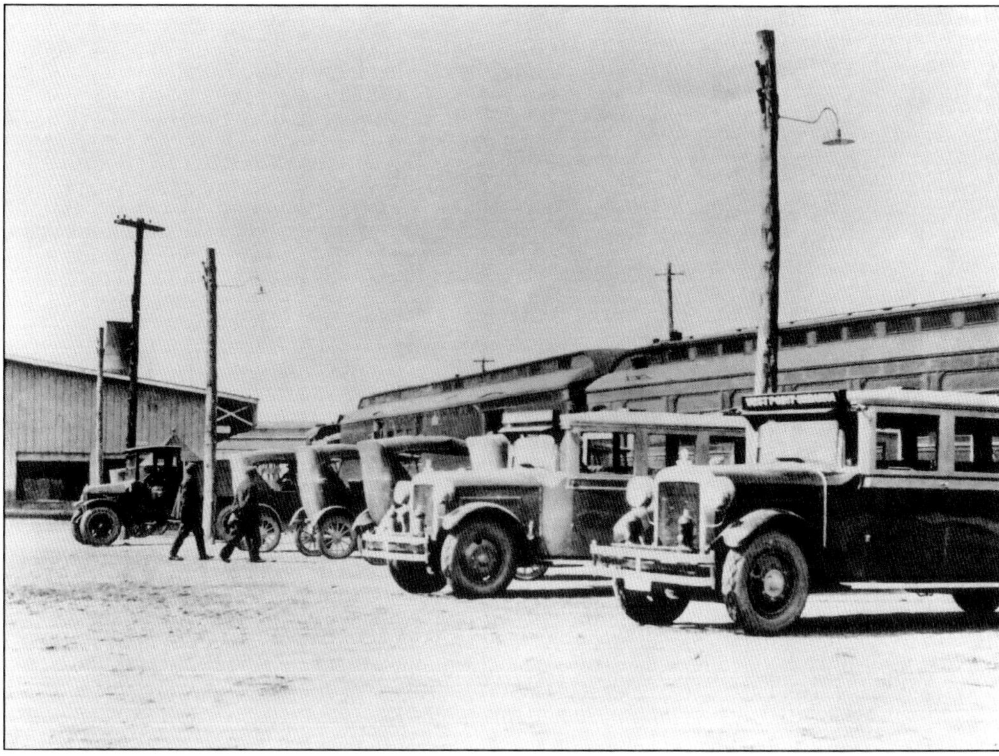

In this photograph from the 1920s, buses line up along the railway tracks at the port. The bus in the foreground shuttled between West Point and Urbanna. (Courtesy of the Mariners' Museum.)

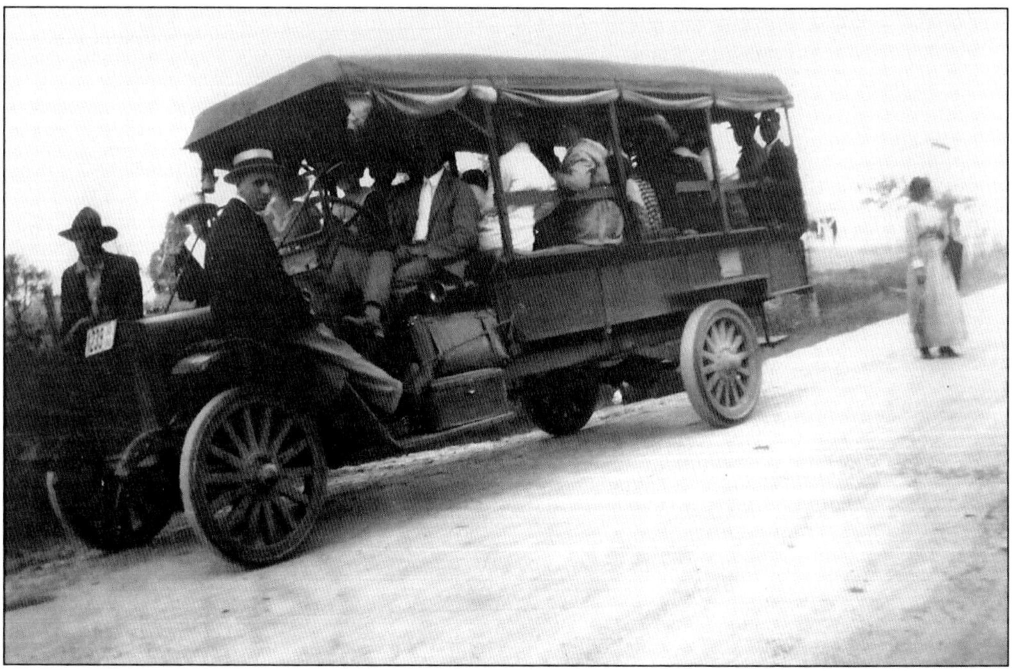

This bus is carrying people to and from the port and rail station at West Point to towns and farms in the surrounding area in the years before World War I.

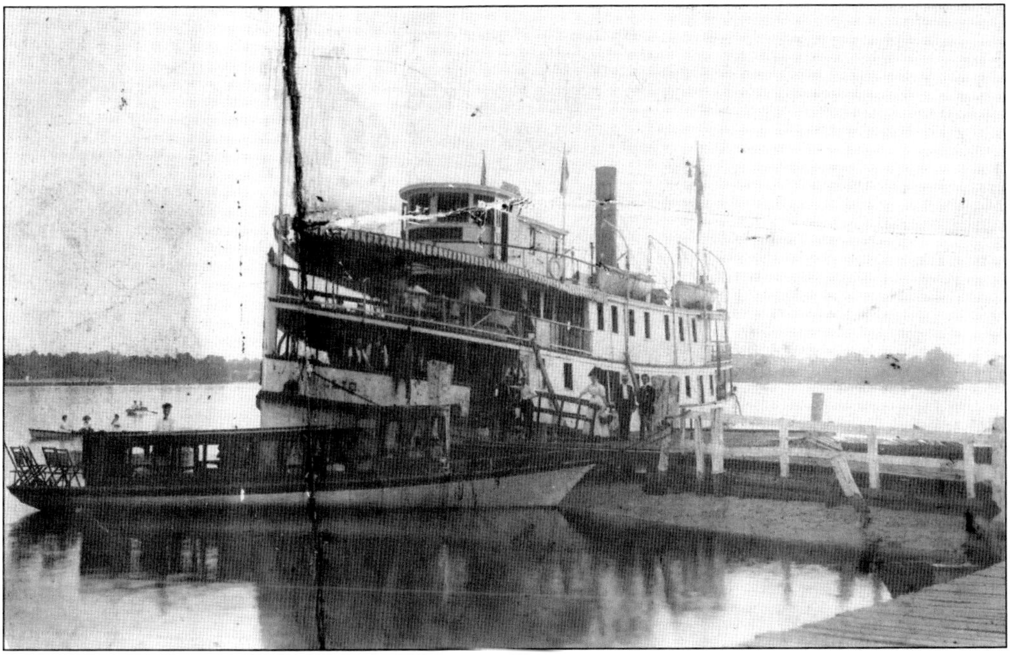

In 1909, passengers disembark from the *Clio,* one of the steamships to ply the three rivers, built in 1889. In addition to the port facilities at West Point, many of the small towns along the Pamunkey and Mattaponi had docks. The steamers could go as far as Walkerton and Aylett, depending on their draft. The *Clio*'s usual route was on the York and Mattaponi. (Courtesy of the Mariners' Museum.)

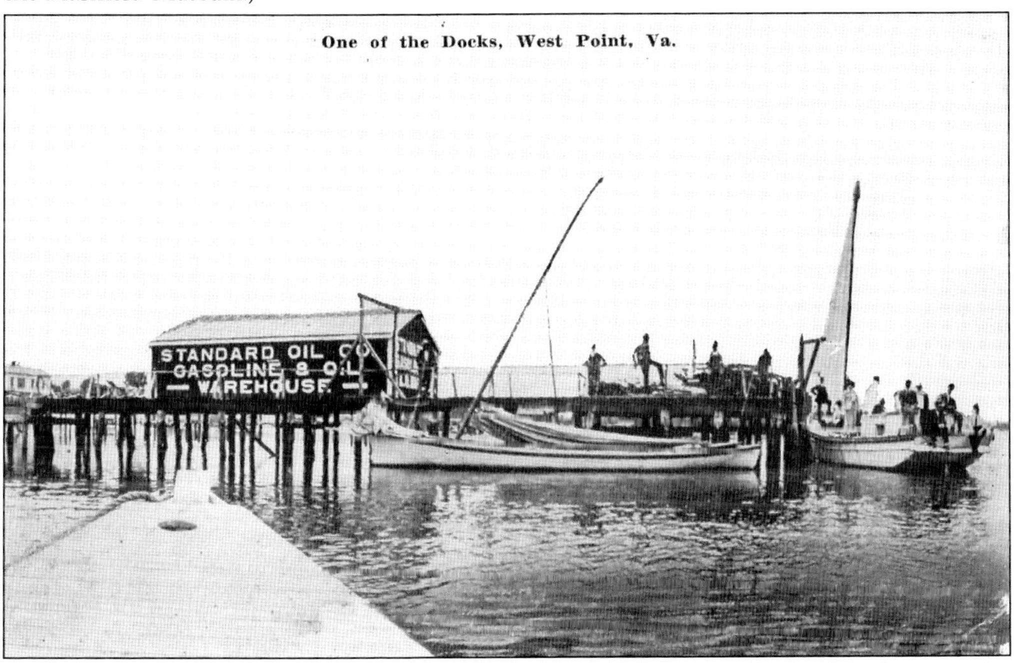

After the Civil War, the wharfs on the Pamunkey River became the focus of the boats in the area; however, there continued to be a few small docks on the Mattaponi River, especially at Glass Island, where the oil companies continue to operate today. (Courtesy of Richard Hosfield.)

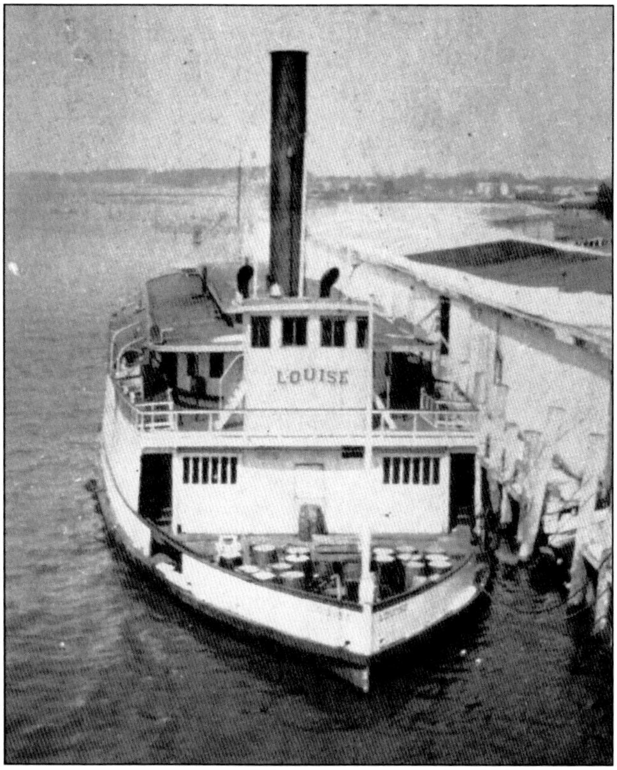

The iron-hull paddle wheeler *Louise*, shown here docked at West Point, was one of the most frequent visitors to the wharfs after 1906, when she replaced the *Elm City*. This *Louise* is not to be confused with another steamer of the same name that ran between Baltimore and Tolcester Beach, Maryland. (Courtesy of the Mariners' Museum.)

Passengers survey the scenery from the upper deck of the *Louise*. (Courtesy of Dennis Roane.)

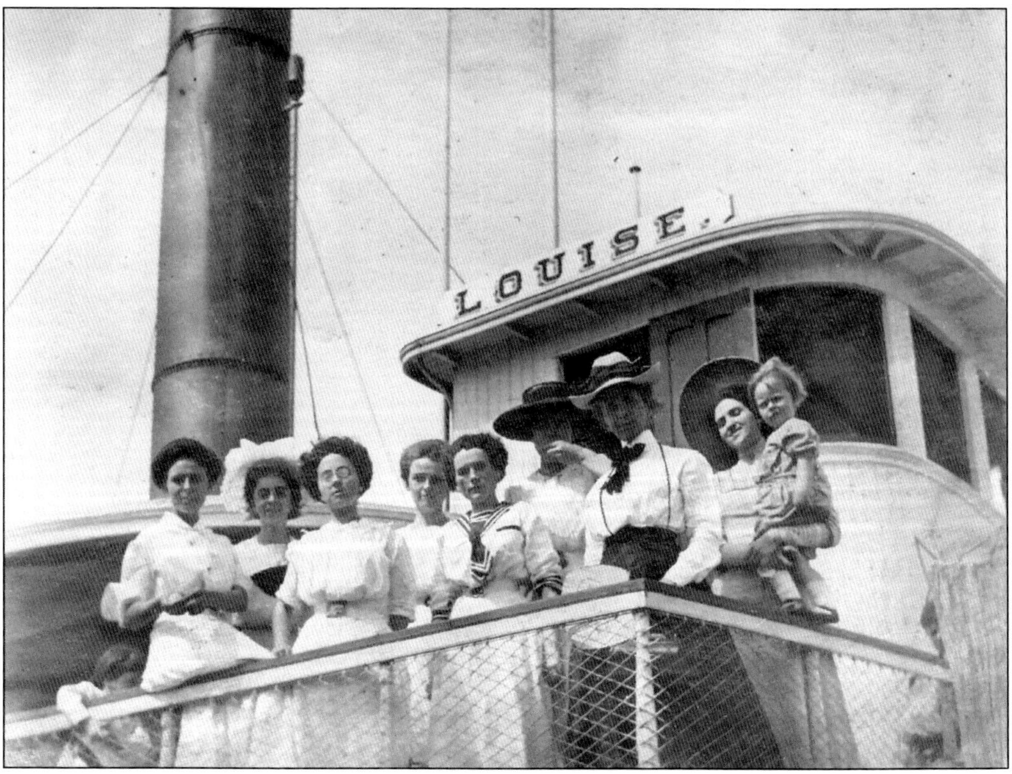

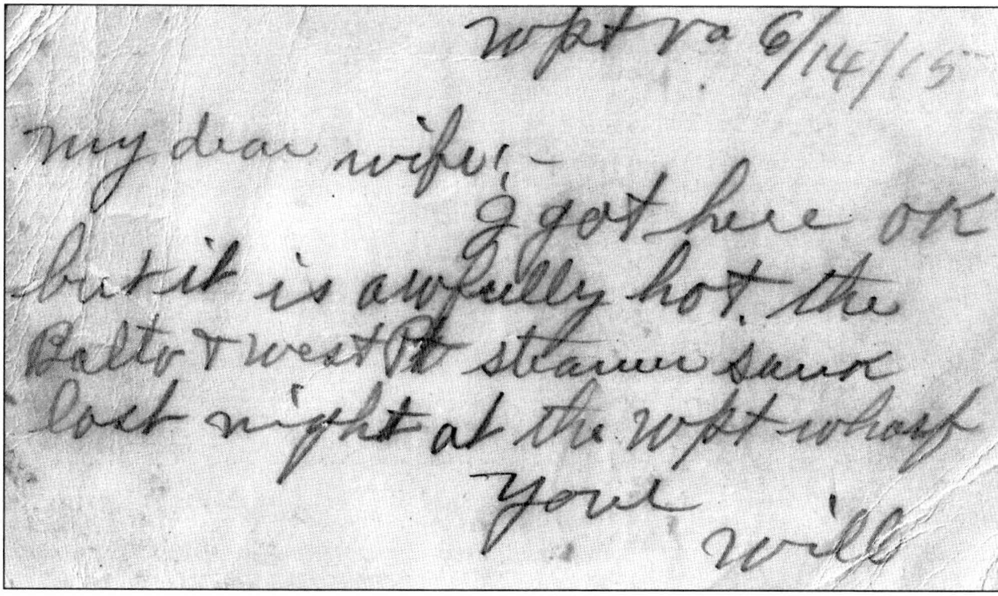
W Pt Va 6/14/15
My dear wife:—
I got here OK
but it is awfully hot. the
Balto & West Pt steamer sank
last night at the W Pt wharf
Your
Will

The message on the back of a postcard from one traveler passing through West Point on June 14, 1915, remarked upon a newsworthy happening. It reads, "My dear wife: I got here OK but it is awfully hot. The Balt. and West Pt. steamer sank last night at the W Pt wharf. Your Will." (Courtesy of William J. Addison.)

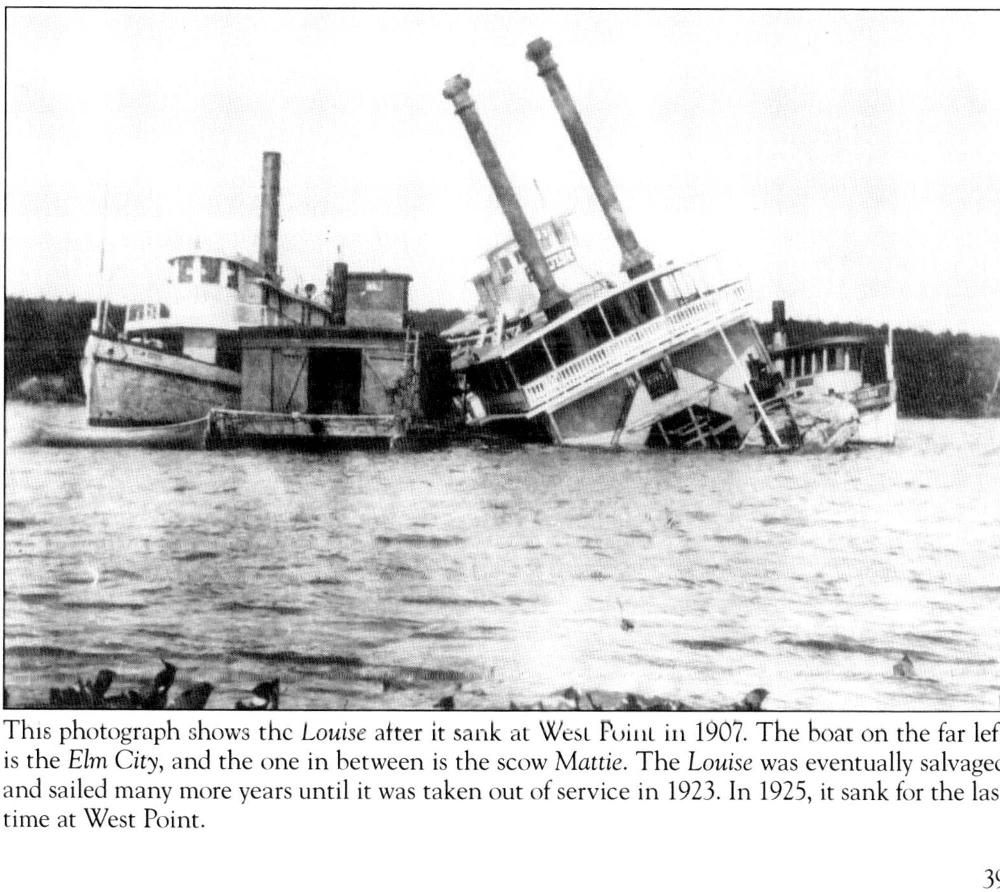

This photograph shows the *Louise* after it sank at West Point in 1907. The boat on the far left is the *Elm City*, and the one in between is the scow *Mattie*. The *Louise* was eventually salvaged and sailed many more years until it was taken out of service in 1923. In 1925, it sank for the last time at West Point.

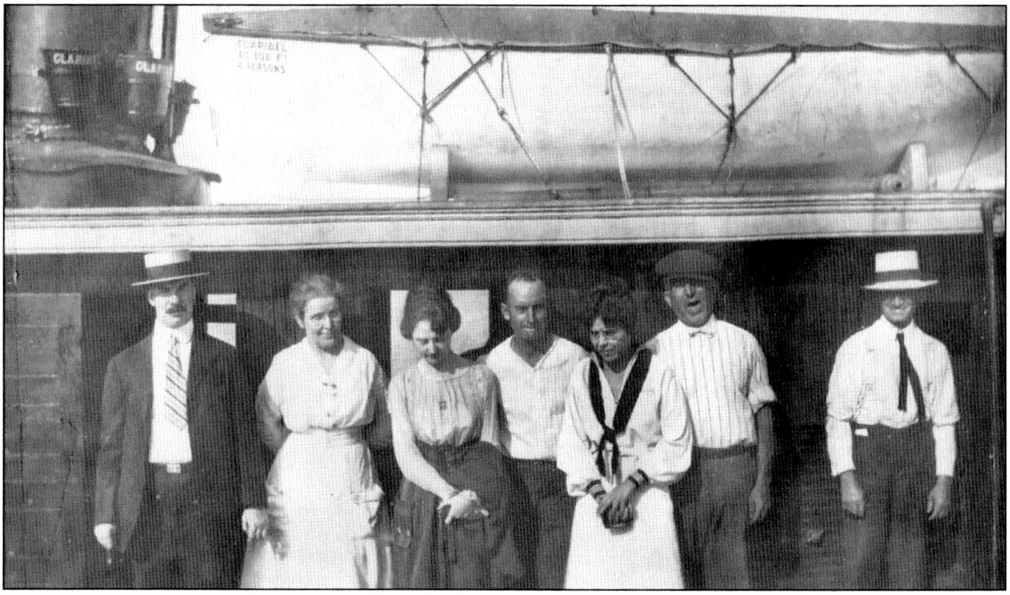

Passengers enjoy watching the launching of the SS *R.L. Newman* at the West Point shipyard in July 1915 from the vantage point of a yacht on the Mattaponi River.

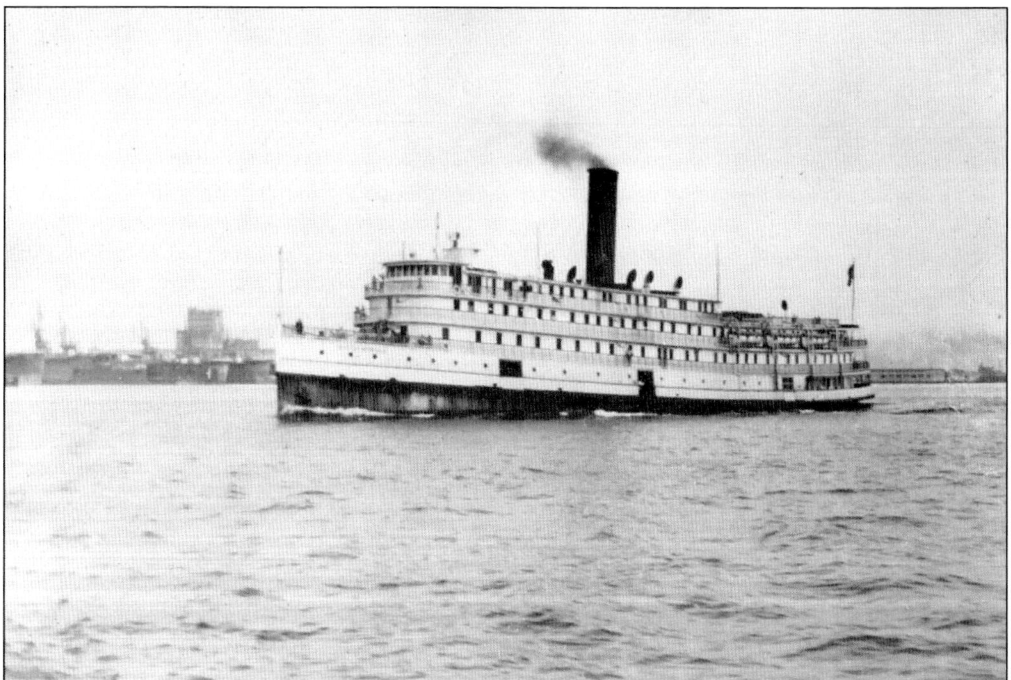

The *City of Norfolk* of the Chesapeake Steamship Company (and later of the Old Bay Line) was one of the steamers to dock at West Point. Ships from the same company with regular service to West Point from cities such as Baltimore and Norfolk would leave the two ports at the same time and cross paths halfway. (Courtesy of William J. Addison.)

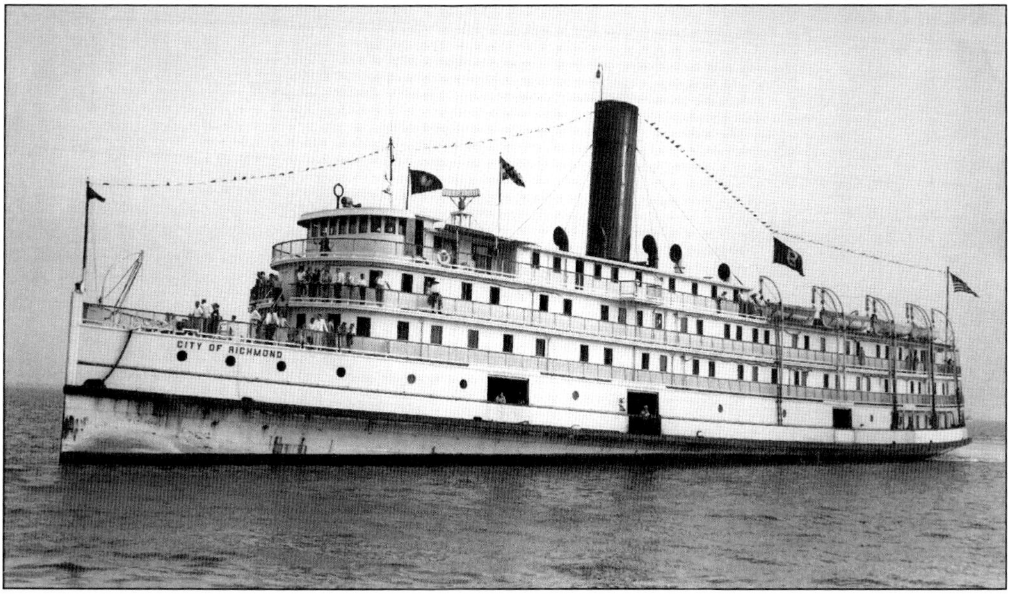

The *City of Richmond* was a regular arrival at West Point. This luckless vessel sank at West Point in 1915. Four months later, she collided with a schooner, and in 1927, she did the same with the steamer *City of Annapolis*. Nonetheless, she was one of the last of the great Chesapeake Bay steamers in service until her final retirement in 1962. (Courtesy of the Mariners' Museum.)

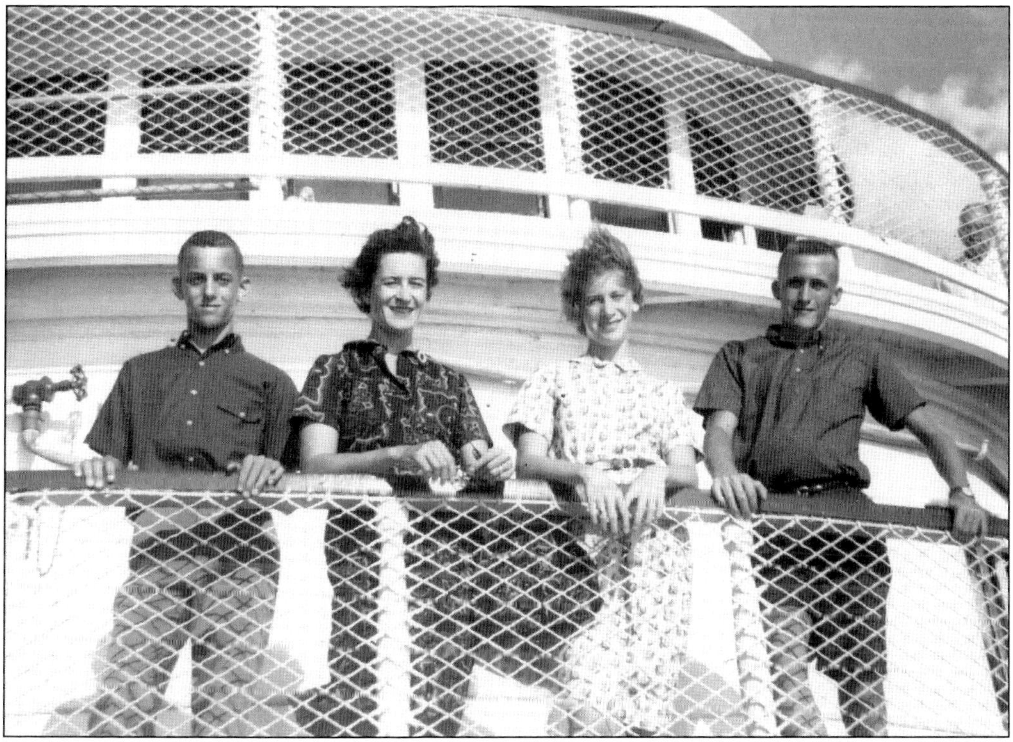

The Bland family from West Point enjoys the last trip of the *City of Richmond*, embarking from Deltaville in 1962. Shown from left to right are Bill, Gertrude, Beverly, and Tyler Bland III. (Courtesy of Tyler Bland III.)

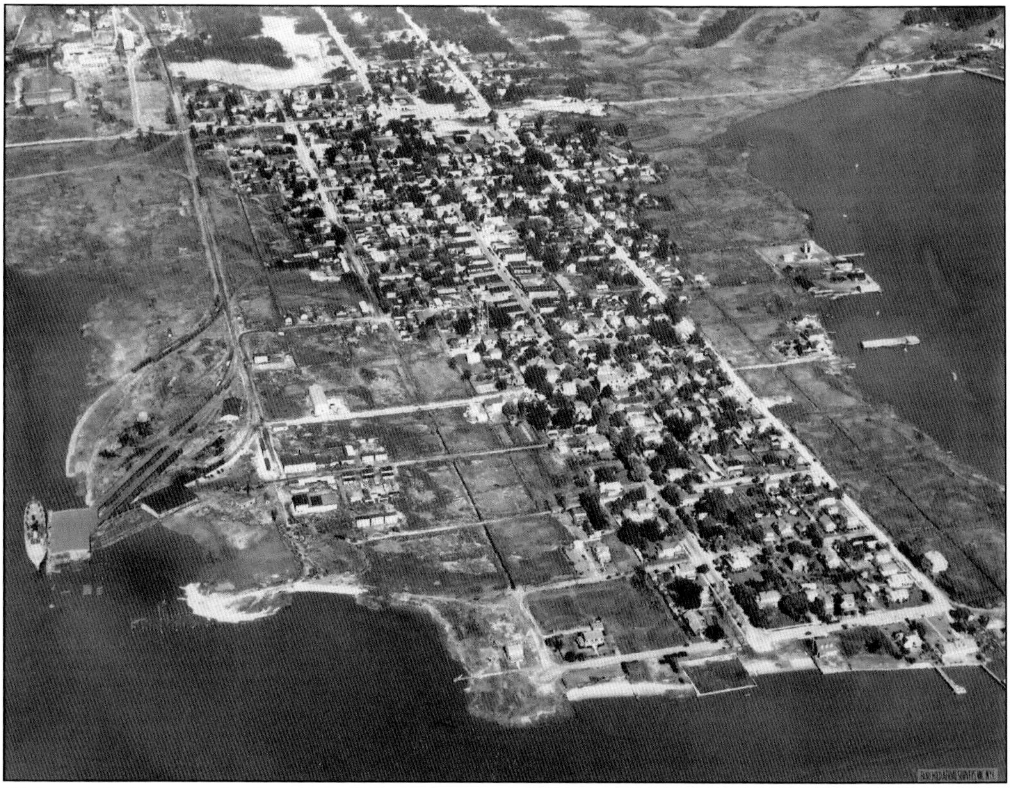

This aerial photograph shows the point of the peninsula in the 1930s. The port, with a steamship docked at the wharf, is visible on the lower left.

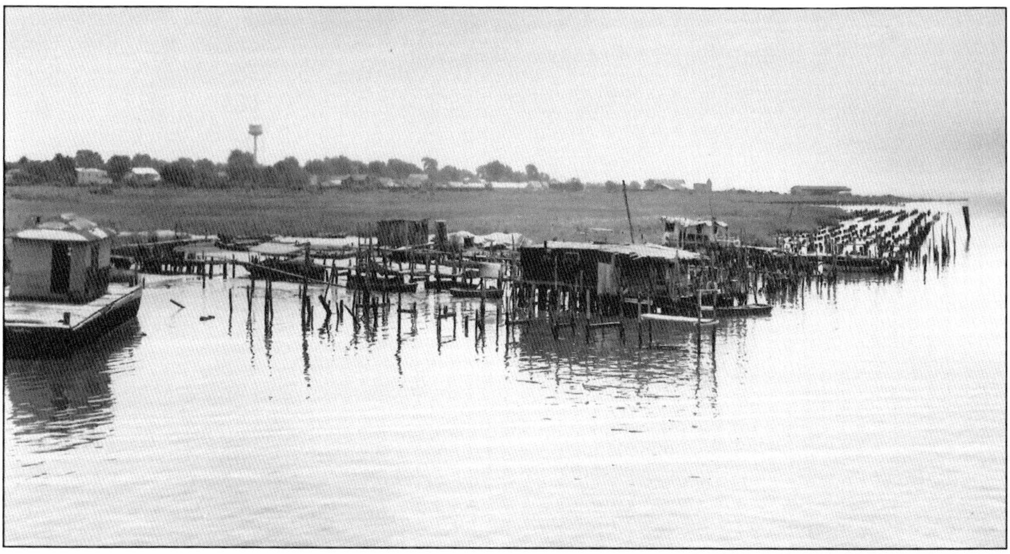

Steamship service to West Point ended in the 1940s. The wharf and other buildings of the port quickly disappeared as a result of storms and fires or were demolished, leaving only pilings and other faint traces of the transportation hub that once brought prosperity to the town. Remnants of the boardwalk complex along the tip of the peninsula are visible just offshore. The small building was a fishing shack.

Four

DELIGHTS OF THE SEA

At the same time that steamboats were coming into use, New York City began to deplete its local oyster beds. Northern suppliers looked south for another source of the delectable bivalve and discovered the bounty of the York River. West Point's oyster industry flourished as faster transportation and commercial icehouses made it possible to provide oysters to restaurants in New York and Philadelphia. York River oysters became famous.

In the late 19th century, a number of small hotels and boardinghouses dotted the town, as did a handful of waterside saloons and establishments that catered to gentlemen looking for a place to gamble. A grand hotel was built at the tip of the peninsula on the site where cannons had been placed during the Revolution and the Civil War. The former site of war machines along the York River bank became a leisure park with a wooden boardwalk. Piers jutted out into the York, allowing visitors to stroll over the water and enjoy the spectacular views. There was a crude swimming pool and a pavilion for picnickers. By the end of the 19th century, a small amusement park with a roller coaster and merry-go-round would be added.

The *West Point Virginian* newspaper was one of several voices for temperance in a town that had 14 saloons and "gentlemen's clubs." When the Prohibition laws banned the sale of alcohol in the 1920s, they effectively destroyed many of the businesses along the riverbanks that catered to sailors and men seeking whiskey and gambling. The rivers still attracted bathers, boaters, and fishermen, but the crowds dwindled. New resorts along the Chesapeake Bay and at the Atlantic Ocean became more accessible and made the rivers seem too tame.

By the mid-1920s, the Terminal Hotel was no more, the saloons and clubs were closed, and Beach Park was losing money. It was subdivided and sold as parcels, and the homes constructed on the old park now grace First Street. The residents could still enjoy the comings and goings of the steamers, crabbers, and oystermen, but the excitement of the boardwalk gave way to the sounds of neighborhood children playing. West Point transformed from being a town based upon the bounties of the sea to one based upon an abundance of trees.

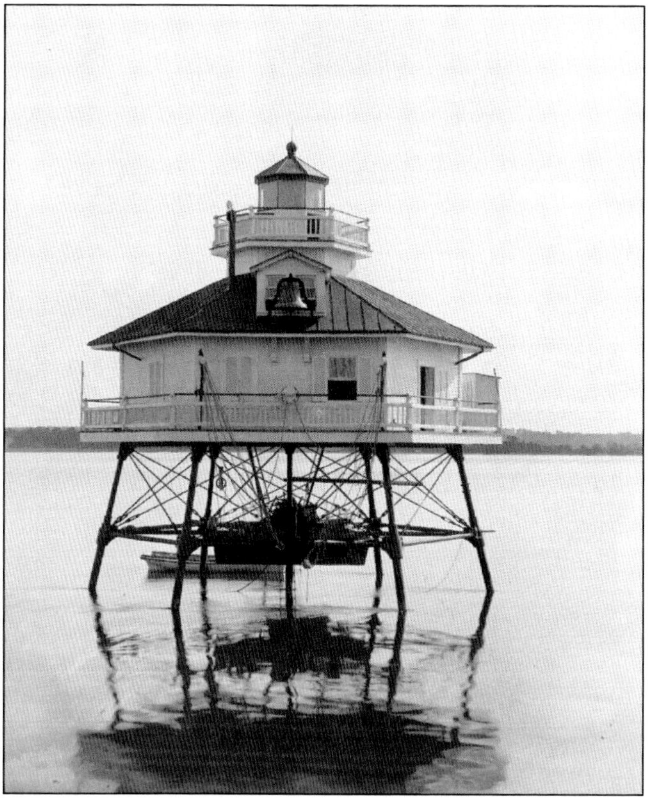

Bells Rock Lighthouse, seen in this 1885 photograph, was erected in 1881 near West Point to assist the York River traffic. The 40-foot-high structure was rebuilt in 1928. The lighthouse keeper, Sam Taliaferro, who lived to be over 105, lived in the upper section and kept livestock on the open bottom deck. The present lighthouse incorporates a portion of the original platform. (Courtesy of the Mariners' Museum.)

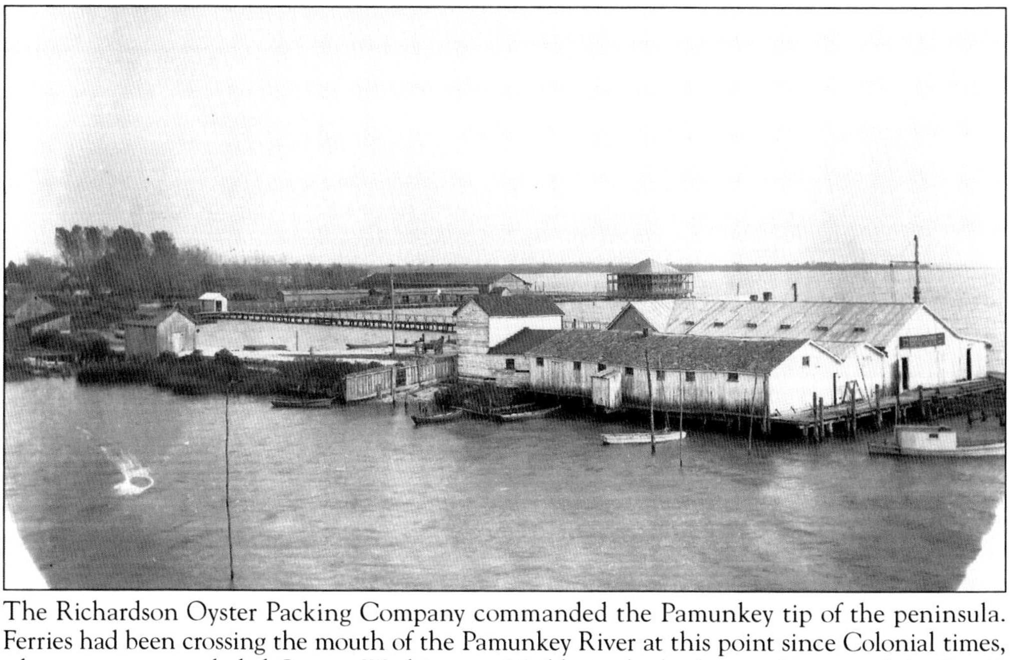

The Richardson Oyster Packing Company commanded the Pamunkey tip of the peninsula. Ferries had been crossing the mouth of the Pamunkey River at this point since Colonial times, when customers included George Washington. Visible in the background is part of the Beach Park boardwalk and a building on it over the water that housed a bar and oyster house. This photograph was taken about 1910.

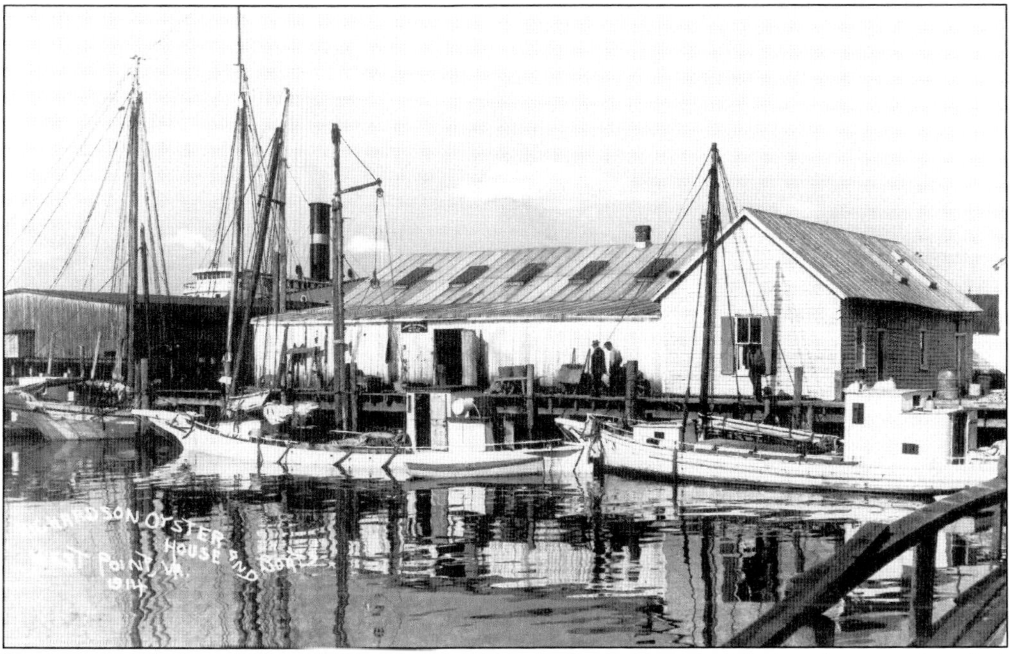

This is another view of the Richardson Oyster House, taken in 1914 by photographer A.F. Graves. The smokestack of a steamship is visible in the left background. (Courtesy of the Mariners' Museum.)

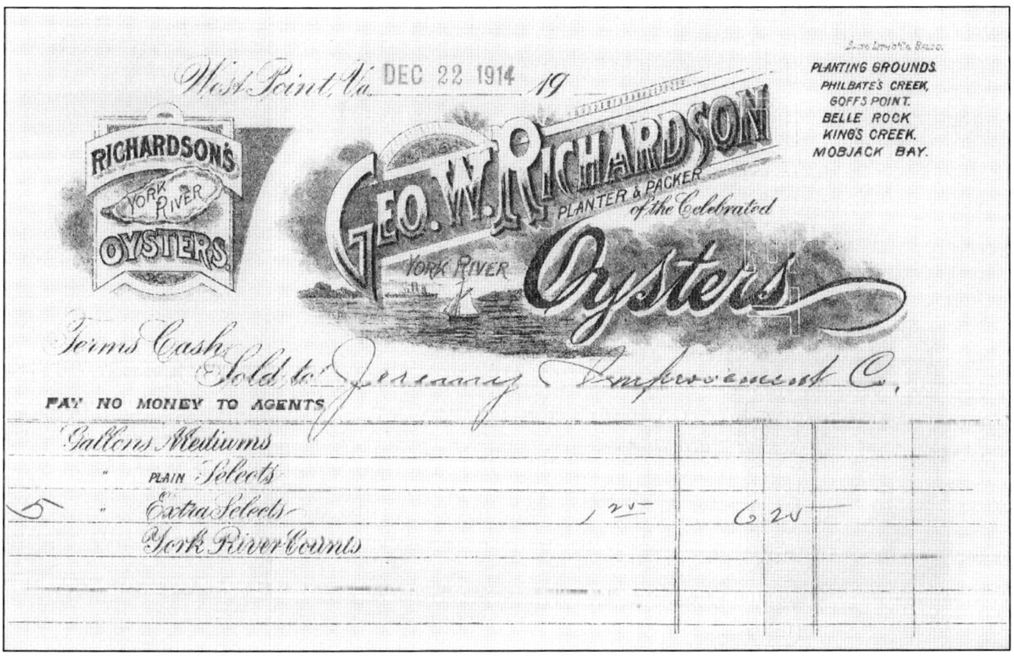

West Point, Va. DEC 22 1914 19

PLANTING GROUNDS
PHILBATE'S CREEK,
GOFF'S POINT.
BELLE ROCK
KING'S CREEK.
MOBJACK BAY.

RICHARDSON'S YORK RIVER OYSTERS

GEO. W. RICHARDSON
PLANTER & PACKER of the Celebrated
YORK RIVER
Oysters

Terms Cash
Sold to Jersey Improvement Co.
PAY NO MONEY TO AGENTS

	Gallons Mediums		
	" PLAIN Selects		
5	" Extra Selects	1 25	6 25
	York River Counts		

This 1914 invoice from the Richardson Oyster House provides, in the top right-hand corner, the exact locations where the oysters came from. (Courtesy of Carol Fetterolf.)

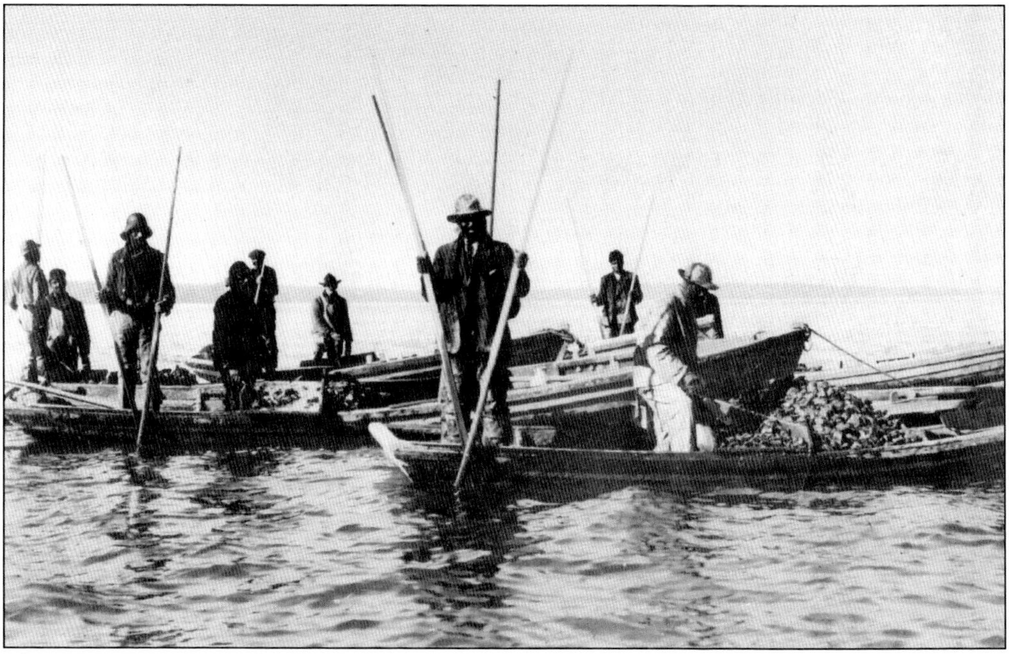

These men are tonging for oysters the traditional way. The oyster industry expanded rapidly in the mid-19th century, when steam travel and ice made it possible to provide oysters to major cities in the north. West Point and the York River became renowned for oysters. (Courtesy of the Mariners' Museum.)

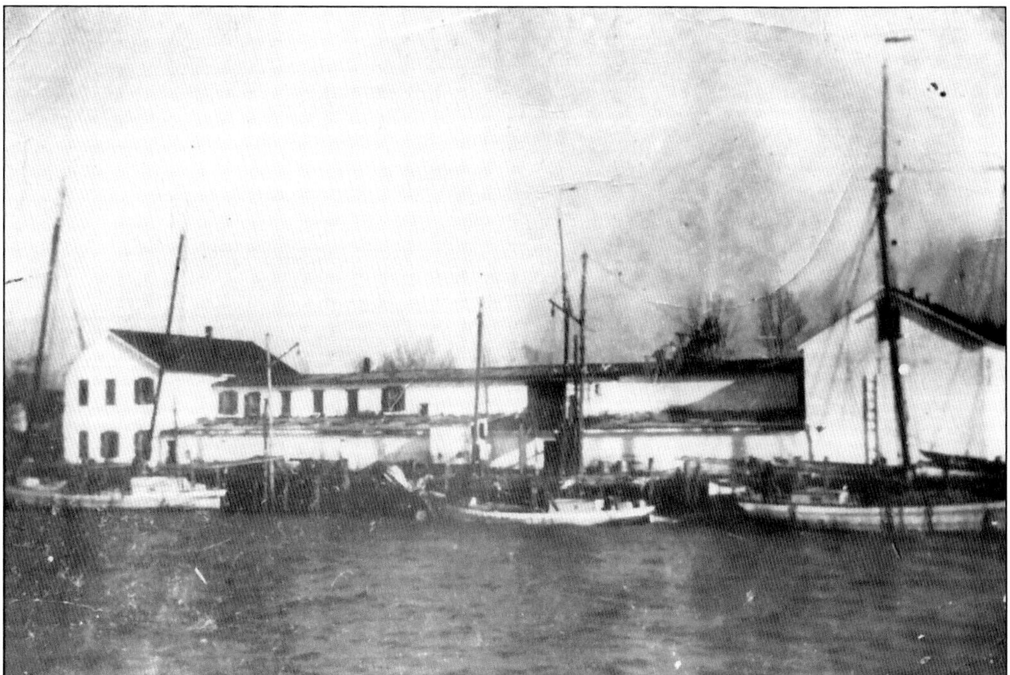

The Marshall Oyster House commanded the tip of the peninsula at the juncture of the Mattaponi and York Rivers. (Courtesy of Juanita Oakley.)

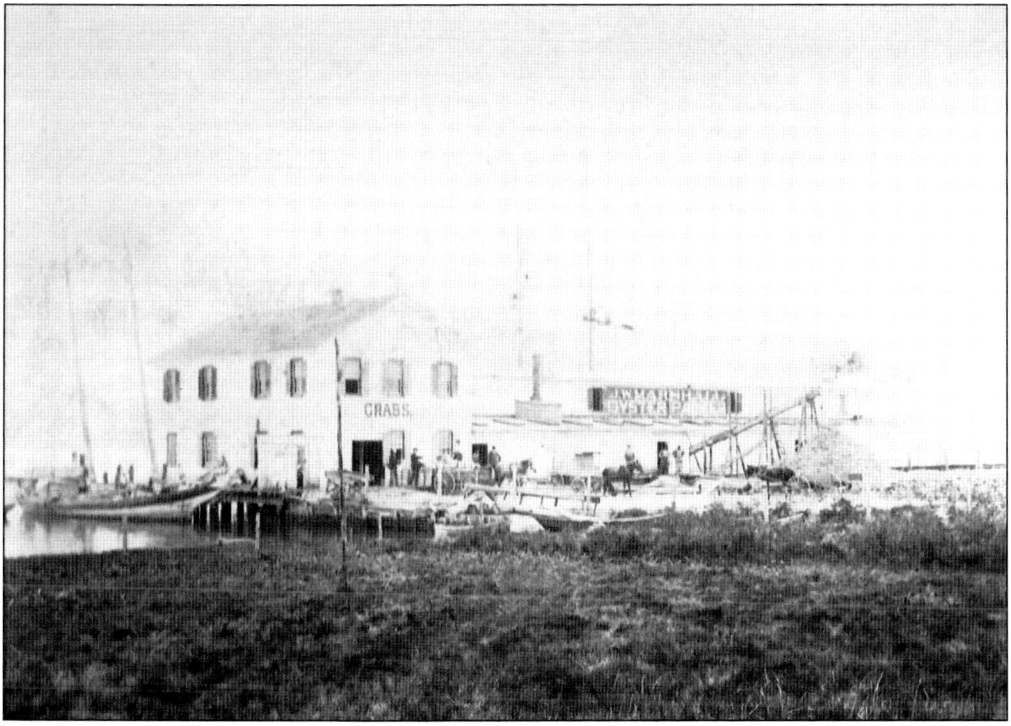

This land view of the Marshall Oyster House is from about 1900. To the right is a large pile of oyster shells, which were sold for paving and to create lime. Unfortunately, not returning the shells to the rivers had a devastating effect upon the oyster populations, which depended upon banks of shells to spawn and grow.

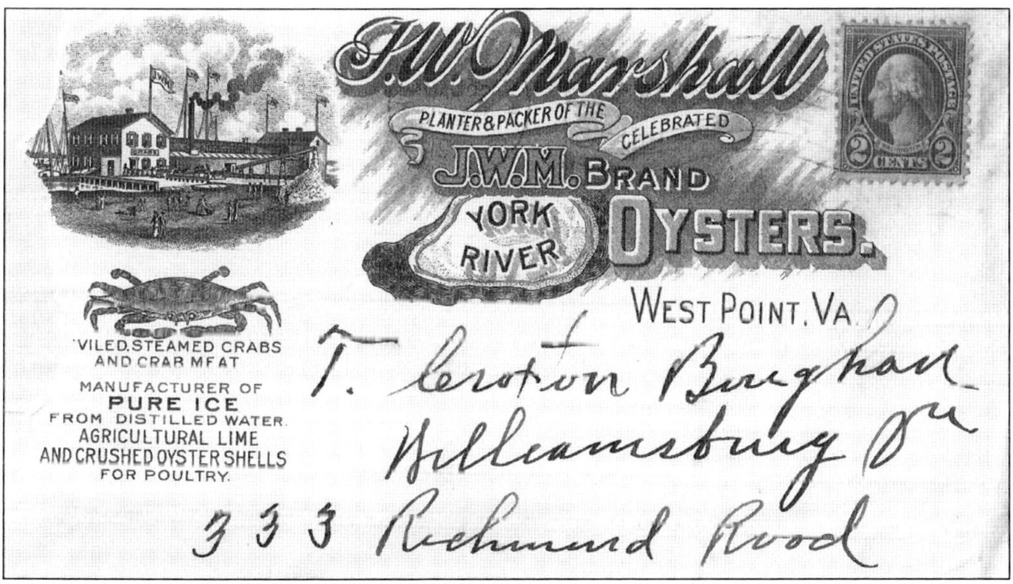

This company envelope from the Marshall Oyster House was also an advertisement. Note that the establishment also sold crabs. (Courtesy of William J. Addison.)

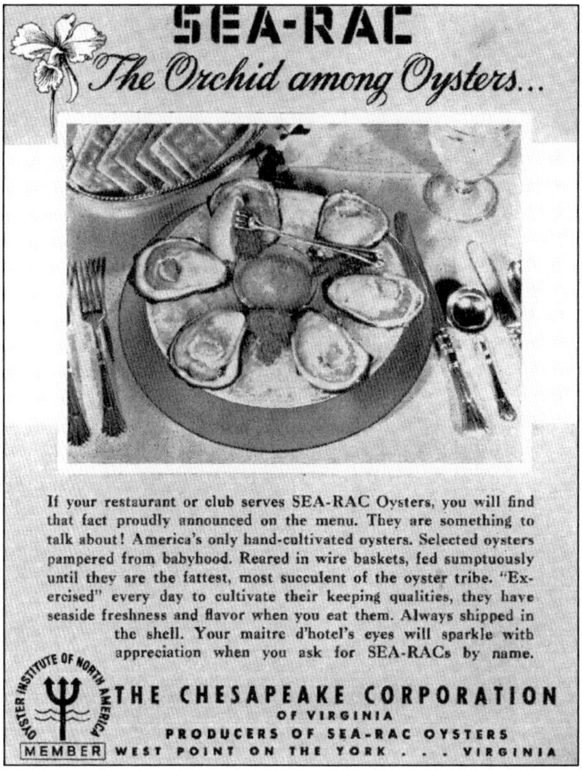

By the 1890s, oyster beds in the area began to decline in large measure from over-harvesting. When this became a crisis in the early 20th century, oystermen blamed water pollution from the paper mill at West Point for their problems. In an effort to prove that the mill was having no effect on oysters, the mill began its own oyster harvesting and marketed them as Sea-Rac oysters to fine restaurants. (Courtesy of Carol Fetterolf.)

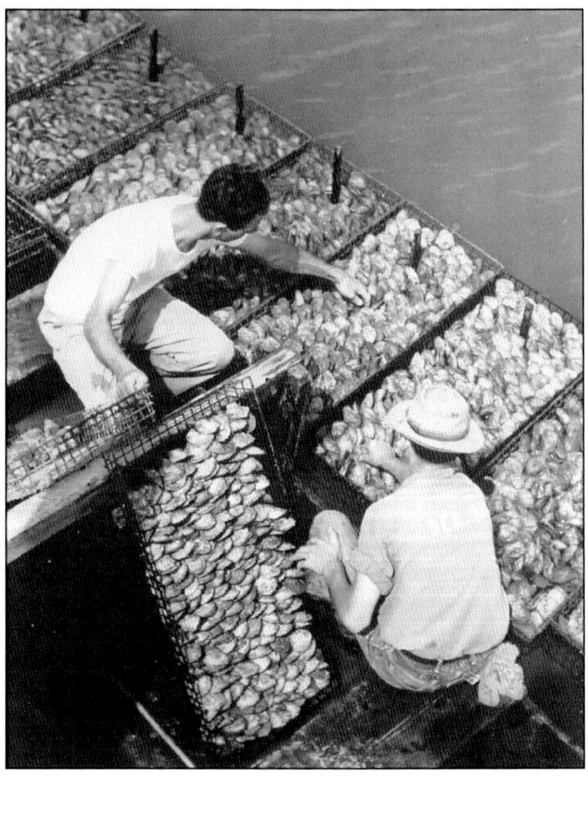

Employees of the mill sort and thin out oysters in a Sea-Rac basket. The man on the left is E.P. Roane, the manager of the Chesapeake Corporation's oyster farm, and to the right is assistant Frank Foster. This photograph was taken about 1943 by William Edwin Booth.

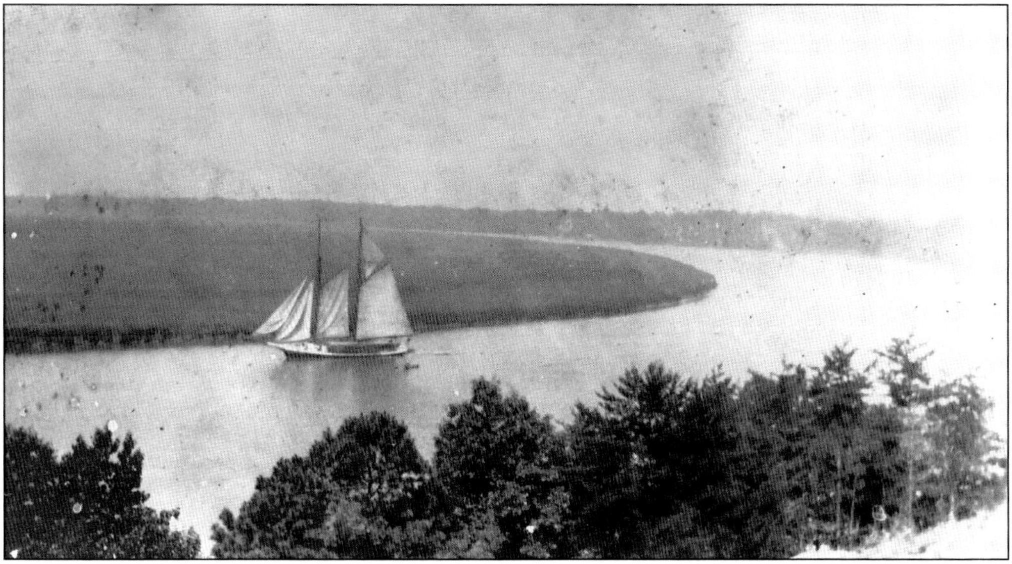

Sailboats often had to resort to poling as they moved up the rivers, especially before internal combustion engines were used on ships. This unidentified schooner navigates the winding Pamunkey River about 1914.

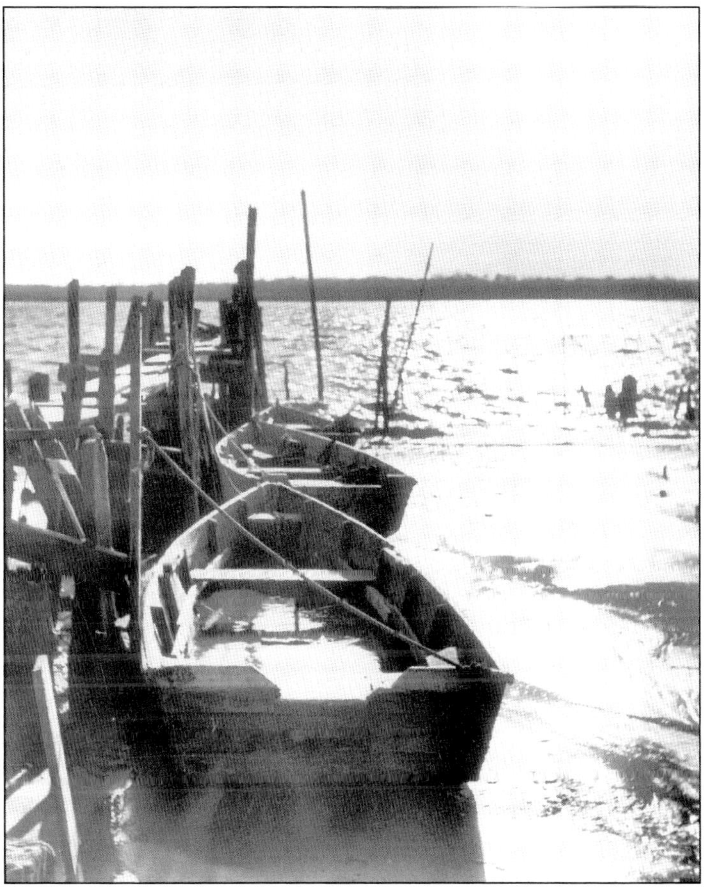

Rowboats tied to a dock at West Point during early March 1963 await fishermen to venture out to fish for shad and rockfish, which are considered early spring delicacies. Rowboats such as these are seldom seen on the rivers anymore. Fish stocks are maintained by hatcheries at the Pamunkey and Mattaponi Indian reservations. (Courtesy of the *Richmond Times-Dispatch*.)

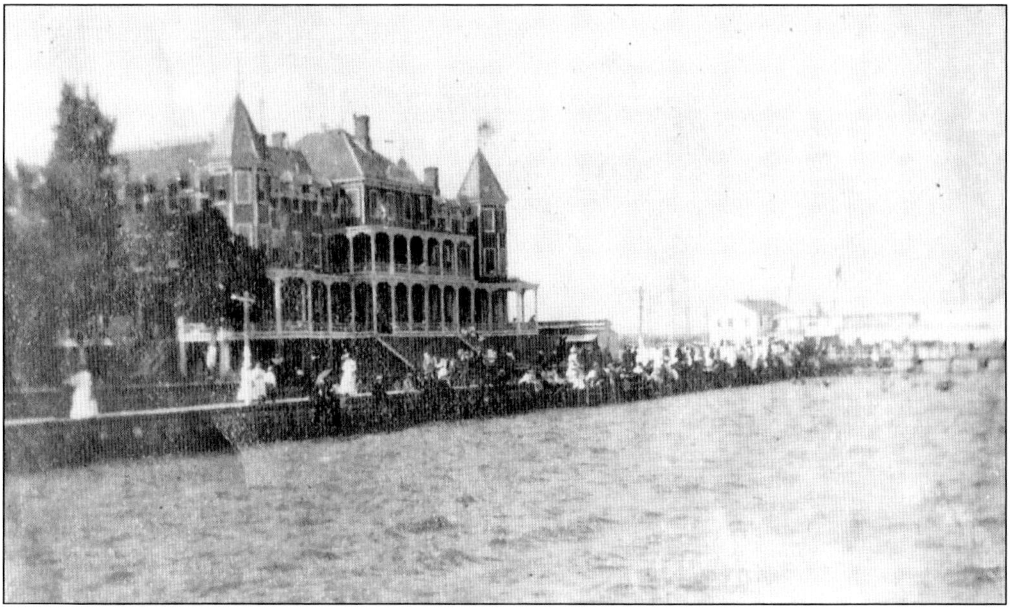

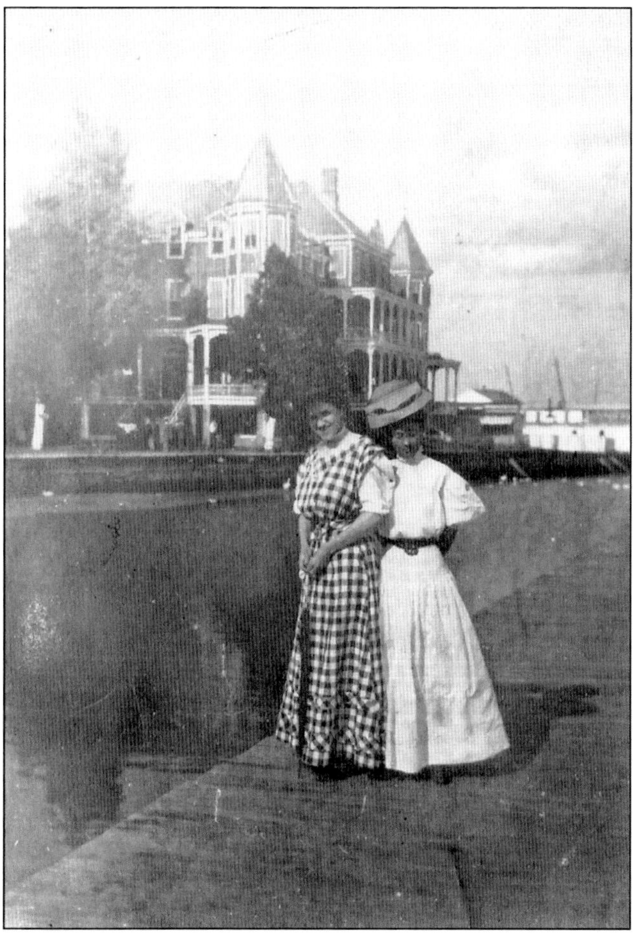

By the 1890s, West Point had become a destination for leisure travelers. The Richmond railroad magnate James Dooley built a 200-room hotel, the Terminal, in 1887. Located on First Street near Lee Street, it sat proudly on the highest ground of the tip of the peninsula where artillery had been placed during the Revolution and Civil War. (Courtesy of Dennis Roane.)

A system of boardwalks was constructed next to and over the waters of the York, allowing vacationers to promenade along the river. (Courtesy of Dennis Roane.)

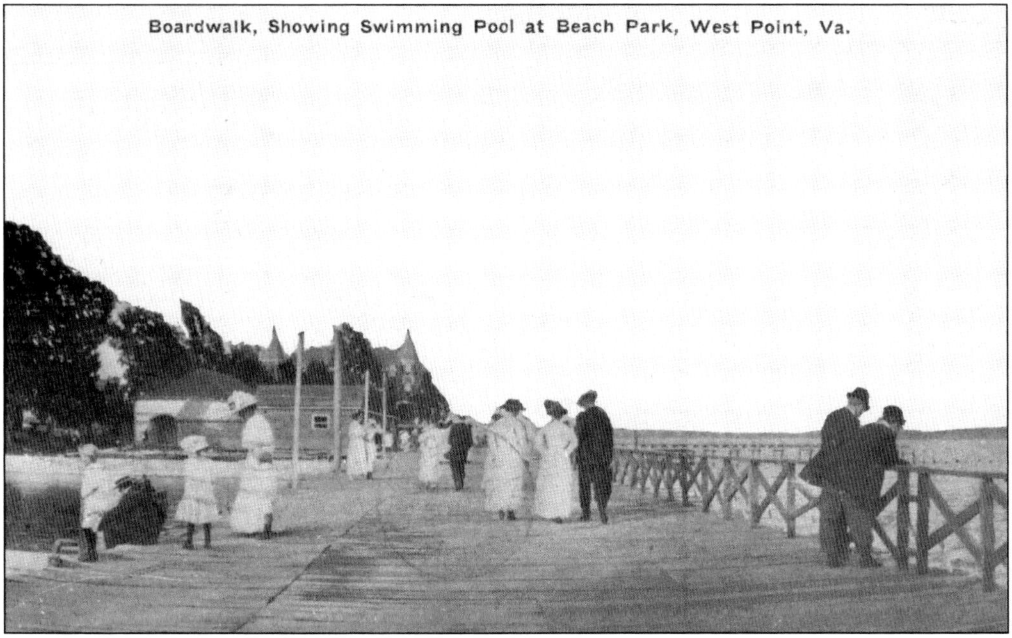

Vacationers enjoy leisurely strolls along the York River at Beach Park. During the early part of the 20th century, the park included an amusement park with a roller coaster and a merry-go-round. On the left, the small building in front of the Terminal Hotel was a movie theater that showed "lantern pictures." (Courtesy of Carol Fetterolf.)

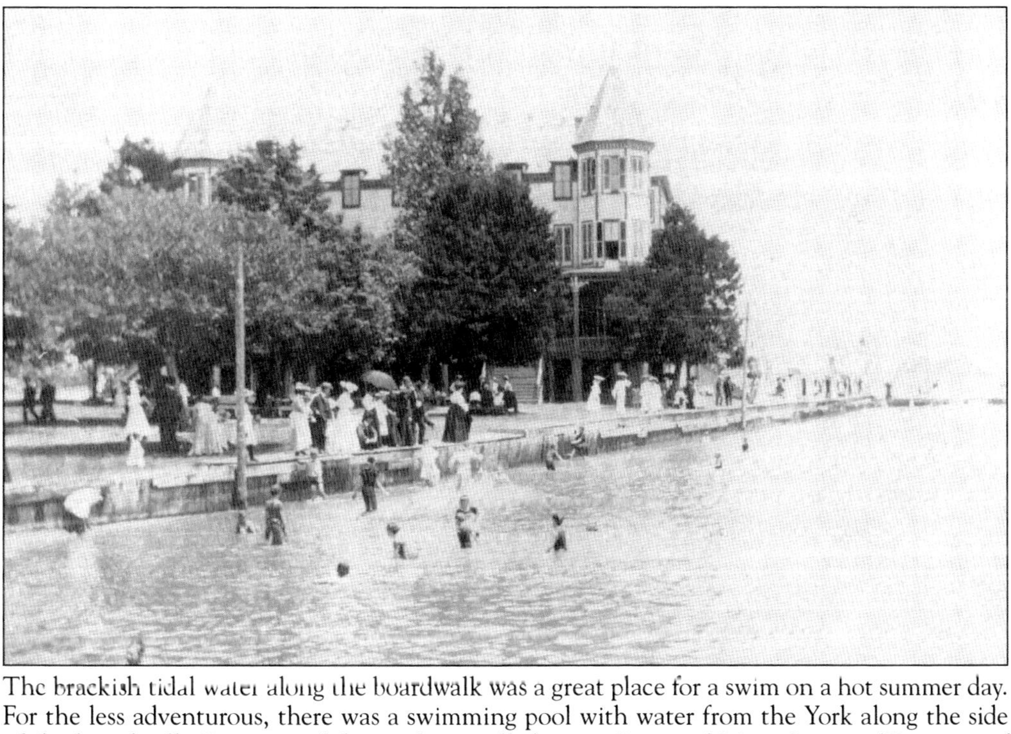

The brackish tidal water along the boardwalk was a great place for a swim on a hot summer day. For the less adventurous, there was a swimming pool with water from the York along the side of the boardwalk. Remains of the pool are still there at First and Main Streets. (Courtesy of Stuart Medlin.)

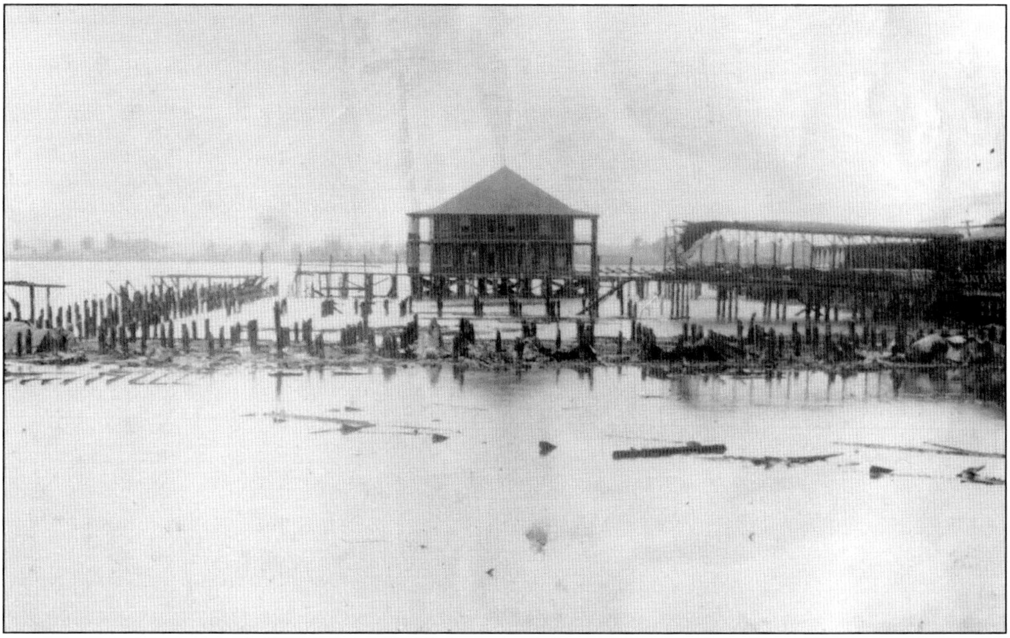

The boardwalk at Beach Park boasted buildings constructed over the waters of the York that were used as saloons and gambling parlors, such as the Beach Park Social Club, pictured here, known for its oysters. The end of the legal sale of alcohol in the 1920s closed these gentlemen's clubs; however, even before Prohibition, much of the boardwalk and its buildings over the York River were engulfed in a fire on July 27, 1910. This photograph depicts the charred remains.

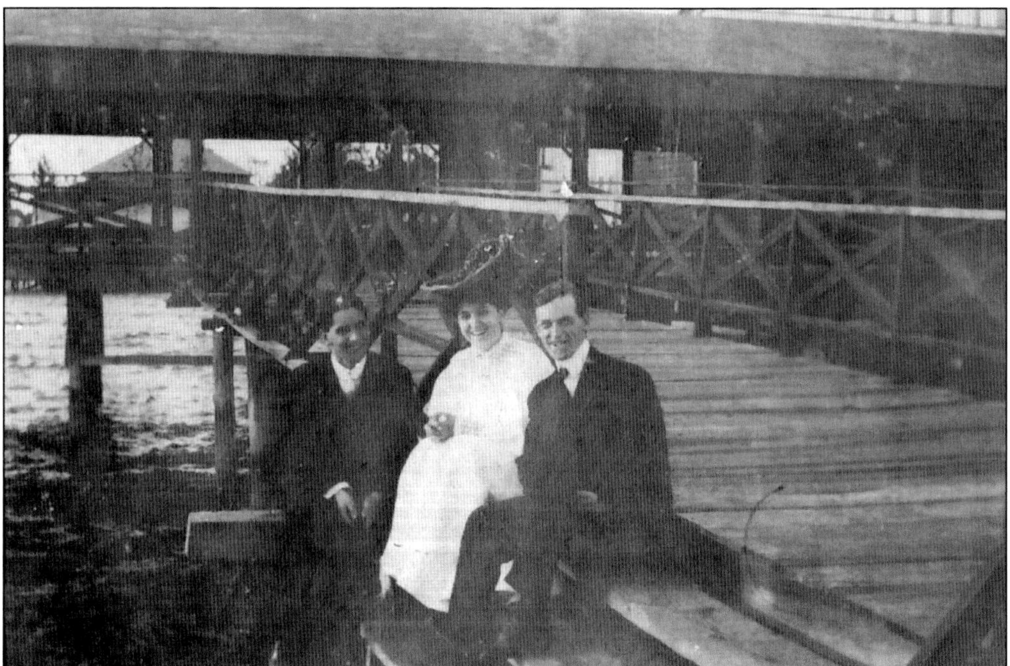

These three young people enjoy the views of the rivers from the boardwalks. (Courtesy of Dennis Roane.)

Boating has always been a popular pastime at West Point. Powerboat races were held for some years at a course along the Pamunkey, where spectators could watch from the riverbanks. (Courtesy of William J. Addison.)

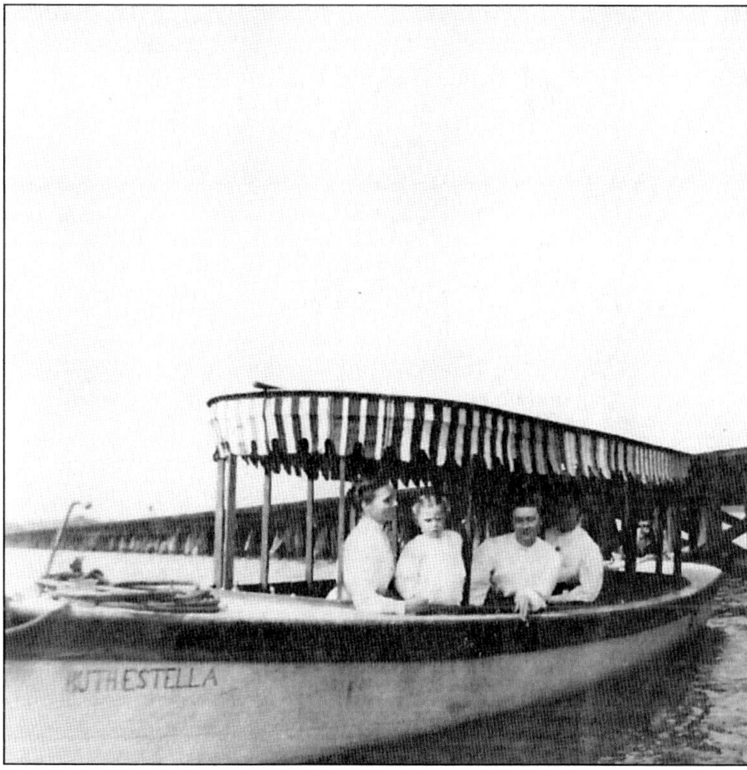

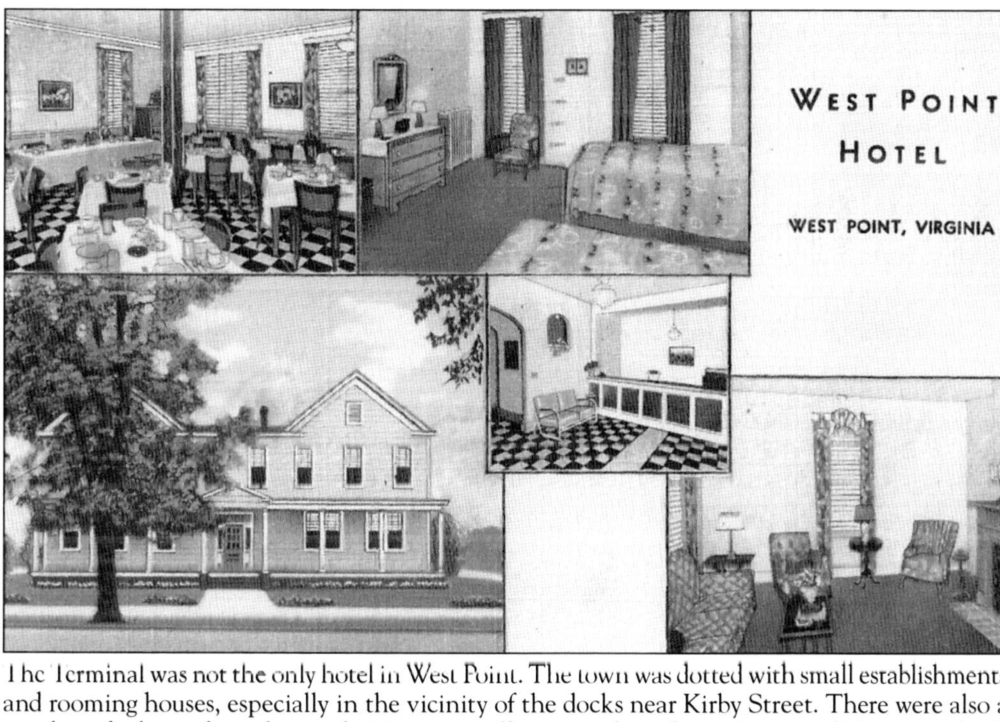

The Terminal was not the only hotel in West Point. The town was dotted with small establishments and rooming houses, especially in the vicinity of the docks near Kirby Street. There were also a number of saloons for sailors and visitors, as well as a number of eateries specializing in seafood. (Courtesy of Janie Wampler.)

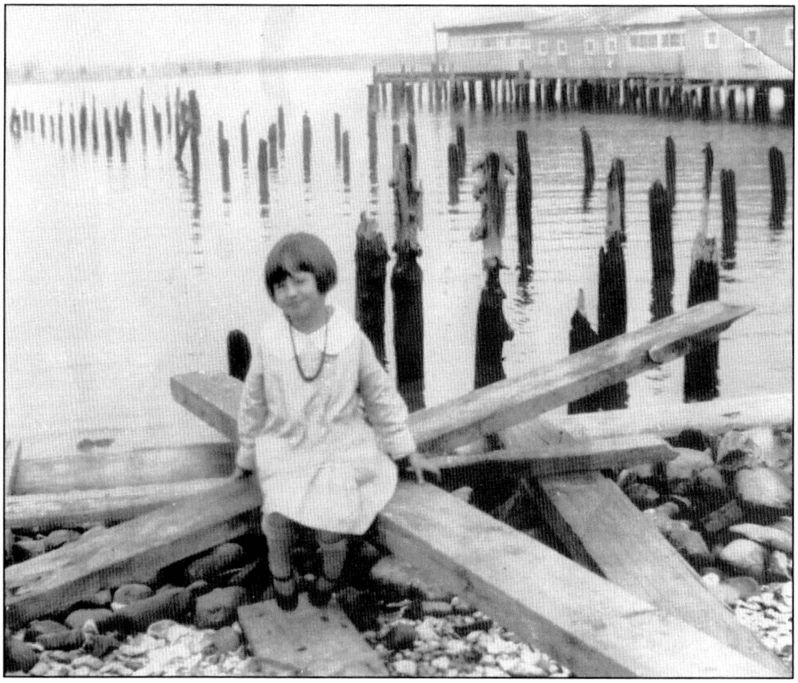

Dorothy Martin Putney plays along the Mattaponi in the 1930s. In the background is the Three Rivers men's club.

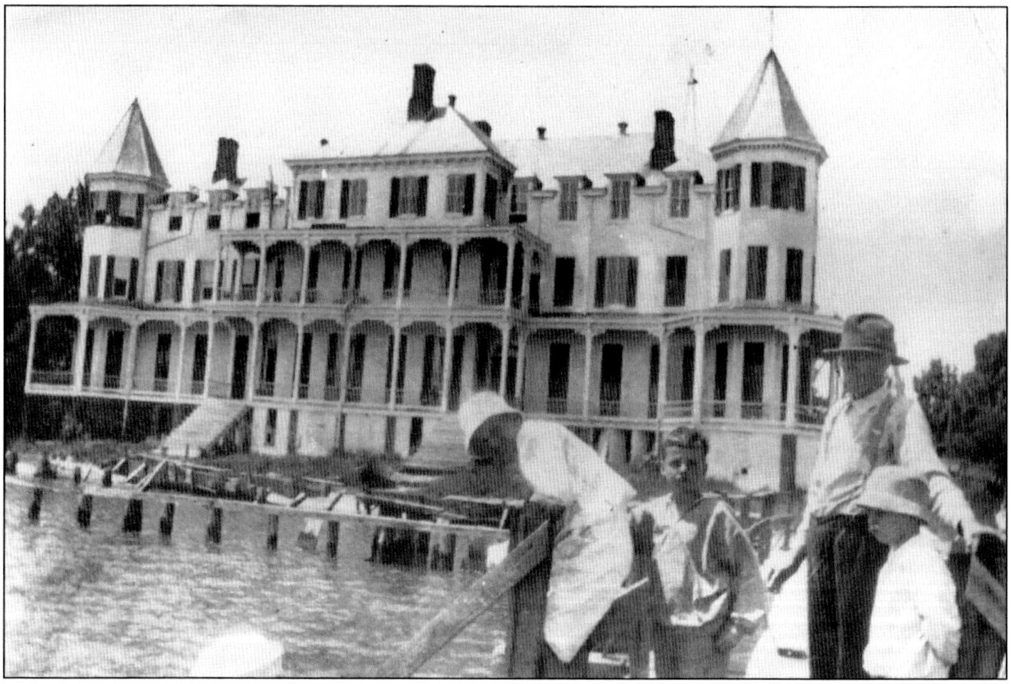

After World War I, holidaymakers came less often to West Point, as competing resorts opened along the Chesapeake Bay and Atlantic Ocean. The boardwalk fell into disrepair, and the Terminal Hotel became a boardinghouse. In 1926, a fire started in the basement of the old hotel quickly consumed the magnificent building that had come to represent the town of West Point. It was rumored that the fire was caused by an exploding whiskey still. Another version claims that dynamite used to eliminate pilings was being stored in the basement.

Five

West Point Becomes a Mill Town

There were a number of light industries in West Point prior to 1900, including a broom factory (which burned down), a toy factory, distilleries, pickle factories, and a furniture factory. Lumber had always been an important product of the area. In 1913, Fox Paper Company of Lockland, Ohio, purchased land on the outskirts of the town along the Pamunkey River and established a pulp mill to supply raw materials for its main processing mill in Ohio; thus, the Chesapeake Pulp & Paper Company was established and ready to begin production in 1914. For the first time, sulfurous clouds wafted from the mill as local pines were refined into the slurry shipped west by rail in tanker cars to become the brown cardboard used for making boxes. It was the pungent smell of prosperity.

Elis Olsson, an ambitious Swedish immigrant and chemical engineer who already had some expertise in papermaking, arrived in West Point in 1918. Through the financing of New York bankers, Olsson bought the West Point subsidiary and renamed it the Chesapeake Corporation. By the 1920s, the company had acquired the machinery needed to produce kraft paper, so it stopped shipping pulp slurry to Ohio.

The company soon owned large tracts of land throughout the region upon where it grew pine trees of the variety needed by the mill. As the town's wharf for the steamships fell out of use, the wharf of the Chesapeake Corporation busily loaded ships from all over the world.

The 1980s would see the company transfer its corporate headquarters from West Point to Richmond. In the ensuing three decades, the company changed owners three times: first to St. Laurant, then to Smurfit-Stone Container, and finally, to TennRock in 2011.

Over the years, the mill and its senior management promoted a number of civic activities and funded many local improvements. For example, it built a baseball stadium and fielded a team. The loss of its corporate headquarters had a great impact on the town. Furthermore, over time, the mill has required fewer and fewer workers through mechanization efficiencies.

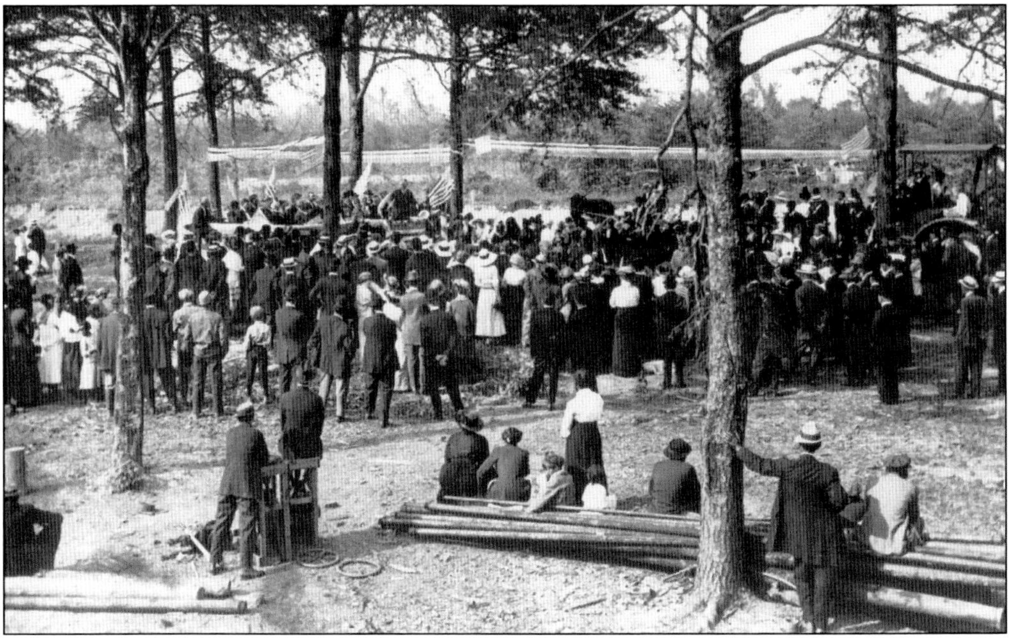

In addition to the fruit of the sea, the other natural resource in abundance in eastern Virginia was pine trees. An Ohio paper mill decided to establish a subsidiary at West Point to provide the raw material needed for its Midwestern plant. Shown here is the 1914 ground-breaking ceremony. The mill provided the needed economic base for the town following the transfer of the Southern Railway terminus to Portsmouth in 1897.

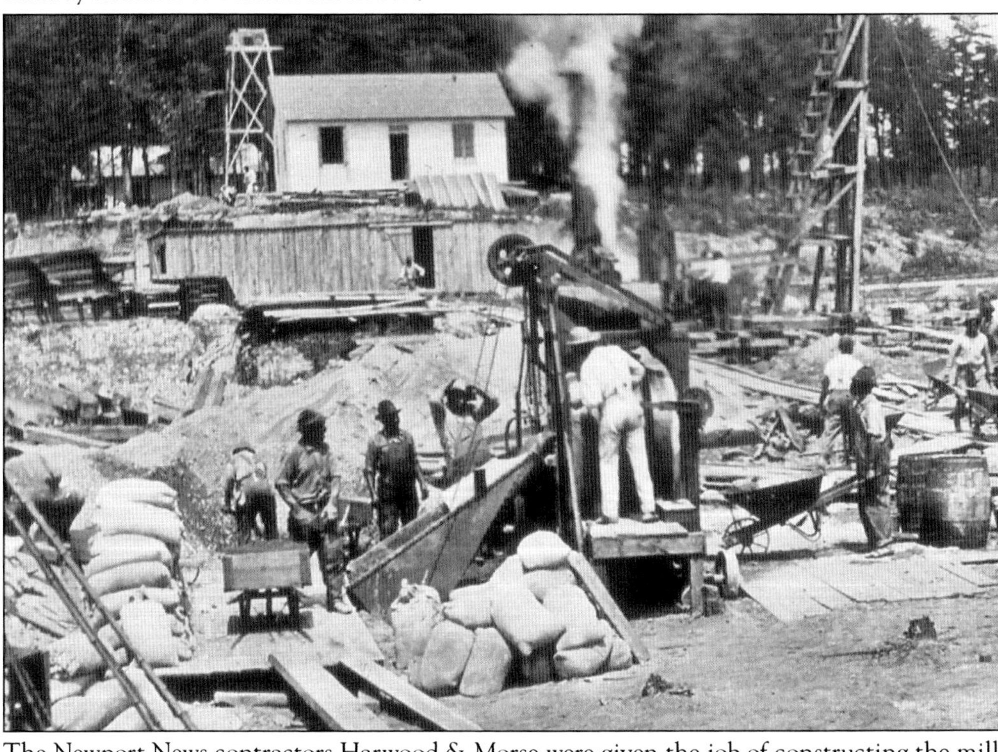

The Newport News contractors Harwood & Morse were given the job of constructing the mill.

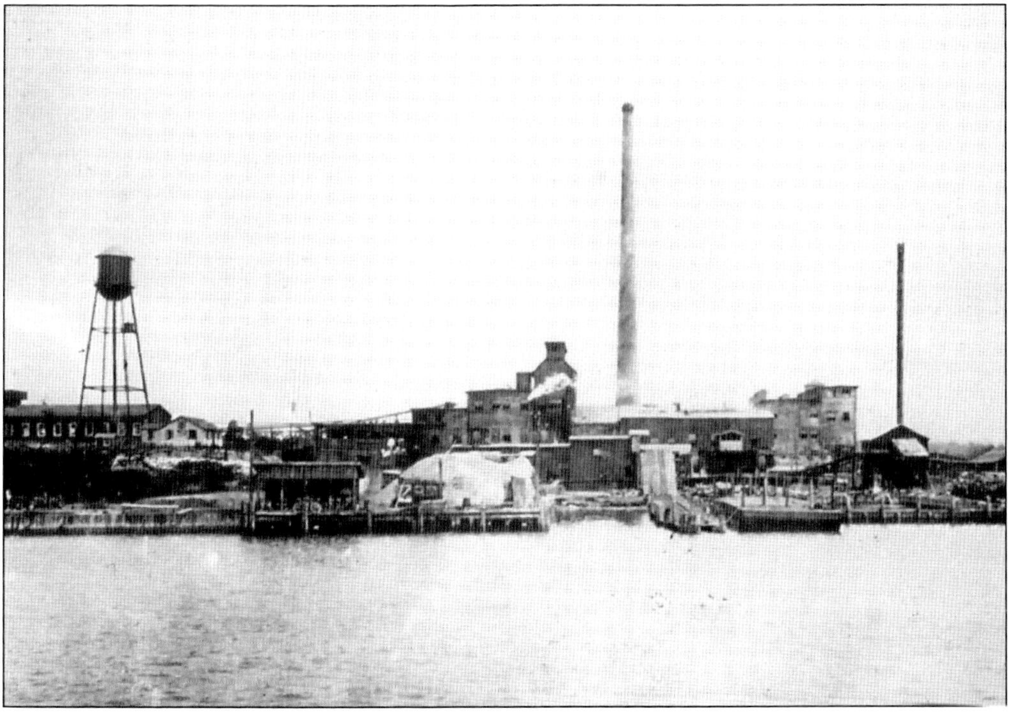

Shown here is the new West Point paper mill shortly after its completion in 1914. At that time, it only produced pulp slurry made from local pine trees. This batter-like slurry was shipped in rail tanker cars to Ohio. The plant did not yet have the machinery necessary to make the finished product of brown kraft paper used for boxes.

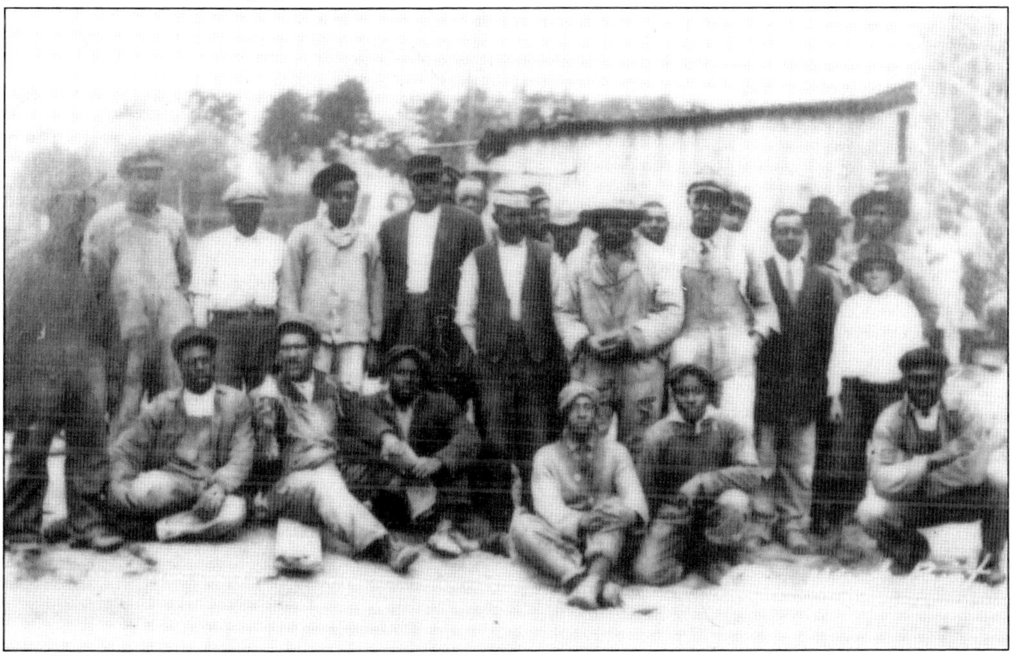

The paper mill provided employment for both African Americans and Native Americans. During its early years, the mill employed about 200 people.

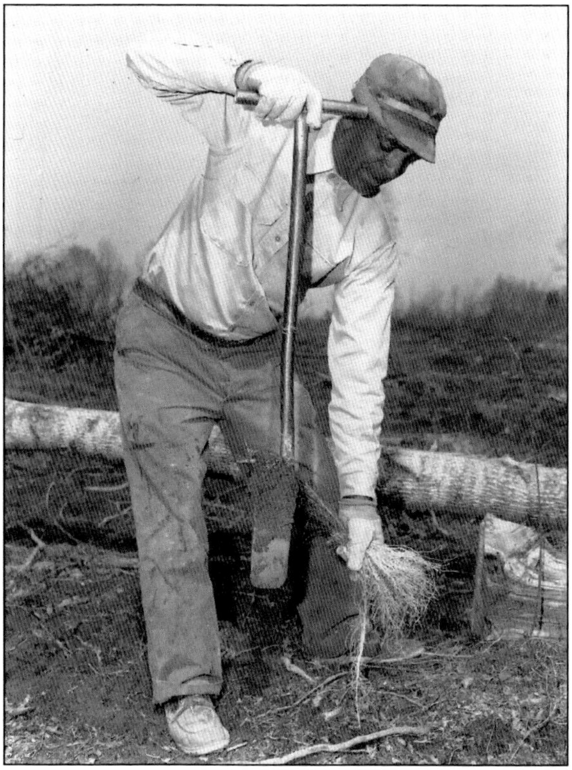

One of the keys to the success of the Chesapeake Corporation was its research and development of strains of pine trees. Problems that had to be solved through experimental nurseries involved tree resin that hampered papermaking and the development of certain varieties of pine trees that grew rapidly. Here, an employee plants a seedling. The mill also owned thousands of acres in the region where its stands of pine trees were grown.

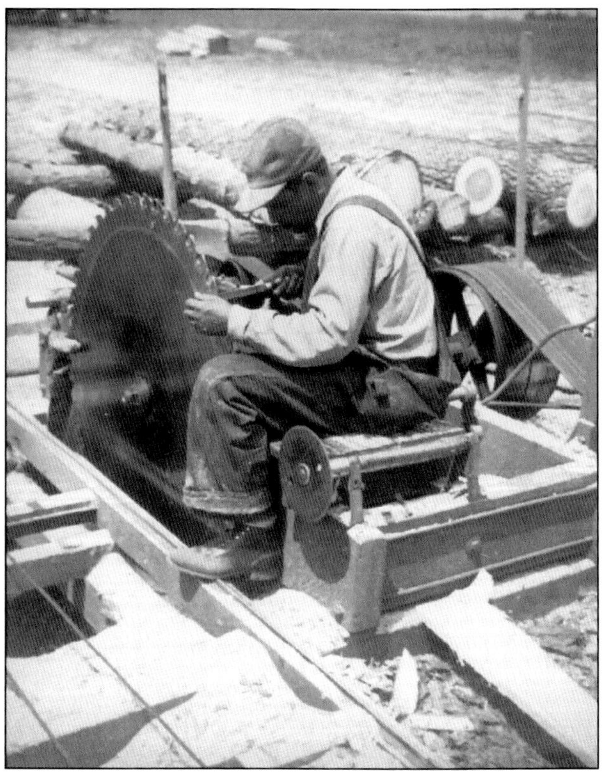

A worker sharpens the saw teeth to cut logs into lumber for the Chesapeake Corporation.

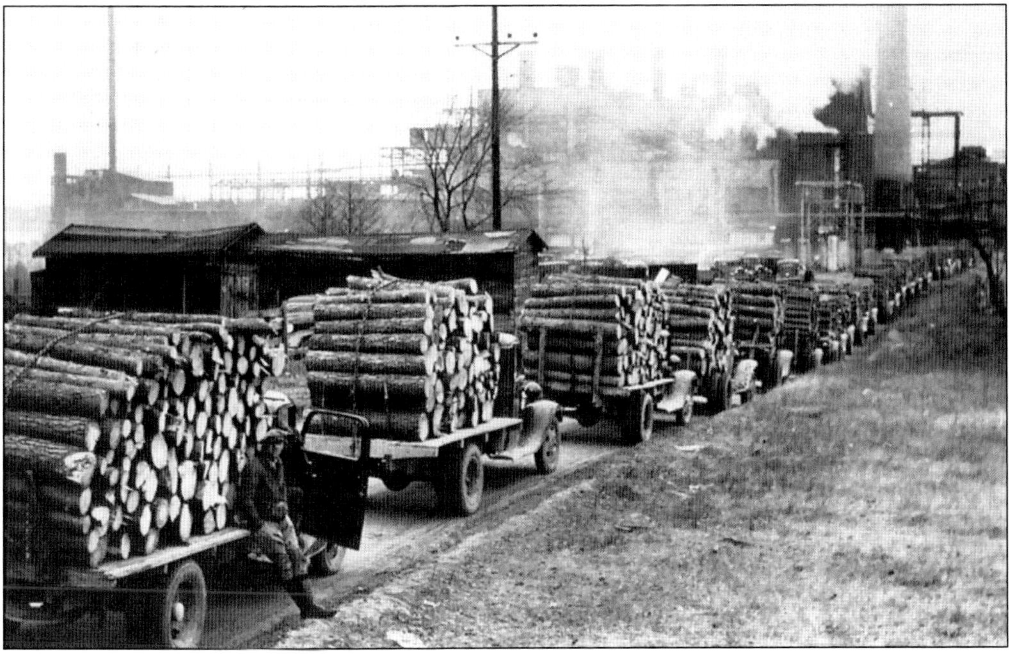

In this 1930 photograph, lumber trucks loaded with pine logs await their turn to unload at the Chesapeake Corporation paper mill. A long line of trucks continues to be a familiar sight at West Point.

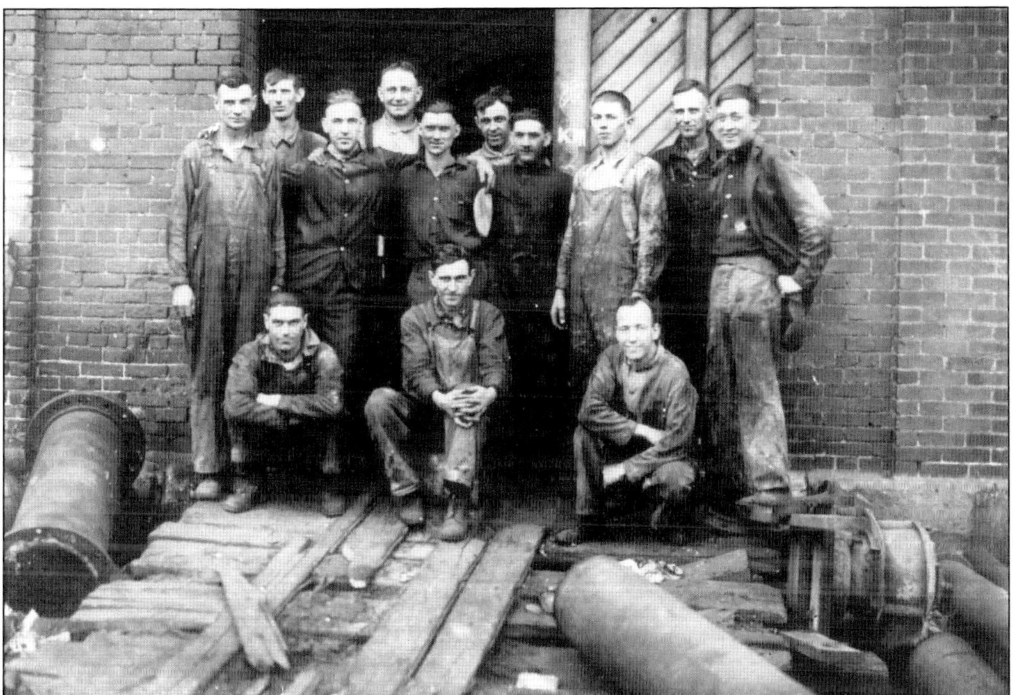

In the mill's early years, oxen were used to move logs around the grounds and at the landings, where the logs were put onto barges. Mill maintenance staff poses for this photograph probably taken in the 1930s.

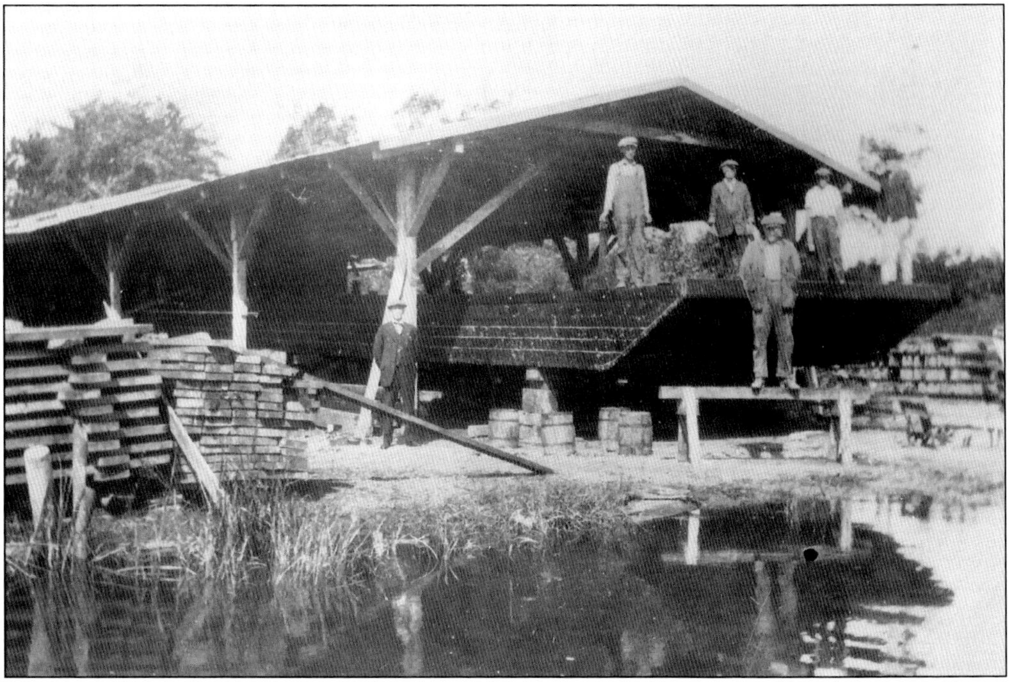

Because many of the logs needed by the mill were shipped by water, the mill built its own barges. Shown here is the construction of one at Mill Creek about 1928. (Courtesy of Virginia Vranian.)

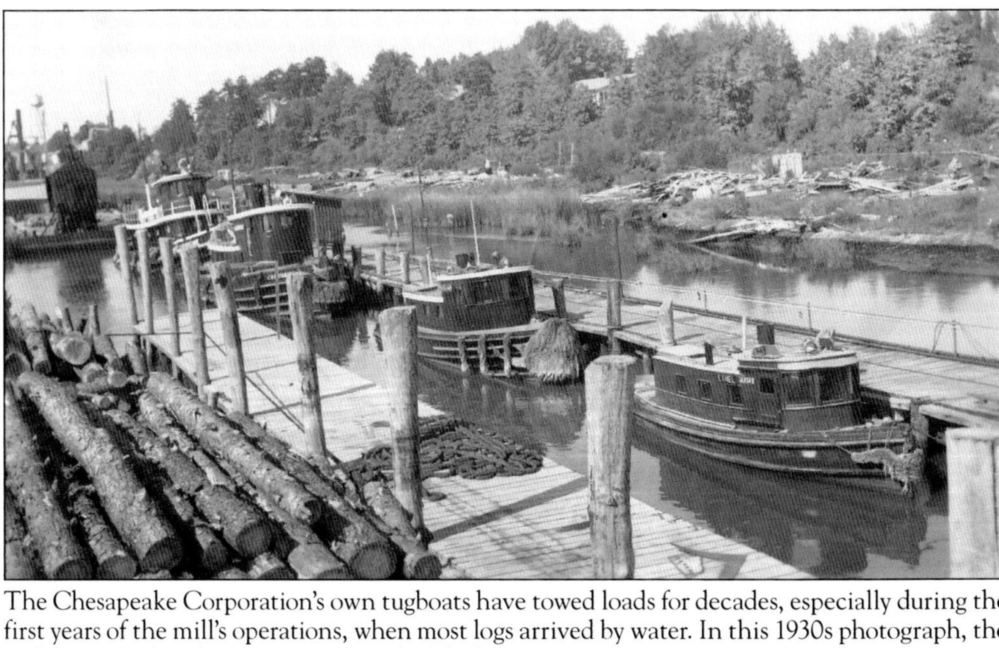

The Chesapeake Corporation's own tugboats have towed loads for decades, especially during the first years of the mill's operations, when most logs arrived by water. In this 1930s photograph, the mill's tugs are lined up at an unidentified dock.

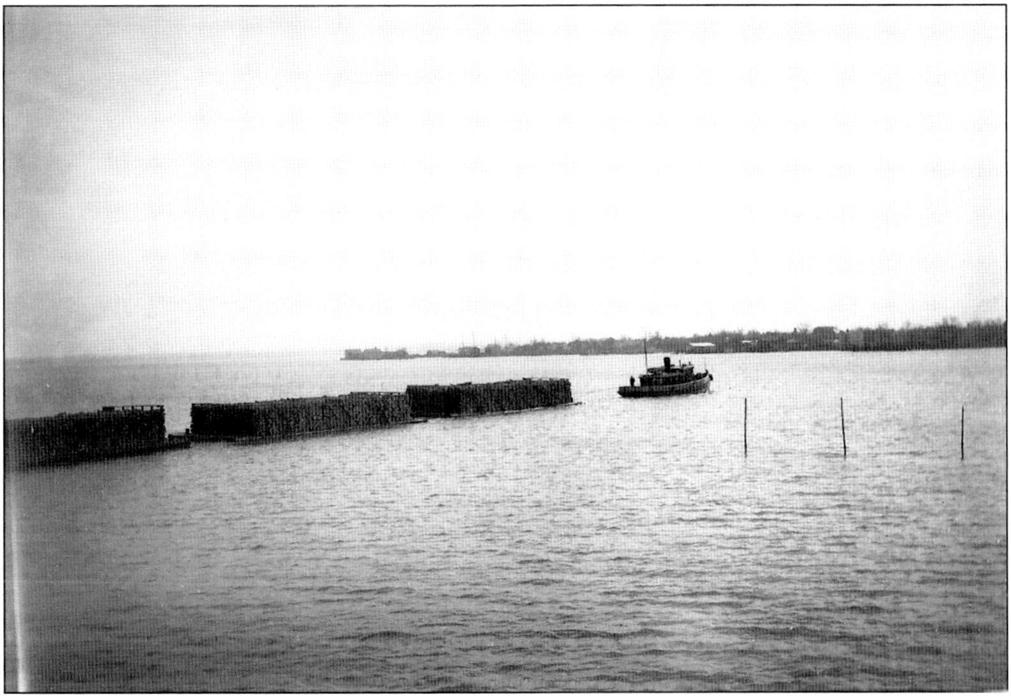

A tugboat pulls a flotilla of barges full of logs toward the mill.

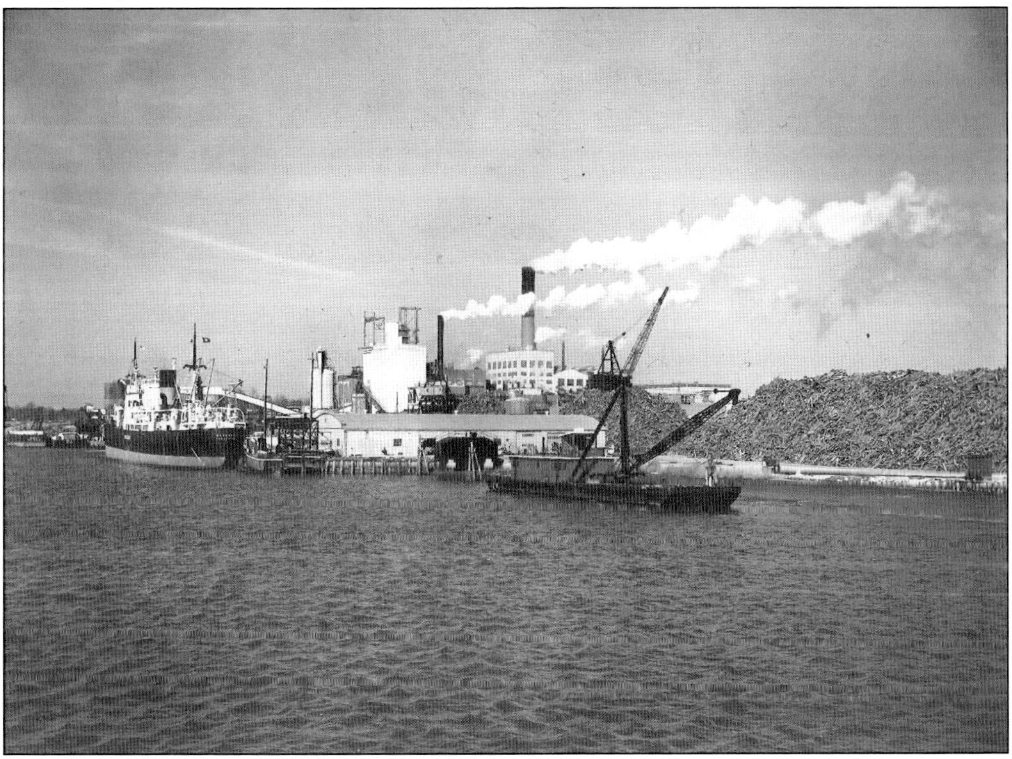

Ships from around the world dock at the Chesapeake Corporation wharf along the Pamunkey River.

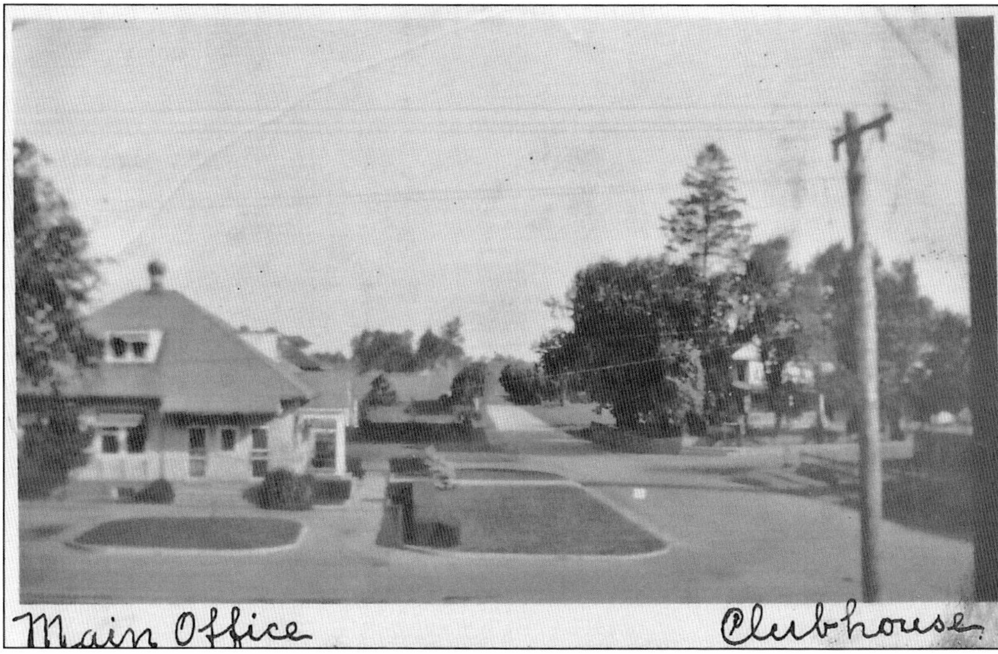

This 1928 photograph shows the first corporate offices of the Chesapeake Corporation. There was also a clubhouse, which was the precursor of the West Point Country Club, in the area of the corporate grounds where some of the executives had homes.

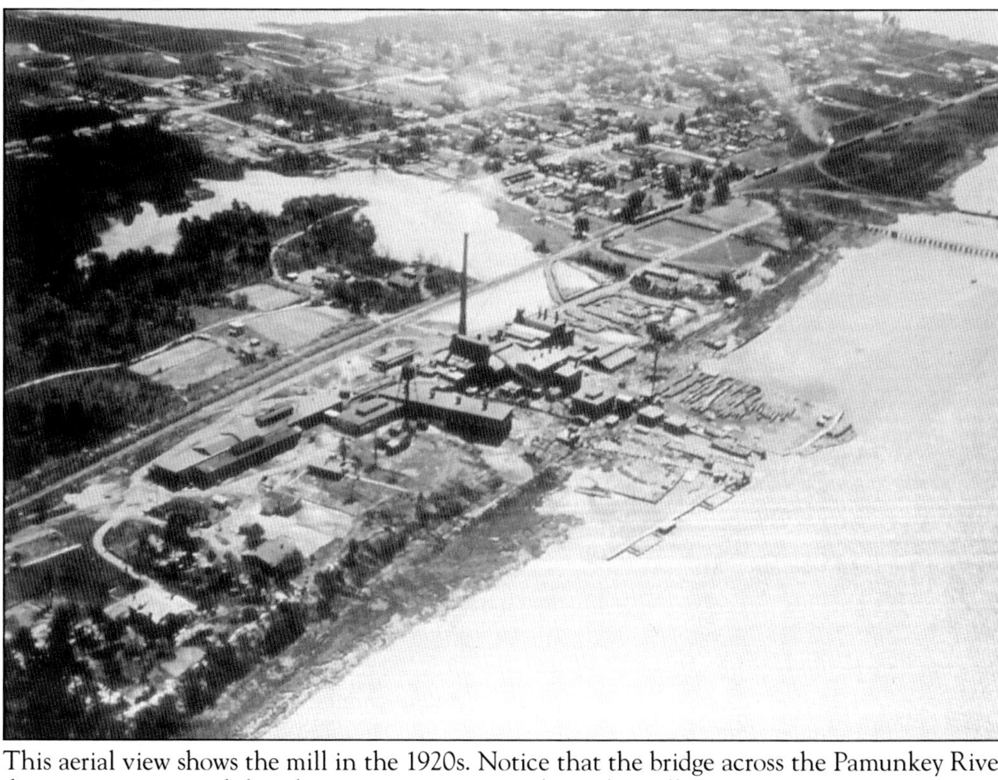

This aerial view shows the mill in the 1920s. Notice that the bridge across the Pamunkey River does not yet exist and that there are extensive ponds on the mill's property.

Elis Olsson, a founder and chief executive officer of the Chesapeake Corporation, is shown here wearing the Order of Vasa, Knights Class medal awarded to him by the King of Sweden. A chemical engineer specializing in papermaking, he immigrated to the United States from Sweden in 1906 and is rightly credited with making the mill successful. He and his wife, Signe, were also driving forces in the town of West Point and generous benefactors of community life, a legacy that his family continued after his passing in 1959.

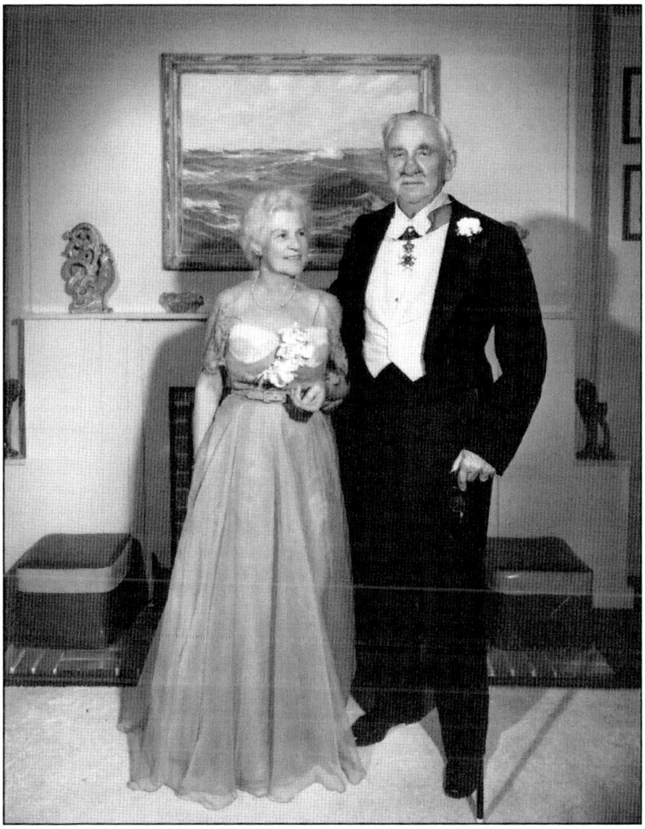

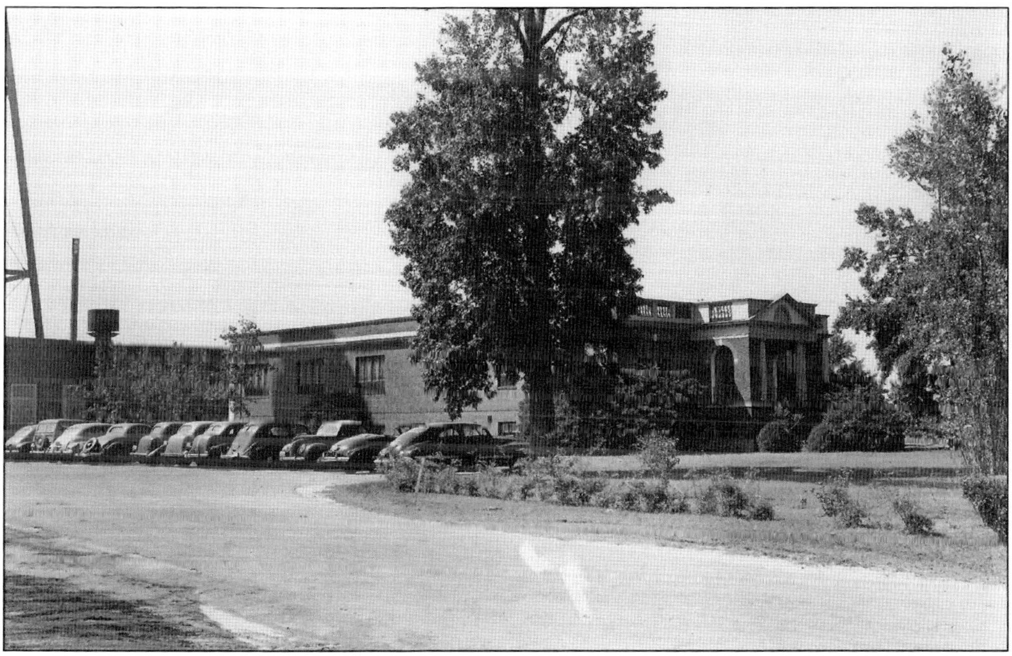

The second-generation headquarters of the Chesapeake Corporation, built in the 1920s, was replaced in the 1960s with the present office building. This photograph was taken in the 1940s.

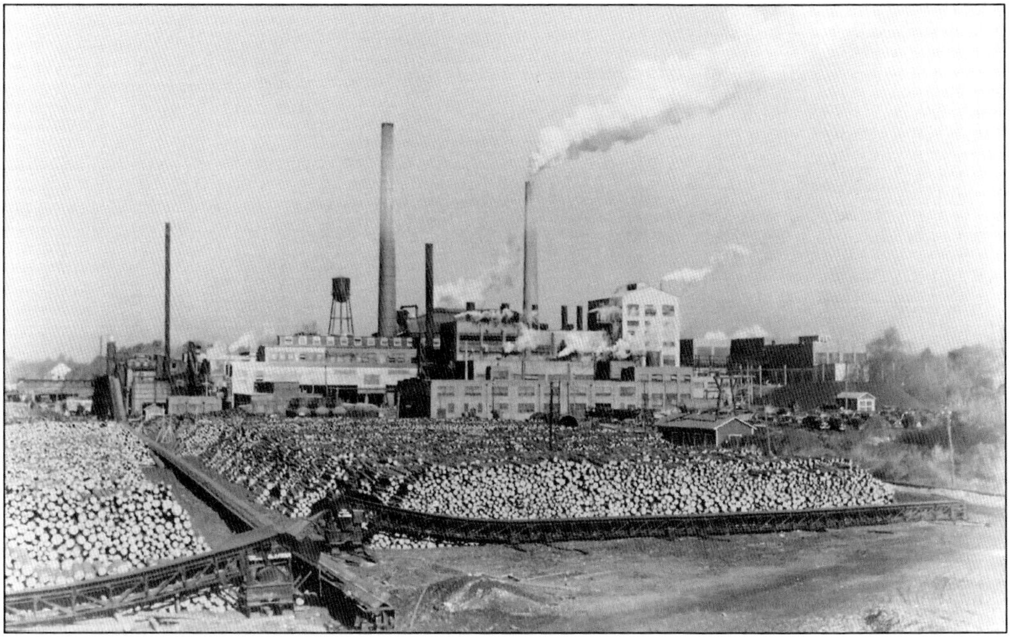

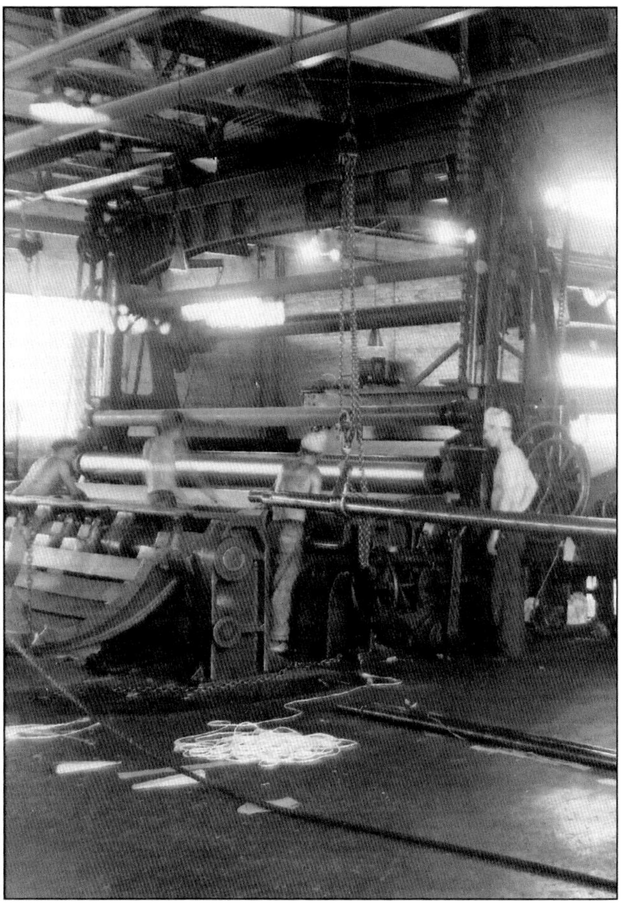

The Chesapeake Corporation in 1963 still had neatly stacked piles of logs before the logs were completely moved by machine. The mill transforms trees into kraft board and paperboard used to make boxes. It has refined its processes so that instead of only producing brown cardboard, it also manufactures white board, which is so white that it has to be softened with a hint of dye.

Workers man the giant papermaker, affectionately referred to as "the big machine," inside the Chesapeake Corporation mill.

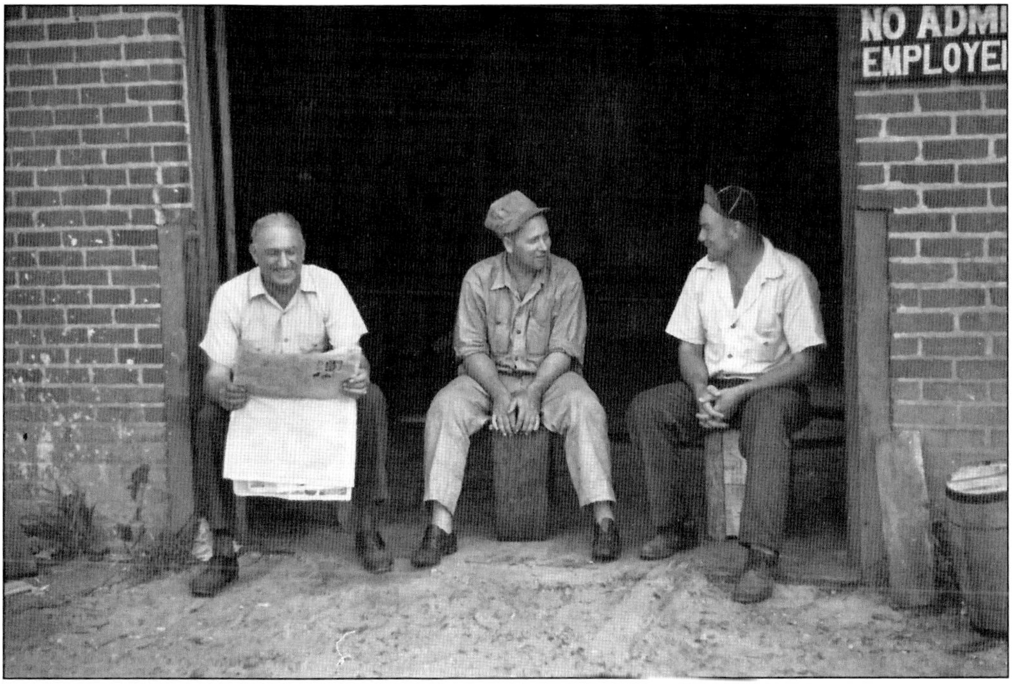

Workers at the Chesapeake Corporation paper mill take a welcomed break.

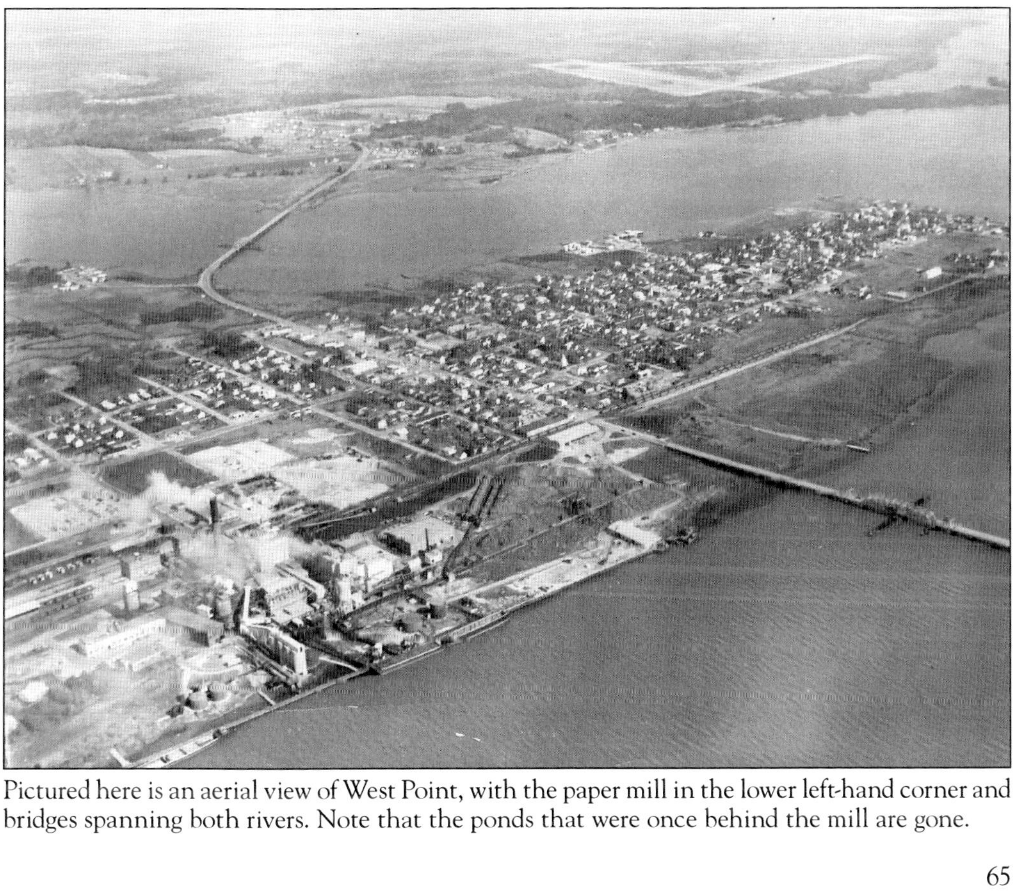

Pictured here is an aerial view of West Point, with the paper mill in the lower left-hand corner and bridges spanning both rivers. Note that the ponds that were once behind the mill are gone.

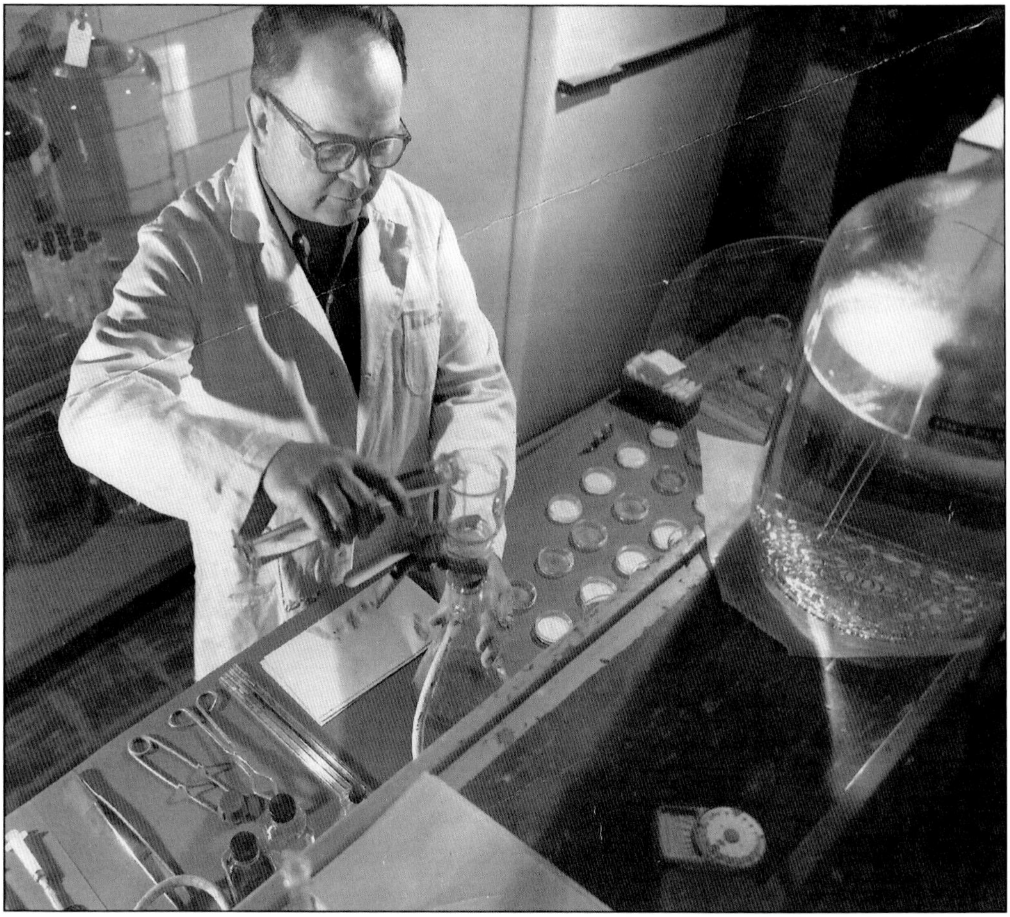

One of the biggest concerns of the Chesapeake Corporation was air and water quality. Here, chemist Stanley Jackowski works to find solutions to the mill's pollution issues in October 1968.

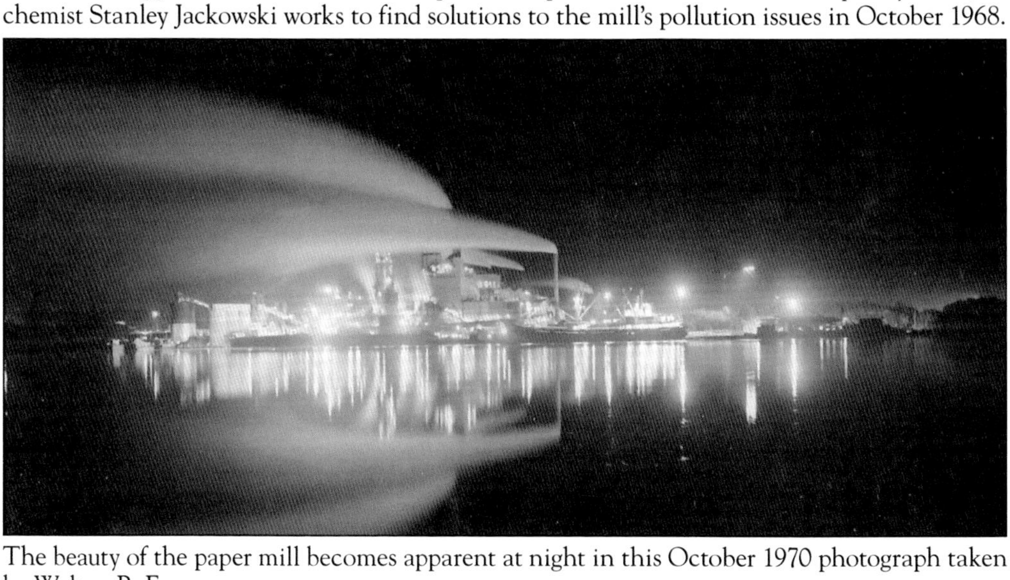

The beauty of the paper mill becomes apparent at night in this October 1970 photograph taken by Walton B. Evans.

Six

Modern West Point and the Military

The same year that the Chesapeake Corporation began construction of the primary industry at West Point in 1914, World War I erupted in Europe. Though not affected immediately, when the United States became embroiled in the conflict, West Point did its part. With America's entry into the war, the demand for merchant ships was unprecedented. The US Shipping Board instituted a crash program to fill the need for Liberty ships. By 1917, a rail spur was built parallel to Euclid Avenue, running east to the Mattaponi River. There, the York River Ship Building Corporation, a new company, began construction of two wooden merchant vessels. The war ended before the enterprise could produce more than one finished ship, but a number of the men brought to work in the shipyard stayed on in West Point when it closed. During World War II, the abandoned shipyard at Port Richmond was used for the military's top-secret research effort to create man-made icebergs capable of supporting landing aircraft.

Thompson Field, an airport built by Crosby Thompson, served the military during the years between World War I and World War II, as did the one that replaced it during World War II, Middle Peninsula Airport. Today, the Middle Peninsula Airport continues to serve the military, especially the bases at the lower end of the York.

While many of West Point's sons served with distinction during the conflicts of the 20th century, Lt. Gen. Lewis Burwell "Chesty" Puller gained international renown for his bravery during both World War II at the Battle for Guadalcanal and the Korean War. He was born in a modest frame home near the corner of First and Main Streets in 1898. While still young, his parents moved across the Mattaponi to Saluda. But with family ties to West Point, he often returned, especially when he attended West Point High School. He remains the most decorated US Marine in American history and is referred to as "the Marine's Marine." The public park along the York close to his birthplace has been named in his honor.

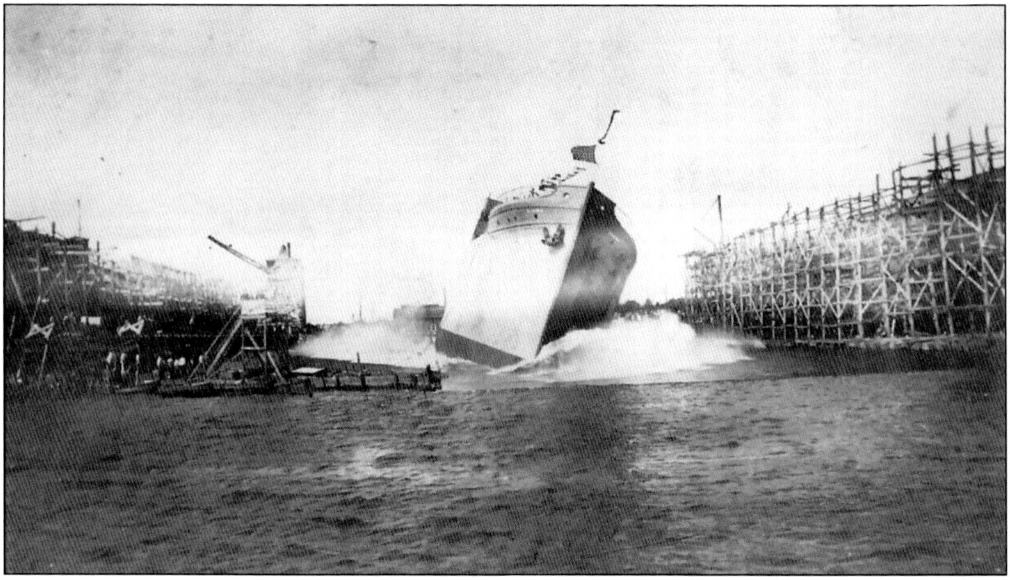

As part of the government effort during World War I to increase shipbuilding, the York River Ship Building Corporation established a shipyard on the site of a defunct cannery on the banks of the Mattaponi. Two vessels were laid, but only one was completed—the *R.L. Newman*—which is shown here being launched in 1919.

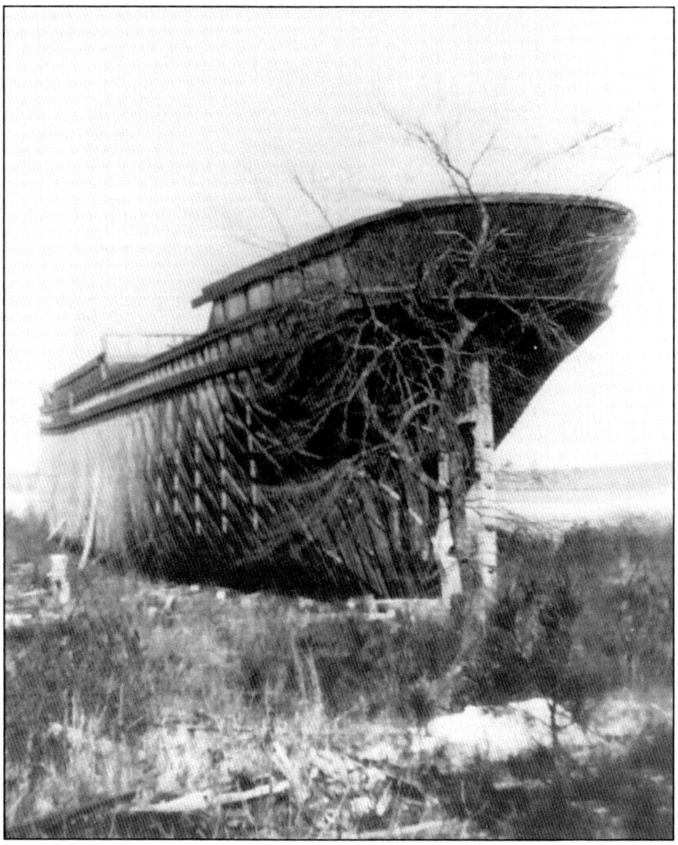

The second ship was still unfinished when World War I came to an end and was never completed. Its empty hulk became a place for local children to explore. The shipyard failed with the coming of peace.

On the eve of World War I in 1914, the town of West Point held a patriotic parade. Note the flags decking the front porch of the home in the background.

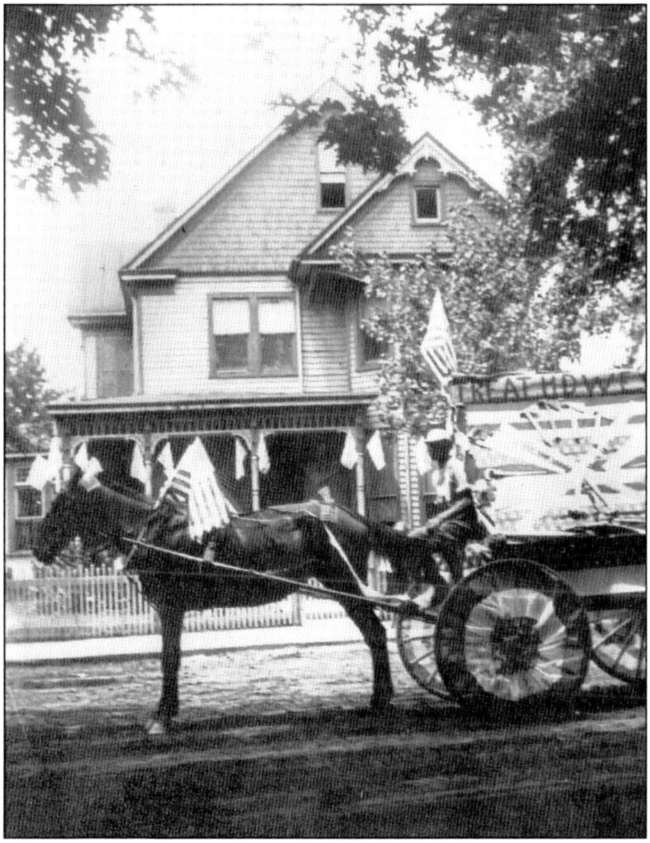

The Olsson family in their military dress uniforms pose with their parents, at Romancoke, the family home, during World War II. Carl and Inga Maja Olsson stand behind their mother, Signe, on the left. Sture Olsson, in his Navy whites and standing on the far right behind his father, Elis, would succeed him as head of the Chesapeake Corporation.

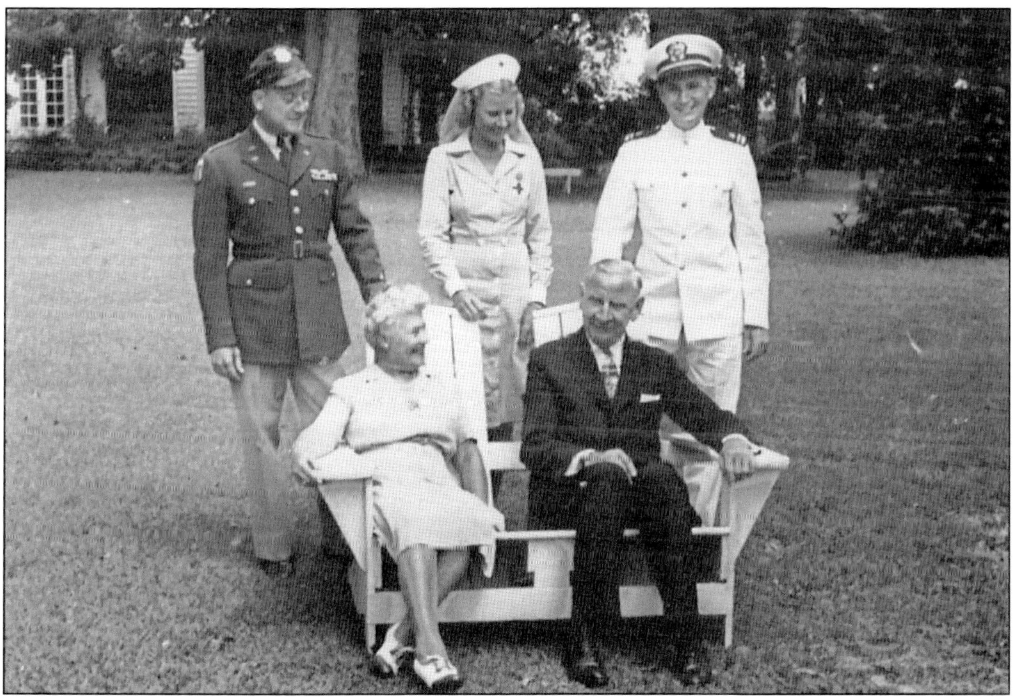

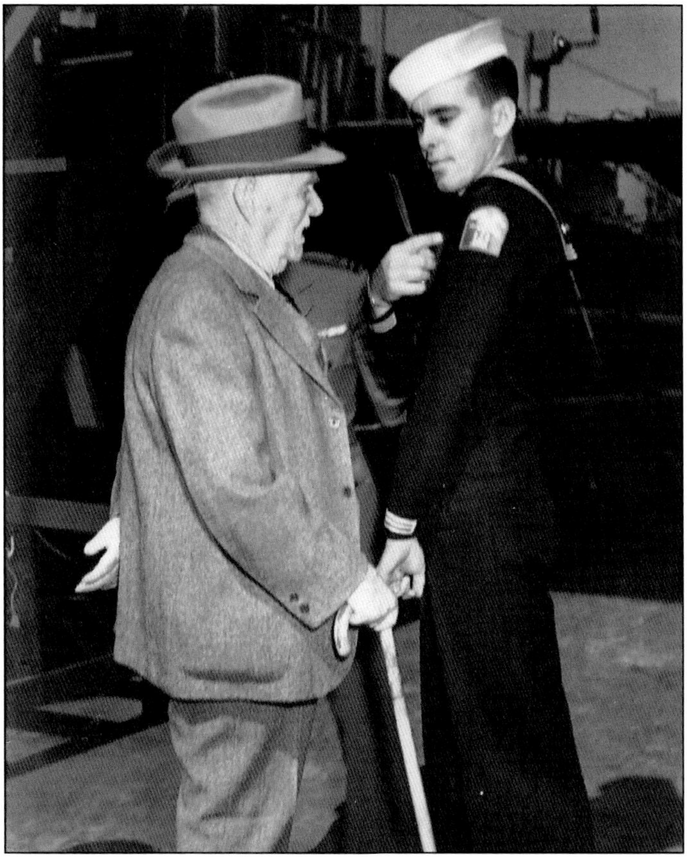

Civil War veteran and West Point native Theodore Norman Mayo inspects the insignia of a World War II sailor. Mayo enlisted in the Confederate army at age 16 and served in Company C of the 26th Virginia Infantry. He passed away in 1948 at 103 years old. (Courtesy of William J. Addison.)

Buses line Main Street to transport servicemen to Camp Perry during World War II. Troops passing through West Point on the way north would fill Highway 33 for days at a time in an unending procession.

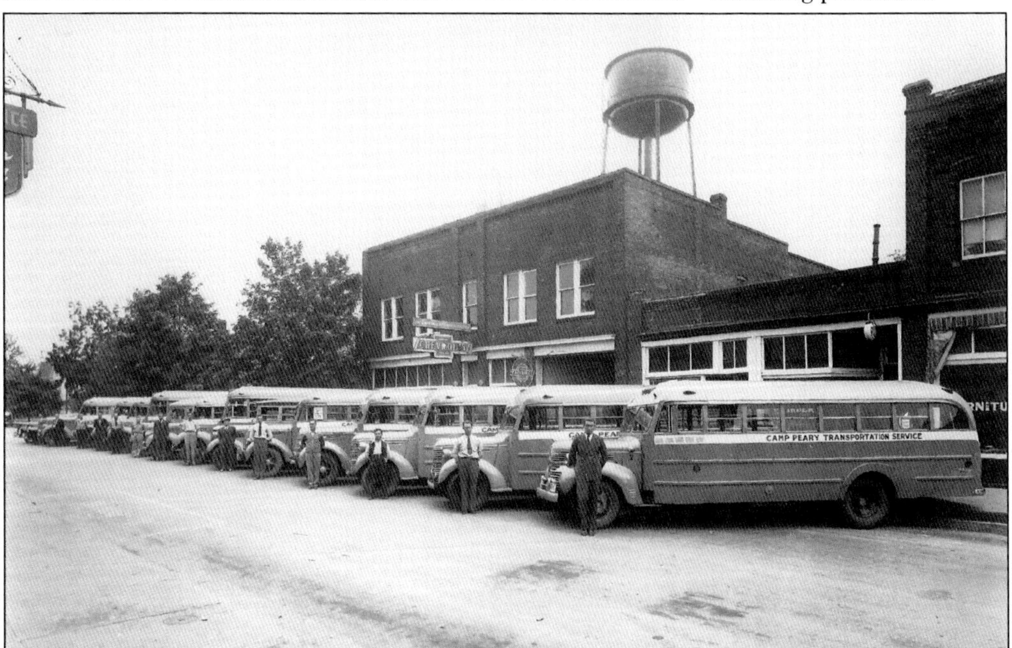

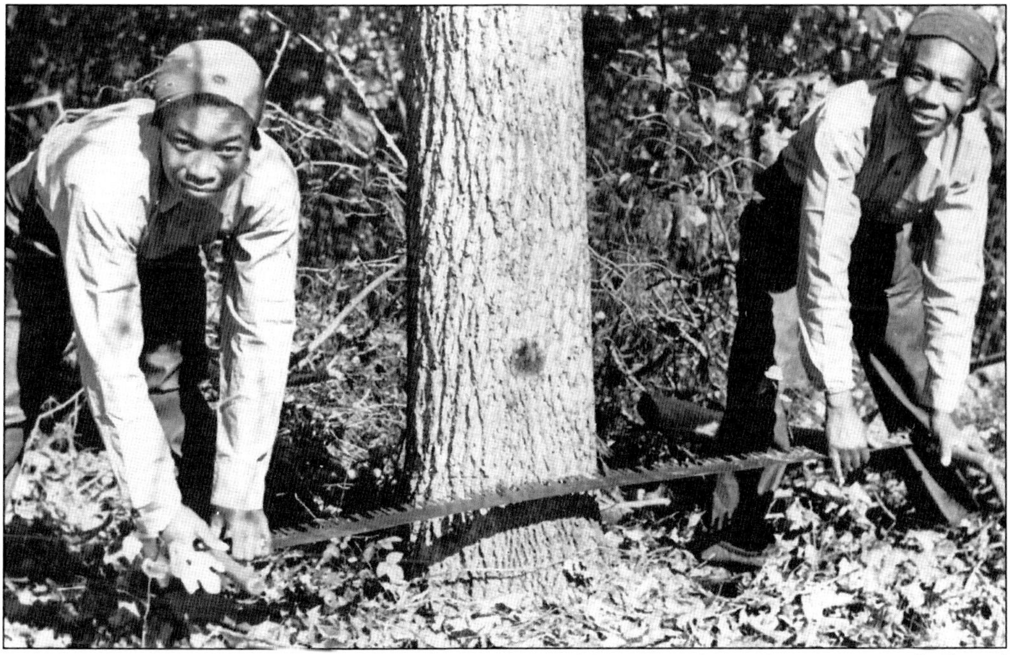

Women took on work usually done by men during World War II. Shown here are Essie (left) and Ida Braxton in about 1943, cutting trees for the paper mill. Pulp was a vital commodity needed in the war effort, so at one point, German prisoners of war were brought to the area to work for the Chesapeake Corporation.

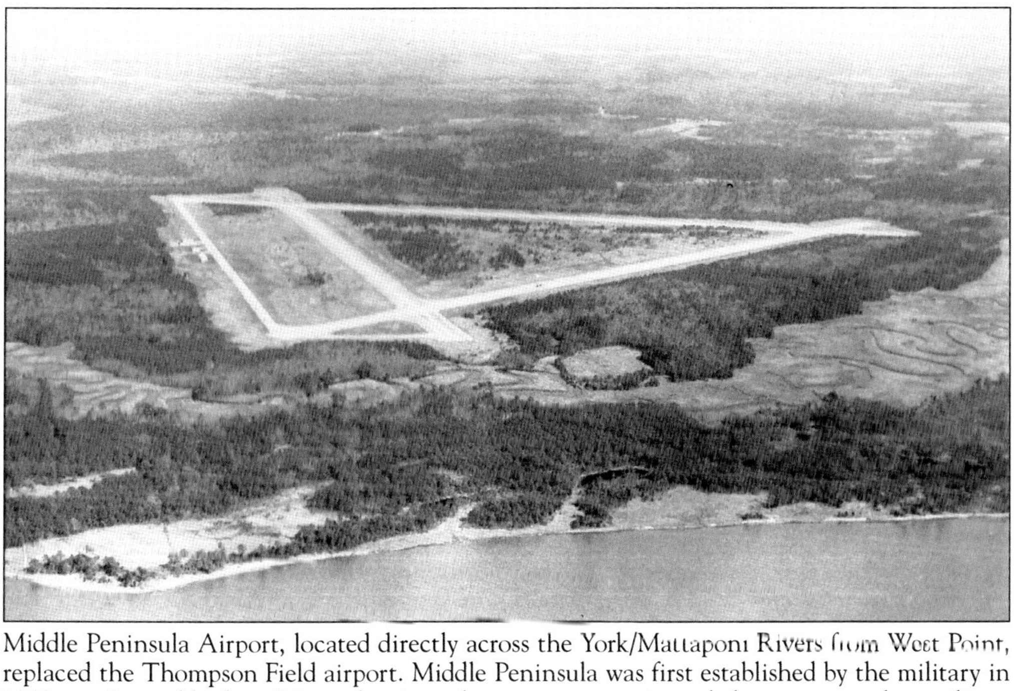

Middle Peninsula Airport, located directly across the York/Mattaponi Rivers from West Point, replaced the Thompson Field airport. Middle Peninsula was first established by the military in 1943 as a "scrambler base." Its early triangular runways were intended to accommodate military aircraft that needed to be disbursed quickly if the East Coast came under attack. It continues to serve both military and civilian aircraft and skydivers.

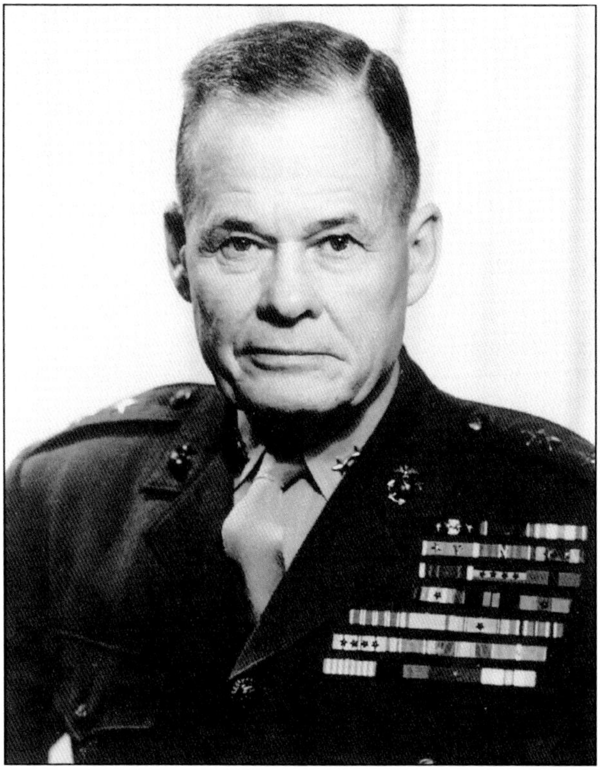

West Point native son Lt. Gen. Lewis "Chesty" Puller was a hero of the Pacific theater during World War II and later a hero of the Korean War. He remains the most decorated US Marine in American history and is known as "the Marine's Marine." He was born in 1898 on First Street and lived in West Point all of his life until he graduated from West Point High and went on to VMI. (Courtesy of William J. Addison.)

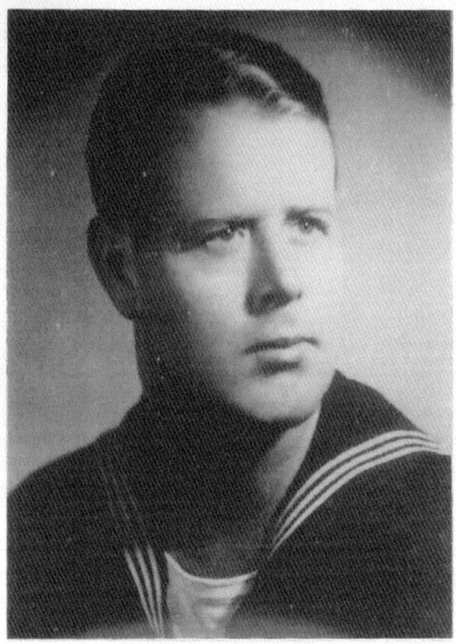

FORREST H. KIRBY

Forrest H. Kirby, was the son of Mr. and Mrs. Walter L. Kirby, was killed in action while serving aboard the U S S EVERSOLE on 10-28-44 during the second battle of the Philippine Sea. The EVERSOLE was a destroyer escort. Forrest graduated from West Point High School in 1929, attended Randolph Macon College where he played football. He was employed by the Chesapeake Corporation until he enlisted in the Navy in 1941. He was a member of the West Point Methodist Church and interested in sports, having been West Point High School's first football coach. He was raised to Master Mason in the West Point Lodge No. 238 AF and AM in 1940.

By: Lynn Perry

Another West Point native, Forrest H. Kirby, was killed in action during the second battle of the Philippine Sea in 1944. Before the war, he had returned home after completing college to teach at his alma mater, West Point High School, where he was its first football coach. A civic-minded young man, he was honored posthumously by the town when it named one of the three main streets Kirby Street.

In this image captured during World War II, soldier Stanley Zuraw poses in front of the Pamunkey Tea Room, which mainly served beverages much stronger than tea. The watering hole was a popular social destination during the war and is now part of the Van den Boorgard Center. (Courtesy of Betty Jenkins.)

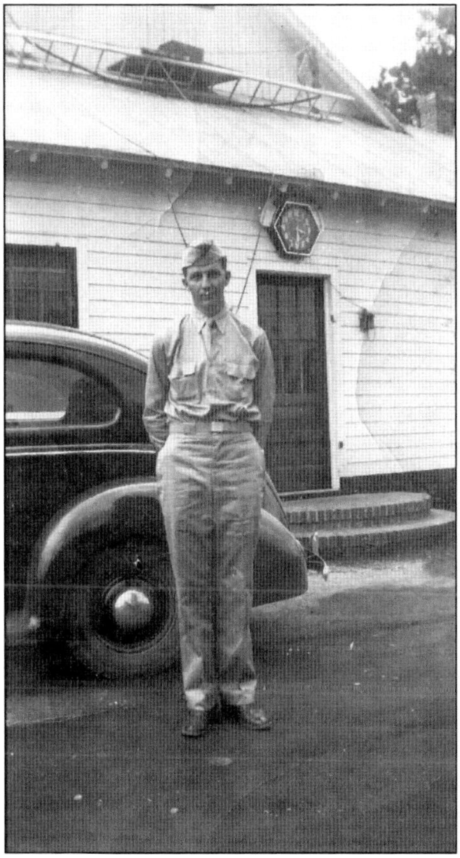

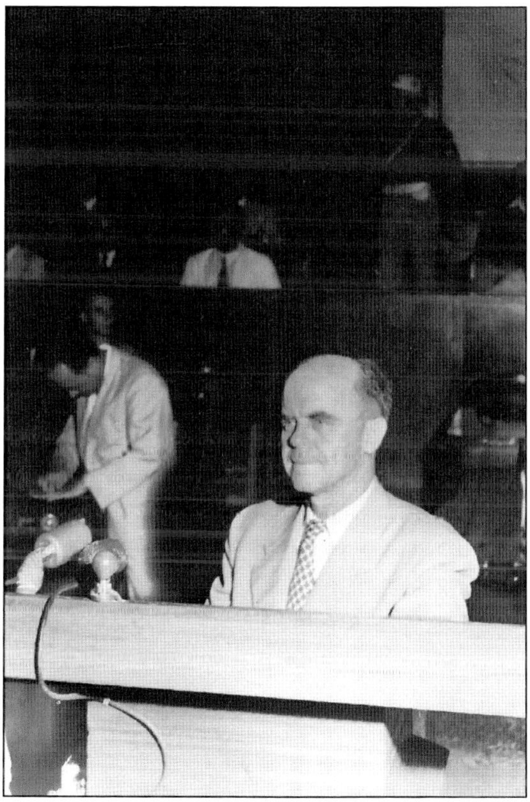

West Point lawyer David Nelson Sutton Sr., a veteran of World War I, is shown serving as an associate counsel for the Supreme Command Allied Powers, Occupied Japan, War Crimes Trial between 1946 and 1948. (Courtesy of William J. Addison.)

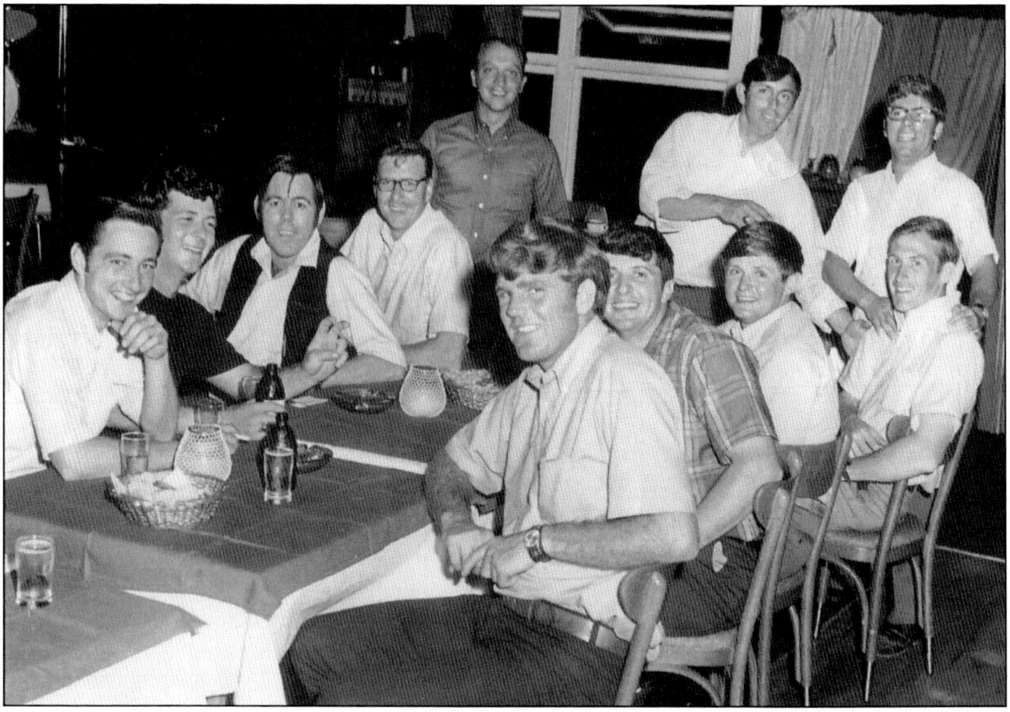

In this c. 1971 photograph, Company D of the 276th Combat Engineer Battalion of the National Guard Unit of West Point relaxes after a long day of work at Fort A.P. Hill. They are, from left to right, unidentified, Steve Bohannon, unidentified, Michael Prince, William Harlow, James Haywood, Billy Kriete, Ty Bland, Billy Wyatts, Johnny Minor, and Lloyd Taylor. (Courtesy of Tyler Bland III.)

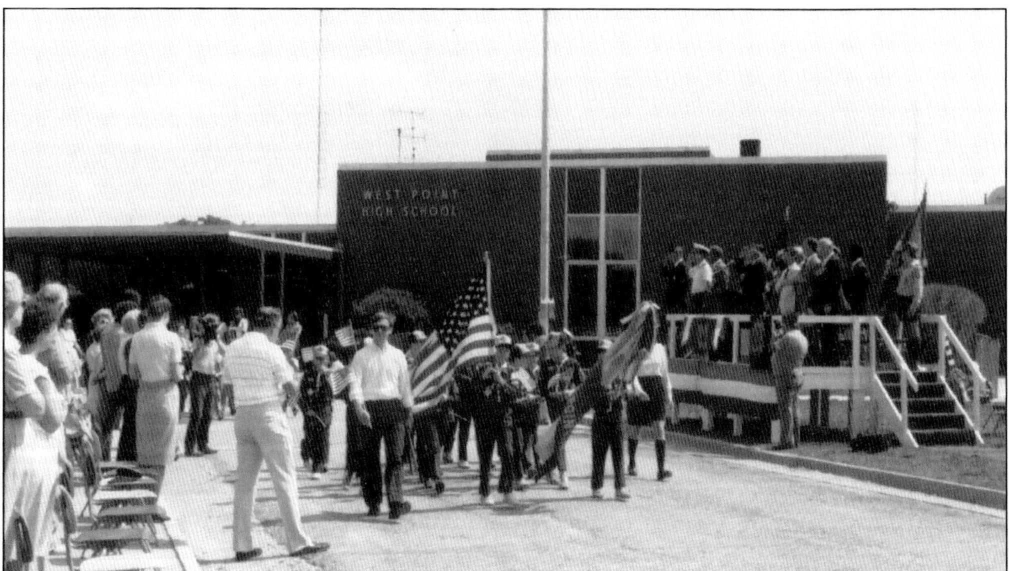

The local chapter of the Veterans of Foreign Wars parades in front of the new West Point High School in the 1970s. (Courtesy of Marianna Chestnutt.)

Seven

Port Richmond

In 1910, an Ohio transplant seeking warmer climates for his health arrived in West Point. Crosby Thompson was not only ambitious and resourceful, he was also a visionary. He saw the vast resources of timber, the deep, navigable rivers, and available rail connections and knew they could be put to good use. He also knew that the nearby city of Richmond needed a shorter shipping route to the Chesapeake Bay and the Atlantic than was afforded by the James River. The short trip overland and then the straight passage down the York would save many miles and cut costs. Therefore, in 1910, he formed the Old Dominion Industrial Corporation with the stated purpose of developing a deepwater terminal for Richmond at West Point. Next, he purchased the Taylor Farm, the last remnant of the West Plantation, and plans for a new community were born.

Thompson started by convincing the Southern Railway to improve passenger service from Richmond. By laying heavier rails and utilizing better equipment, the travel time between West Point and Richmond was reduced to 50 minutes. ODI Corporation encouraged the establishment of a pulpwood mill by donating its first timberlands. Furthermore, Thompson was determined to have a bridge cross the Mattaponi, so ODI Corporation financed the bonds to build the Gresham Bridge, finished in 1914.

Thompson's attempts to establish a deepwater terminal came to an end in 1916, but his promotion of industry in his newly founded town of Port Richmond never ceased. He was instrumental in the establishment of a shipyard during World War I and an airport after the war.

In the ensuing years, Port Richmond grew and prospered as a separate community with its own post office, school, and merchants. Its population included many recent immigrants from Eastern Europe, who formed their own Catholic community in the area. As time passed, however, the mutual needs of the two towns made unification necessary, which led to Port Richmond's annexation by West Point in 1963. A new school and much-needed water and sewer improvements benefited both communities, but Port Richmond as an autonomous village was no more.

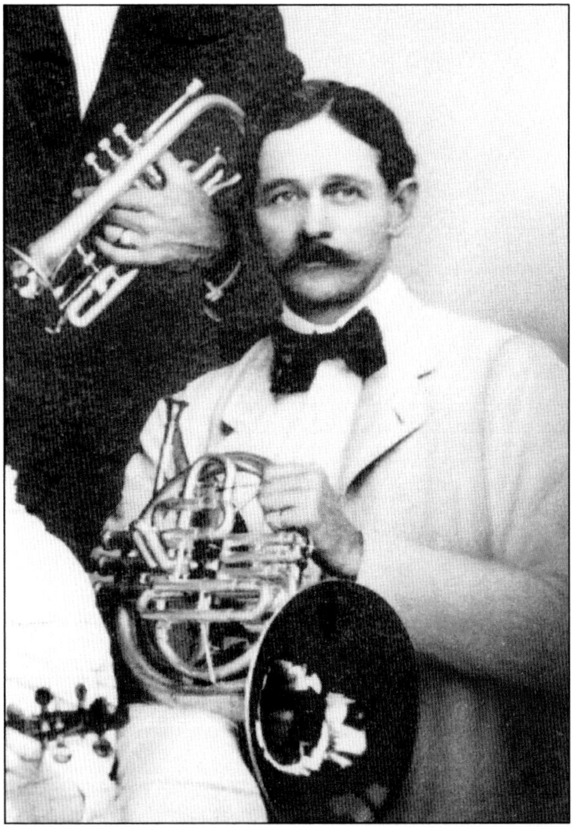

Crosby Thompson, the man behind the idea of Port Richmond, was born in Ohio in 1868. He moved to West Point in 1911.

Thompson built a home on the bluffs of the Pamunkey River, an area now informally referred to as "the Gold Coast," which he then named Euclid Heights, a suburb in his native Cleveland. This was the site of native villages and the first homes of English settlers. Thompson's home was one of a handful constructed in West Point using kits from Sears, Roebuck and Co. (Courtesy of William J. Addison)

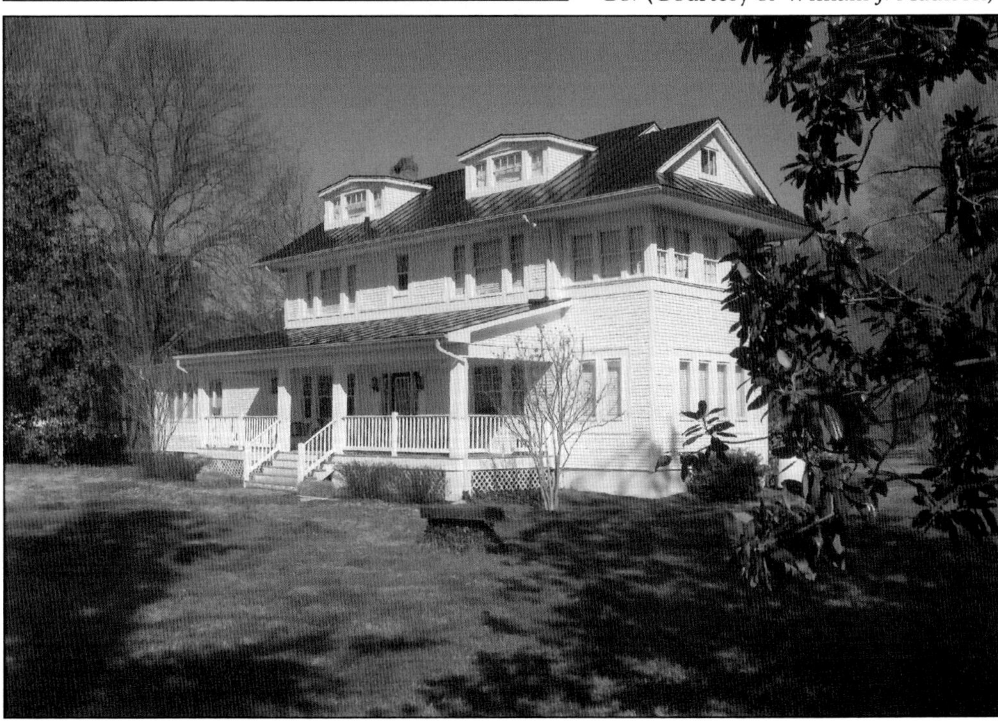

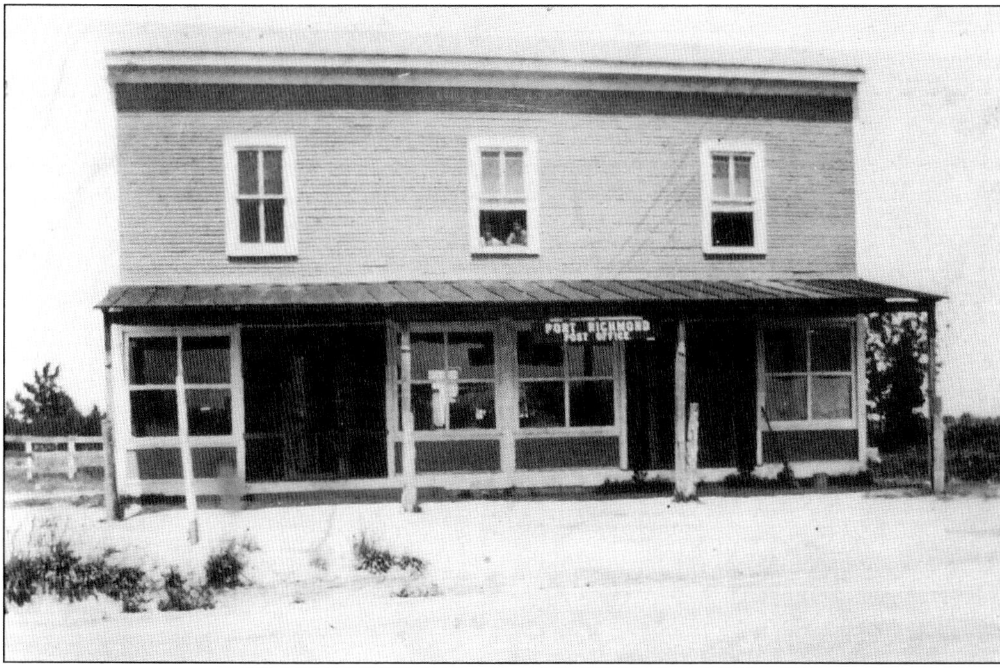

Until 1934, the Port Richmond post office was part of the Robbins General Store, shown here in the 1920s.

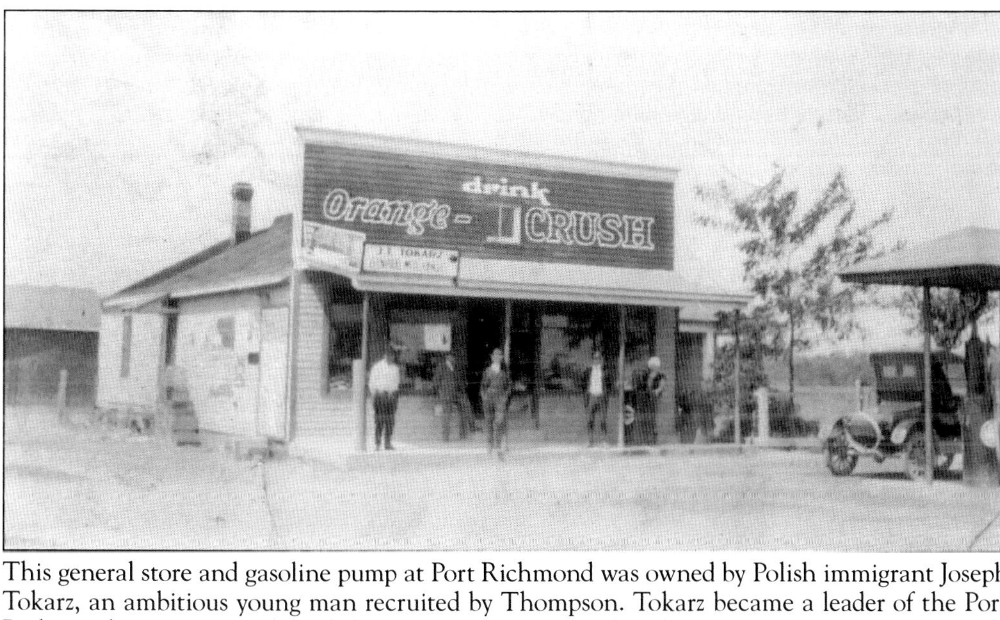

This general store and gasoline pump at Port Richmond was owned by Polish immigrant Joseph Tokarz, an ambitious young man recruited by Thompson. Tokarz became a leader of the Port Richmond community. The Polish immigrants that settled in that section of West Point brought with them a taste for foods not usually found in Virginia but available in the Tokarz store.

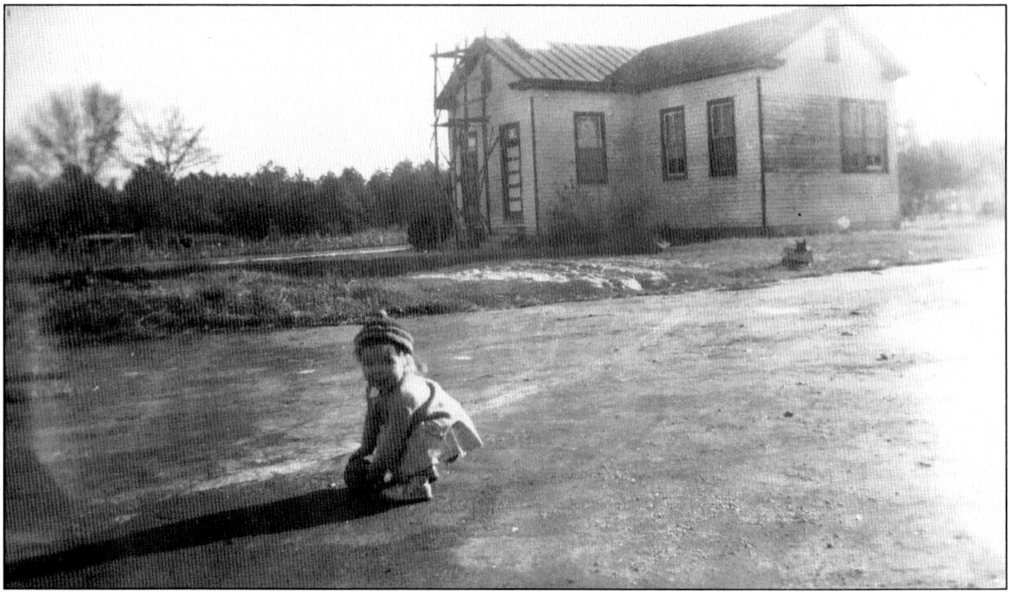

Toddler Betty Buch Jenkins plays outside of the Port Richmond School in the early 1940s. This small public school had two classrooms for grades one through seven. (Courtesy of Betty Jenkins.)

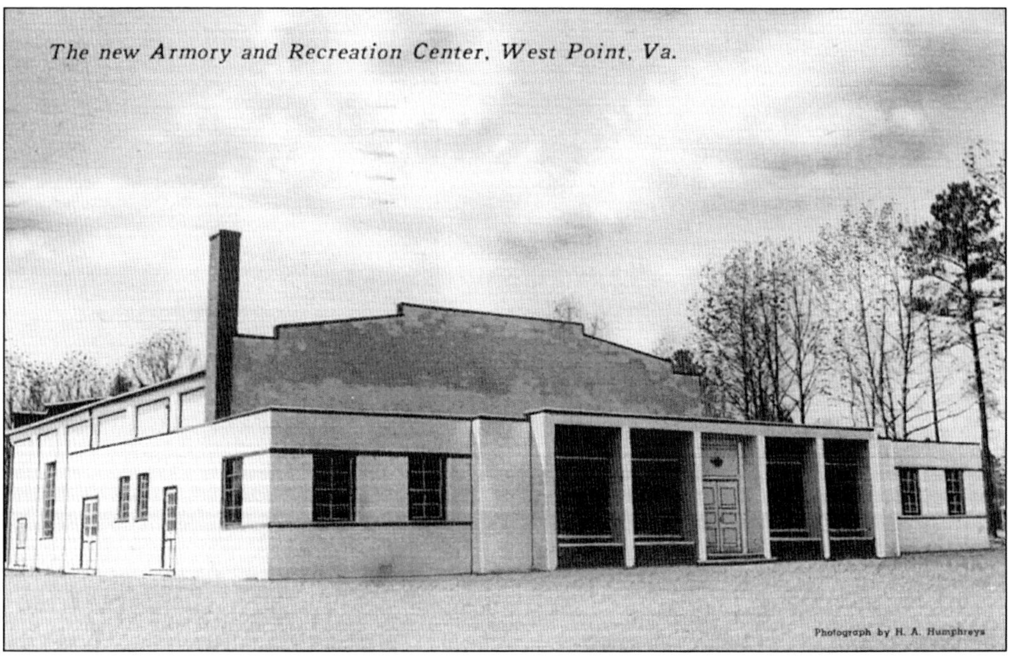

The National Guard Armory built in Port Richmond in 1953 also served as the West Point area's primary community center. It was the main location for basketball tournaments. (Courtesy of Richard Hosfield.)

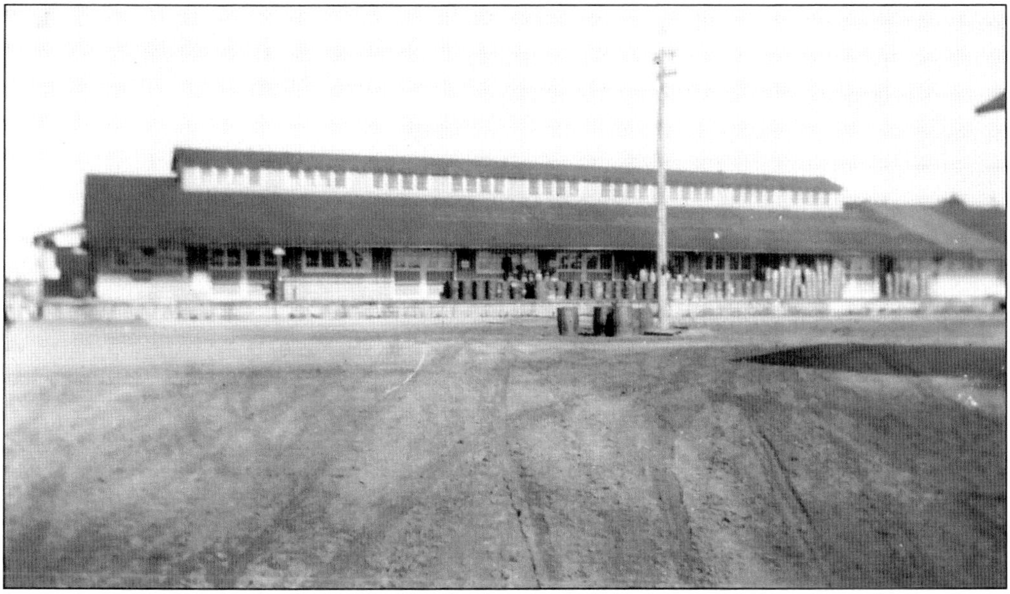

Port Richmond had a pickle factory that sold its products under the name Lord Baltimore Pickles. The factory, shown here in 1928, was a boon to local farmers who grew cucumbers, watermelons, and peppers. (Courtesy of Carol Fetterolf.)

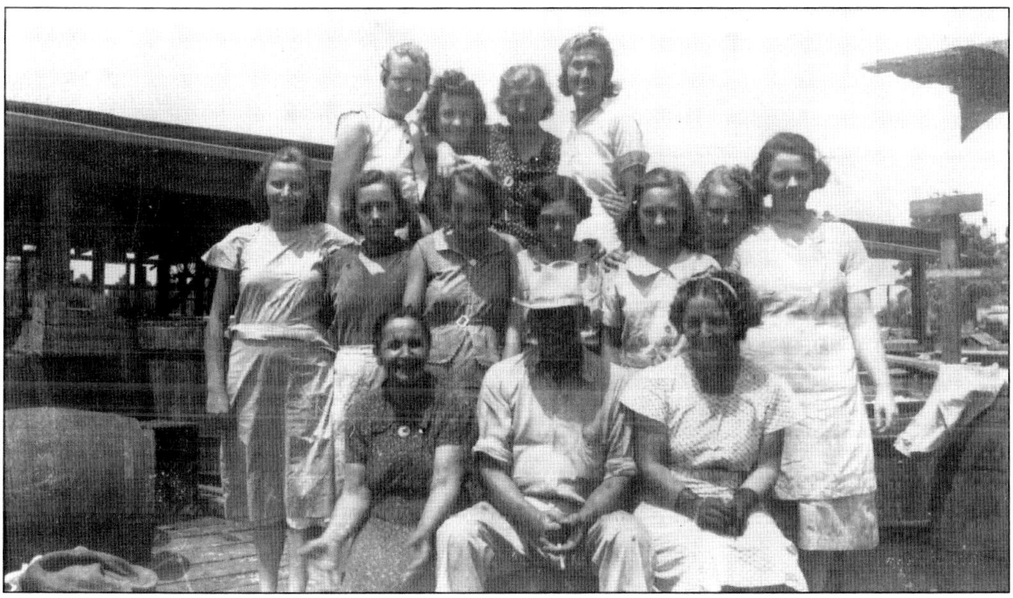

A group of workers from the pickle factory pose amid the barrels about 1940. Note that several ladies have rubber gloves on. (Courtesy of Carol Fetterolf.)

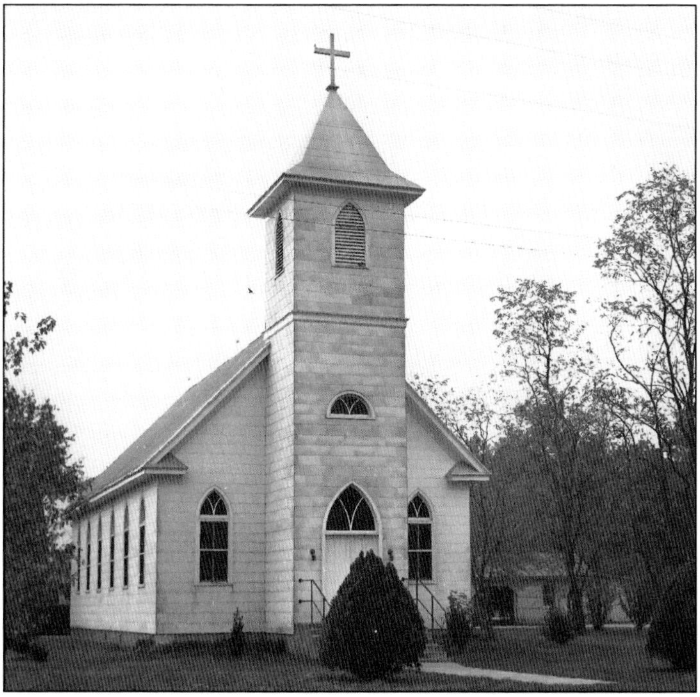

Prior to the founding of Port Richmond, St. Theresa, a small mission Catholic congregation in West Point, was established in 1906. With the coming of Eastern European immigrants to Port Richmond, there were enough Catholics for the first time to form a large congregation. Our Lady of the Blessed Sacrament Catholic Church was established in 1925 at Port Richmond. This first building for that congregation was demolished in 1968 and replaced with a much larger church on Route 30, after the consolidation of the two congregations.

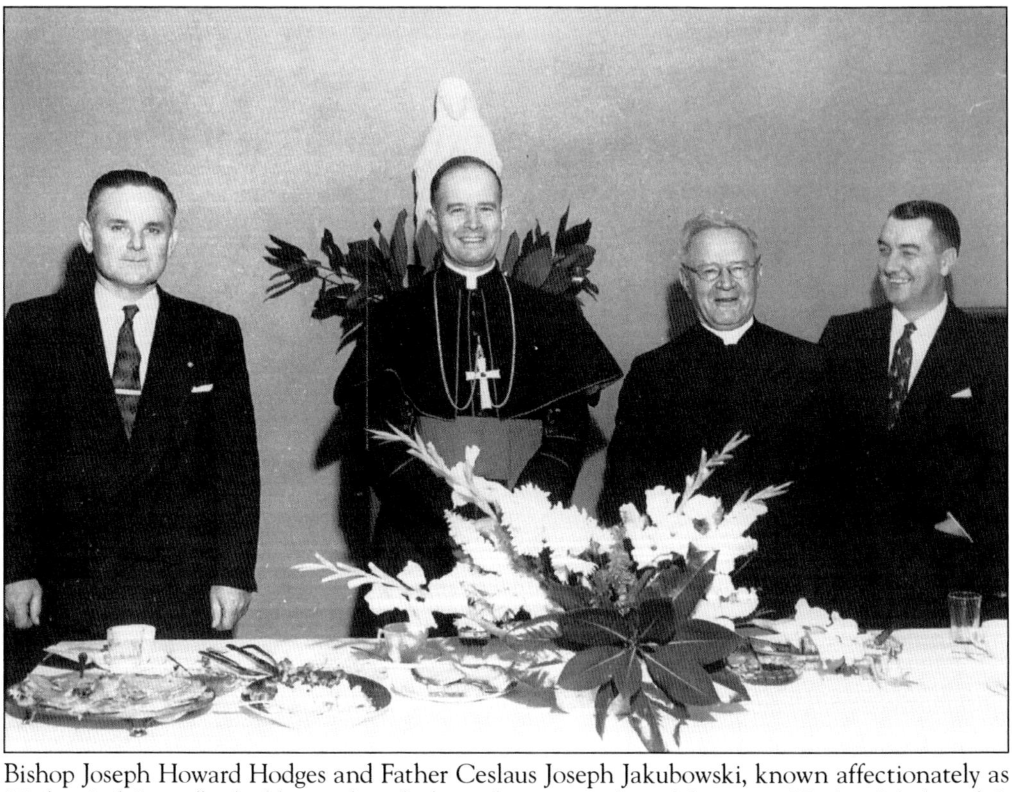

Bishop Joseph Howard Hodges and Father Ceslaus Joseph Jakubowski, known affectionately as "Father Jack," are flanked by unidentified parishioners at the celebration of Father Jakubowski's 35th anniversary as a priest. He served the parish from its founding in 1918 until 1961.

The Catholic community established its own parochial school for the area, the Blessed Sacrament School, in 1931. Students from that school crowd in front of Father Adolph Snella, who, among his many other duties, drove the school bus. This photograph was taken in the 1950s.

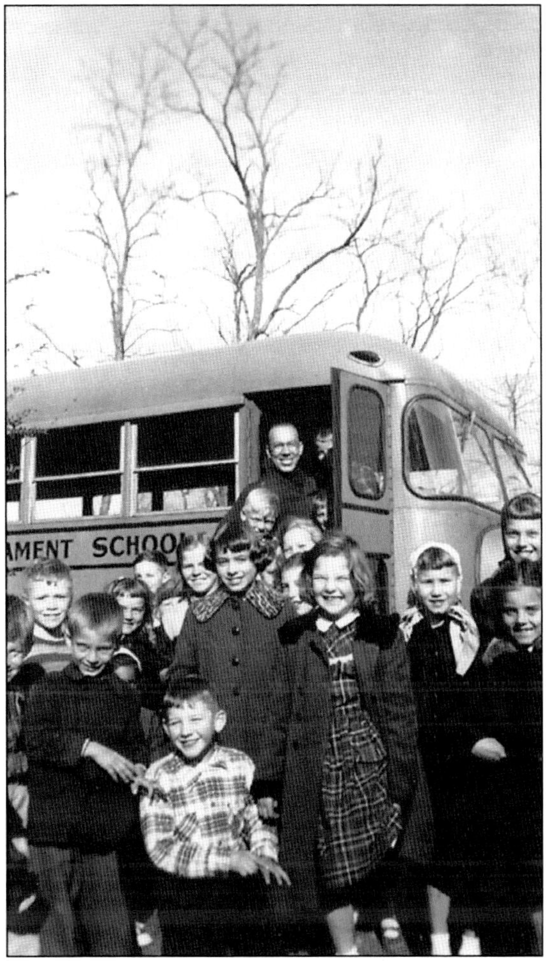

The convent building was also the location of the Blessed Sacrament School. At one time, 10 nuns from the Sisters of Mercy order of Baltimore made up the majority of the faculty. The school closed in 1968, in large measure because teaching sisters were no longer available to staff it. (Courtesy of Carol Fetterolf.)

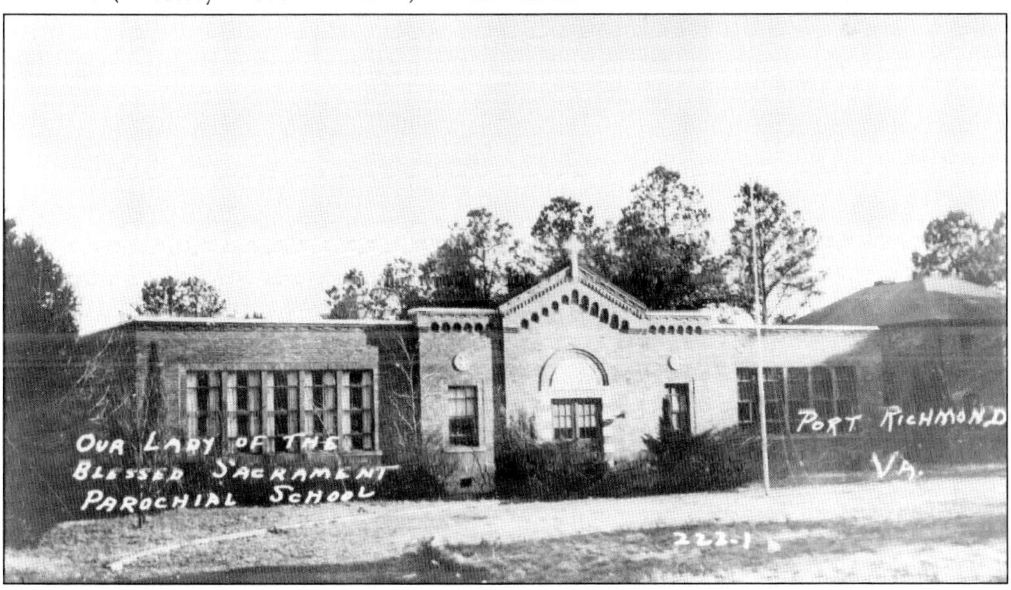

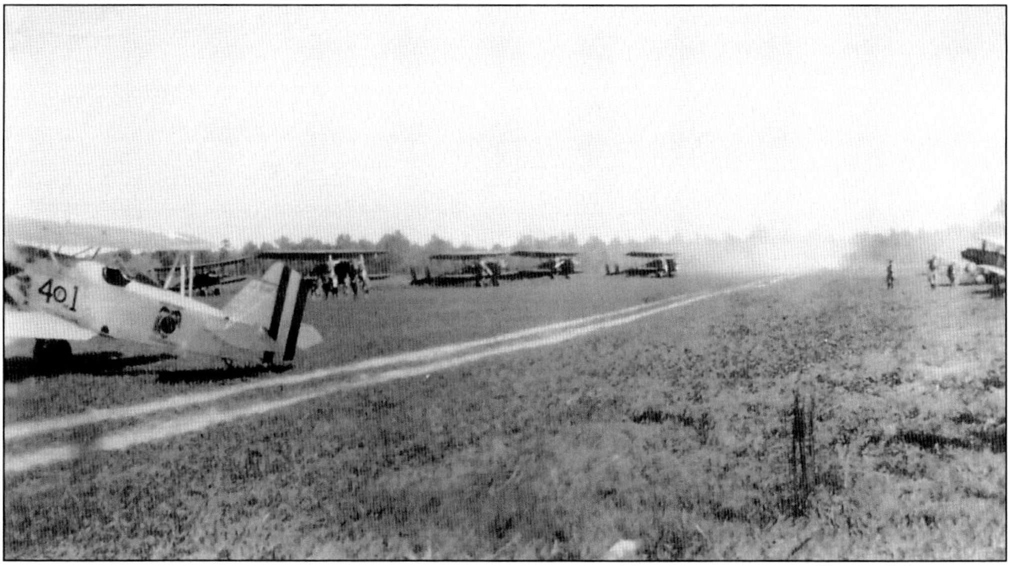

One of Thompson's dreams was that West Point would regain its place as a transportation hub. When his idea of it becoming the deepwater port for the city of Richmond did not come to fruition, he conceived the idea that it could be a center for air travel and constructed a small airport in the vicinity of the present country club on land formerly owned by the Custis/Washington/Lee family. Thompson Airfield at Port Richmond was used by the US military until warplanes became too large for its runways. (Courtesy of Ellis Olsson.)

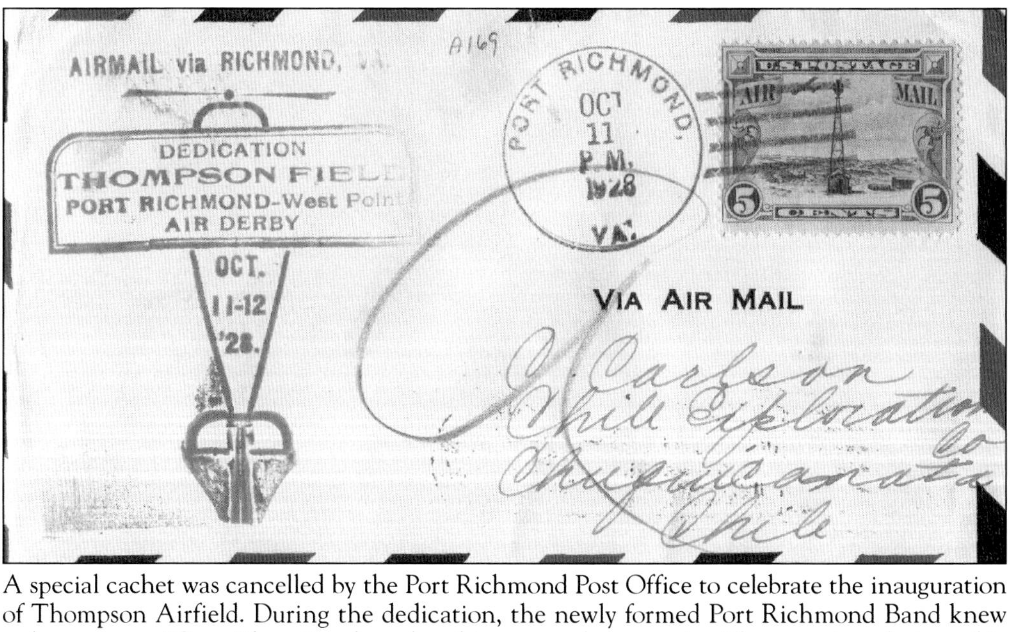

A special cachet was cancelled by the Port Richmond Post Office to celebrate the inauguration of Thompson Airfield. During the dedication, the newly formed Port Richmond Band knew only one tune, "Over There," and so played it over and over again. That evening, during a big party celebrating the day's events, Thompson suddenly died of a heart attack. In an instant, Port Richmond lost its founder and most tireless promoter. (Courtesy of Carol Fetterolf.)

Eight

Downtown Businesses and Community Services

When the town was laid out yet again, in 1860 by J.M. Daniel, it was given three long perpendicular streets, each called by a letter of the alphabet, and short cross streets bearing numbers. Over time, C, D, and E Streets became Kirby, Main, and Lee Streets, respectively. The layout of West Point made it well suited for pedestrians, and its short blocks provided numerous street corners for businesses. Residences were mingled among merchants. The mild climate produced many good days for sitting on porches or strolling the sidewalks. A dense urban environment was developed in the midst of rural beauty.

Before the removal of the terminus to Portsmouth, West Point had ship chandlers, a number of newspapers, banks, saloons (of course), and a wide variety of merchants. Always a conservative town, it did not begin to install water and sewer systems until the Great Fire of 1903 made it obvious that they were necessities. Paved sidewalks were installed in the 1930s and 1940s.

For at least a century, West Point residents never needed to leave town to shop; everything they wanted was readily at hand. People from the surrounding region came to West Point for goods and services, but that changed during the latter part of the 20th century, when new trends in the retail business caused the shuttering of many small stores across the country. As retail chain stores and restaurants opened in surrounding towns, others closed in West Point. Walking to a business was no longer as desirable when everyone had an automobile. Old commercial buildings were put to new uses or torn down. The vibrant town center that once was a shining example of small-town America was superseded by shopping centers and the lure of larger cities easily reached by car. During the 1960s and 1970s, Fourteenth Street became the center of shopping for a time, usurping the older business district on Main Street. But that too was short lived, as a shopping center and strip malls were constructed in old Port Richmond along Route 30.

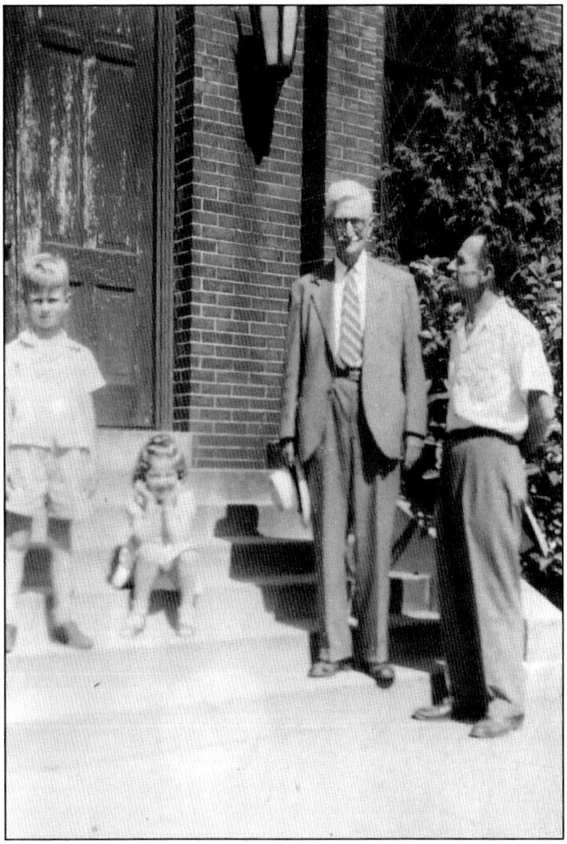

Leonard Slater Cottrell, owner and editor of the *West Point Virginian* newspaper, poses with his son Walter Cottrell and grandchildren David and Susan Cottrell in front of the Methodist Church of West Point in 1939. Cottrell began his journalism career in 1889 with the *West Point Star* newspaper when he was only 19 years old. He later changed its name to the *Virginian*. He was forced to move his paper to Newport News in 1896 after the economy of West Point was devastated by the 1895 move of the railway terminus. One of a handful of newspapers in West Point in the early 1890s, the *Virginian* promoted the temperance movement and modernization of the town. Cottrell was the state editor of the *Richmond Times-Dispatch* newspaper at the time of this photograph. (Courtesy of Frederick F. Jewett.)

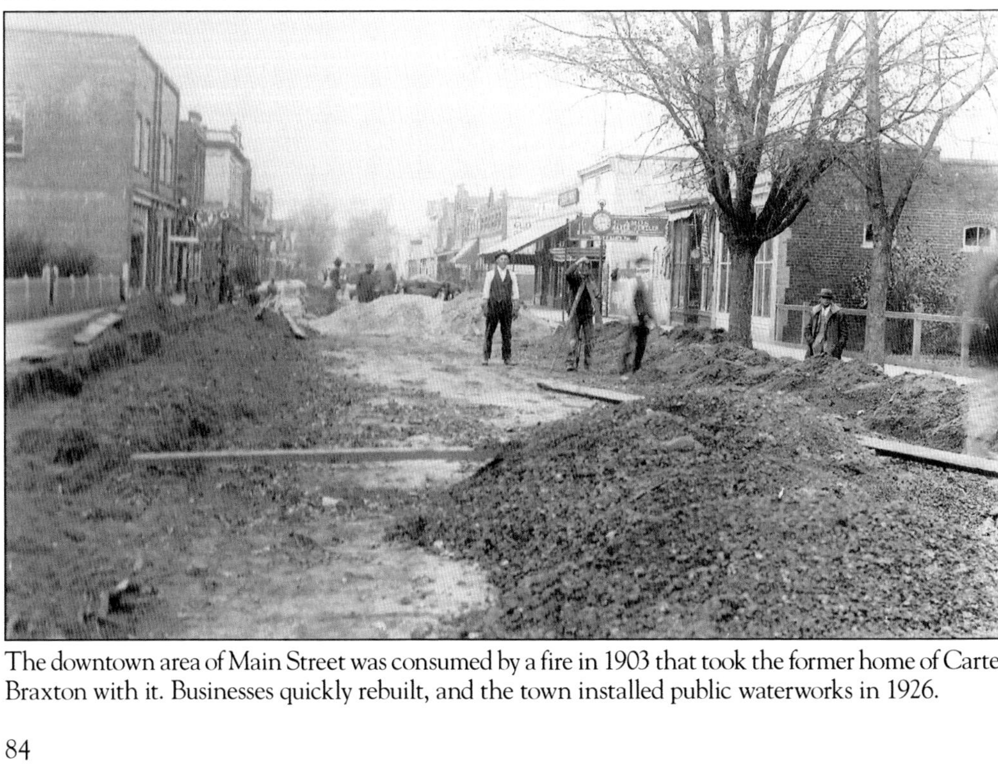

The downtown area of Main Street was consumed by a fire in 1903 that took the former home of Carter Braxton with it. Businesses quickly rebuilt, and the town installed public waterworks in 1926.

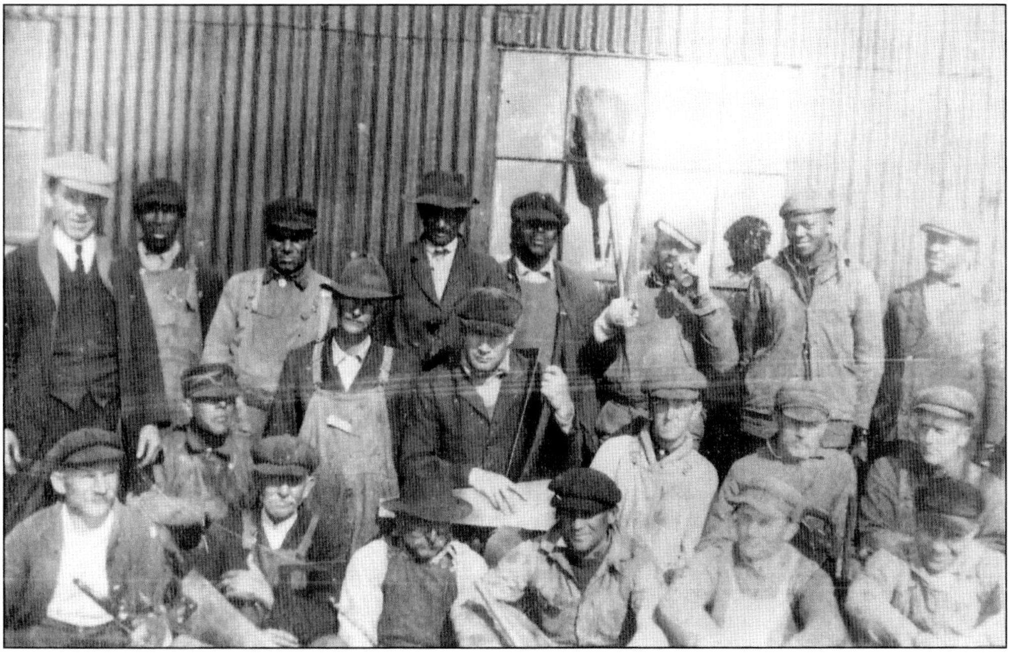

Workers at a West Point lumber mill pose for a photograph about 1900. (Courtesy of Carol Fetterolf.)

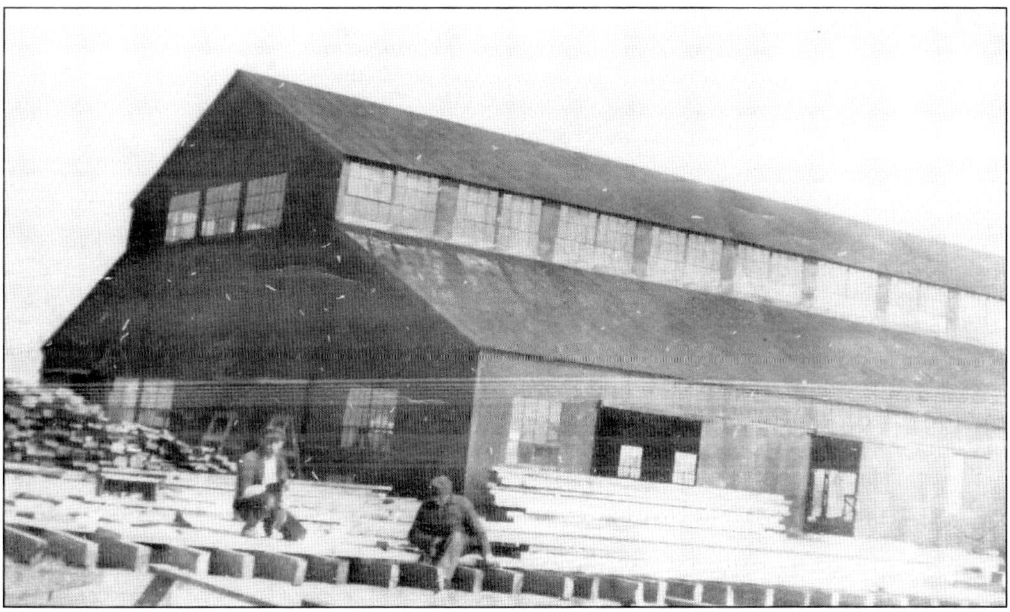

A West Point lumber mill at the port is shown about 1900. Forests in the area supplied more than pulp for paper; the town also had a furniture factory, and lumber was shipped from West Point. (Courtesy of Carol Fetterolf.)

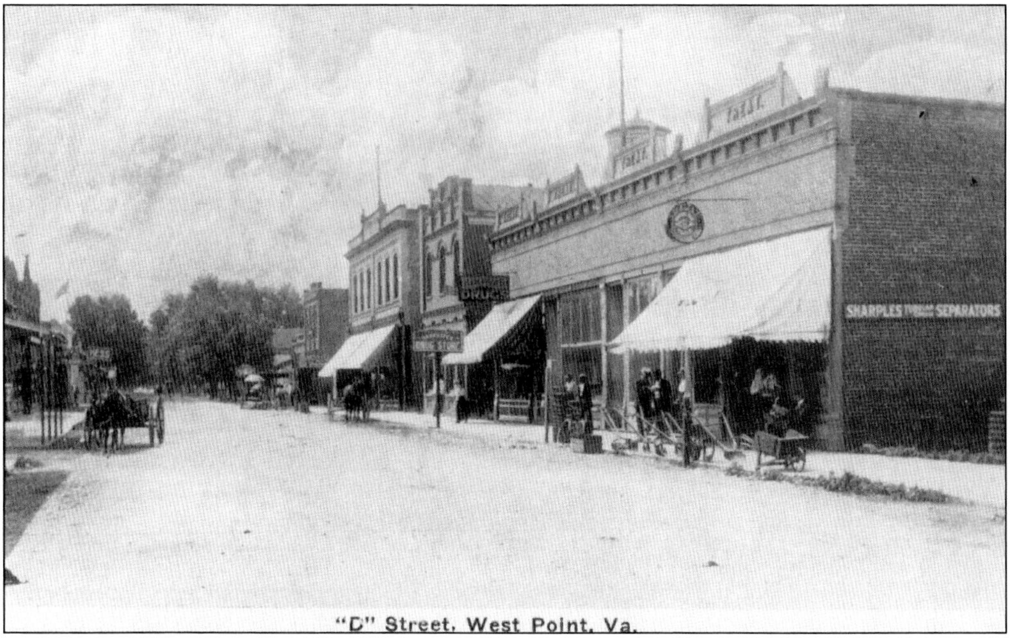

This view of Main Street, called D Street during the early years, looks south about 1900.

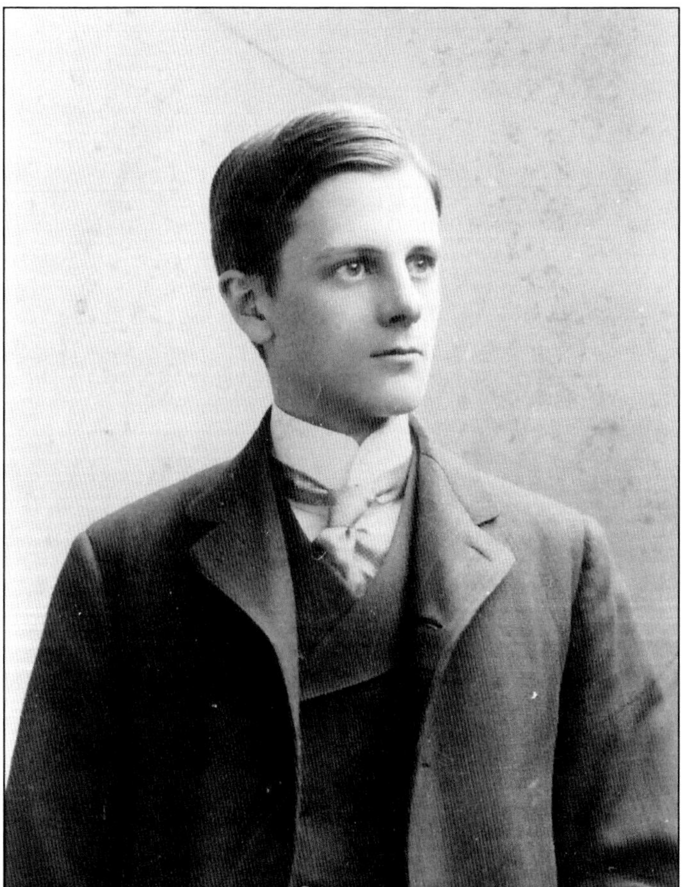

Dr. Barthurst Browne Bagby was the town's primary physician for many decades during the late 19th and early 20th centuries. He insisted that the town council install a sewage system to prevent typhoid outbreaks. He made major breakthroughs in the medical understanding of hookworm and also wrote a detailed history of the town. Dr. Bagby is remembered with a street named in his honor.

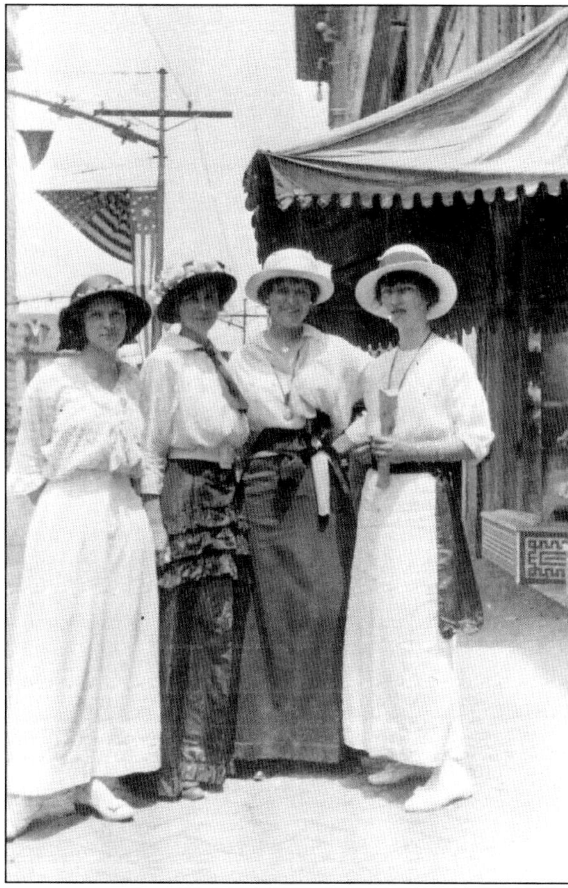

Four young women pause during a stroll on Main Street. The woman second from the left is Martha Puller, mother of the town's "favorite son," Gen. Lewis "Chesty" Puller.

This is an early view of downtown looking south.

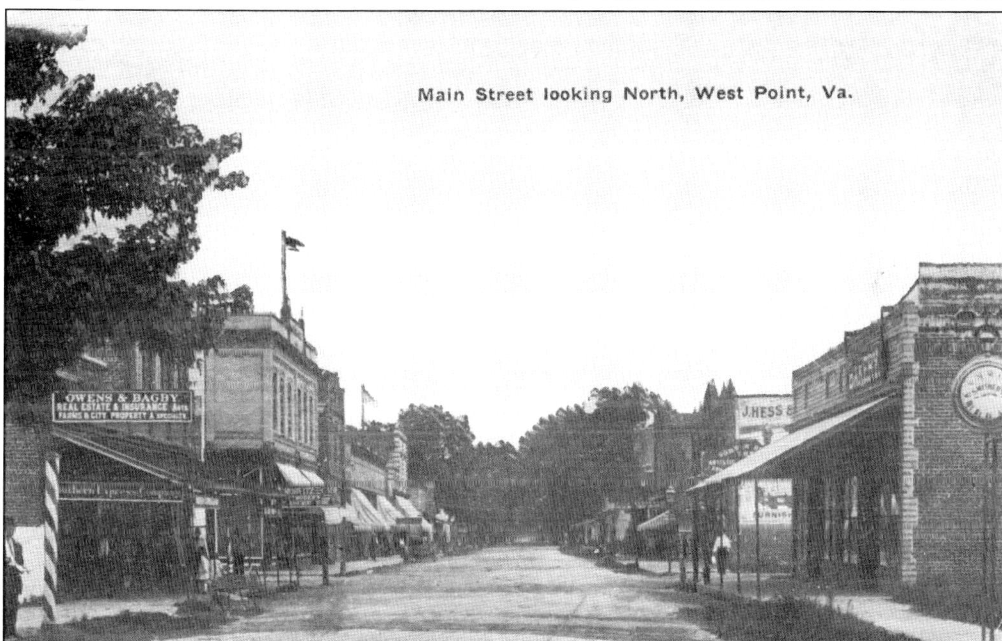

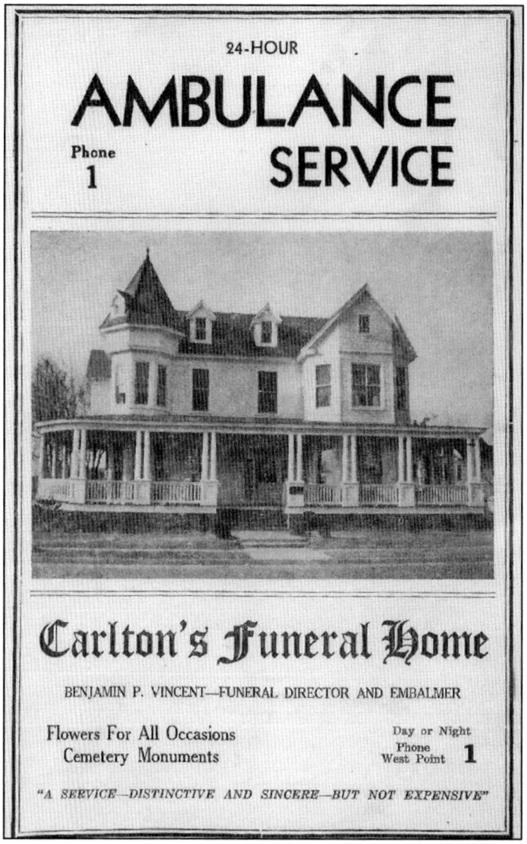
24-HOUR
AMBULANCE SERVICE
Phone 1

Carlton's Funeral Home

BENJAMIN P. VINCENT—FUNERAL DIRECTOR AND EMBALMER

Flowers For All Occasions
Cemetery Monuments

Day or Night Phone West Point 1

"A SERVICE—DISTINCTIVE AND SINCERE—BUT NOT EXPENSIVE"

This advertisement for Carlton's Funeral Home on Lee Street appeared in the early 1900s. The owners, the Vincent family, lived in the building. It is a private residence today, and the Vincents continue to operate a funeral home business on Eleventh Street.

Charlie Clark (right), also known as "Charlie the Barber," was a favorite of the townsfolk. Shown here with his brother Howard Clark (standing in the center) and an unidentified customer in the 1940s, his was one of a number of small businesses owned by African Americans. Another was Bray's Seafood, owned by descendents of James Armistead Lafayette who continued to use their famous ancestor's secret recipe for crab cakes to delight customers, including diners at the restaurants of Richmond department stores. Other African American businesses included a laundry, shoe repair, plaster contractor, restaurants, and general stores.

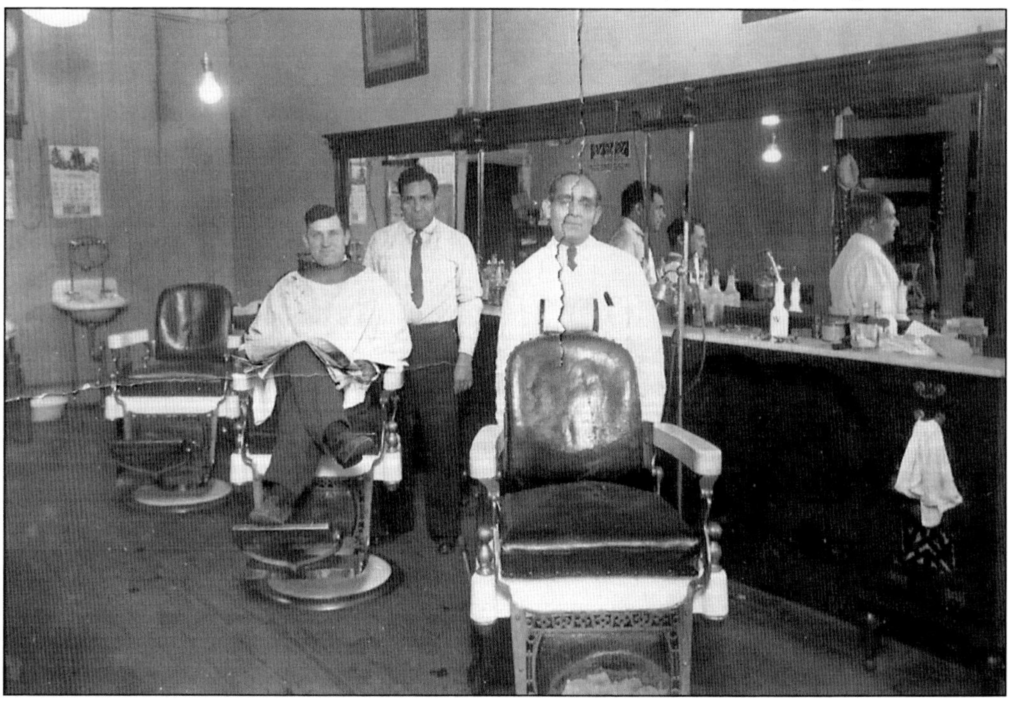

Hunter Virginia Marshall Smith, shown here as a teenage bride, was an early businesswoman. The daughter of the owner of the Marshall Oyster House, she ran a Pepsi bottling plant out of an old carriage house behind her home at the corner of Sixth and Lee Streets about 1910. (Photograph taken at William Foster Studio, courtesy of Juanita Oakley.)

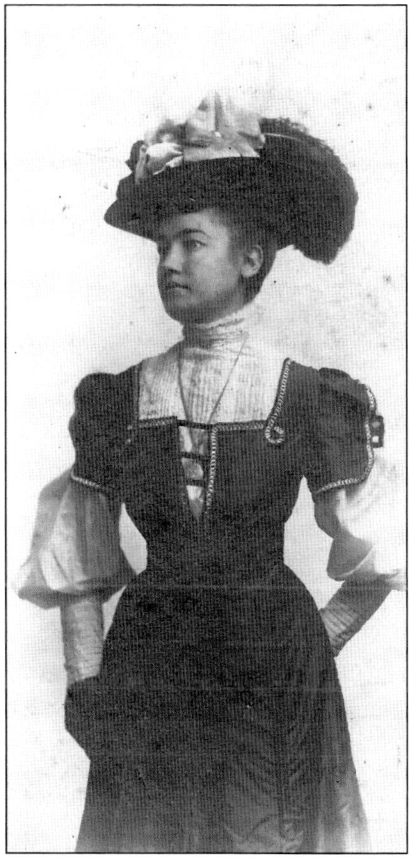

This photograph shows the carriage house where the Pepsi bottling operation was located. Smith also bottled other sweet beverages. The house to the right was built prior to the Civil War and had a larger home attached to it in the 1890s.

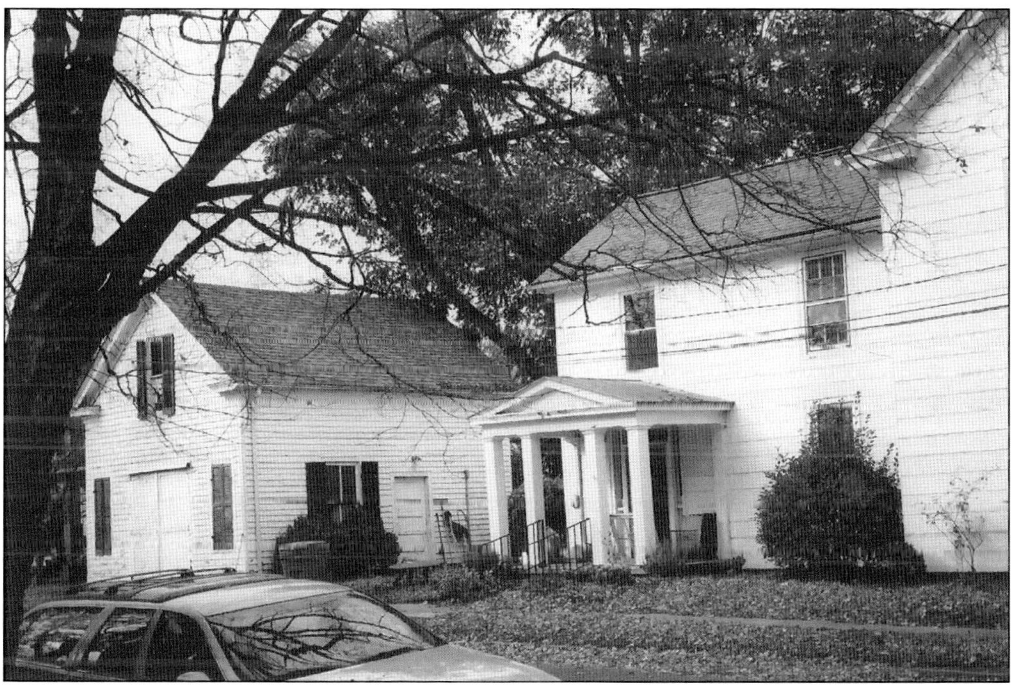

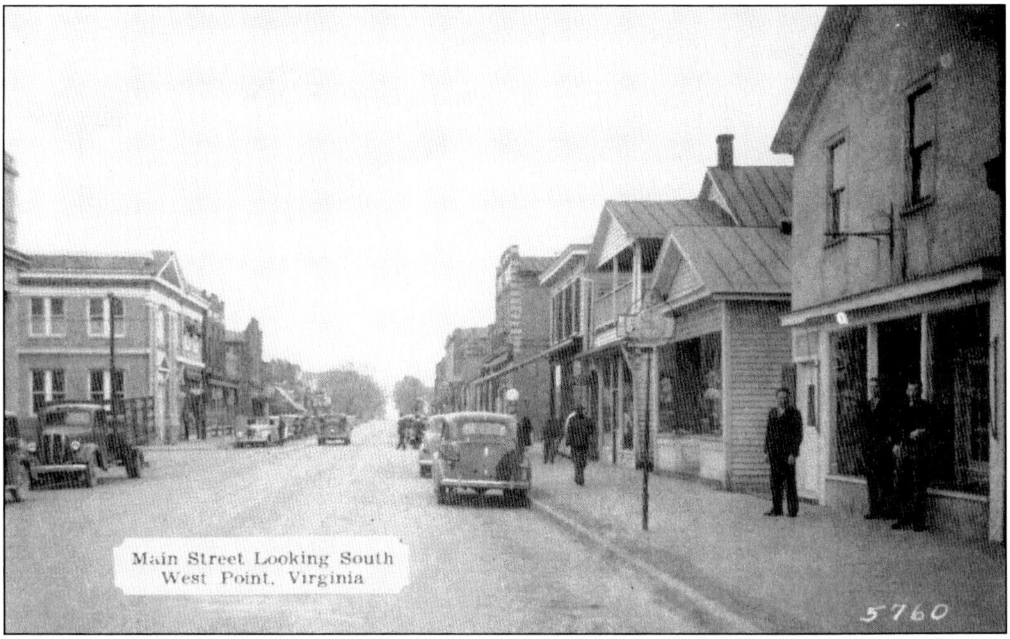

This view of downtown in the 1930s looking south includes the two bank buildings: Farmers and Mechanics Bank on the left, established in 1927, and the former State Bank on the right, whose building was later used by Thrift Insurance Company.

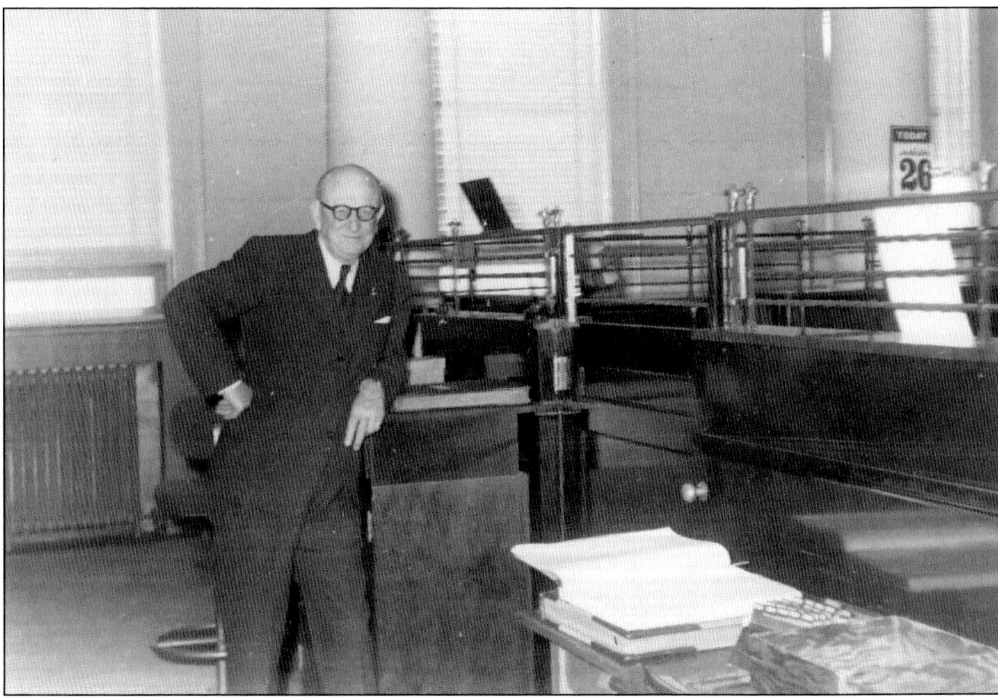

West Point native J. Marshall Lewis first served as president of Farmers and Mechanics Bank from its inception and then as president of Citizens and Farmers Bank when the bank merged with Citizens Exchange Bank & Trust Company in 1933. At the same time, he served as president of the Bank of Gloucester. He retired in 1961.

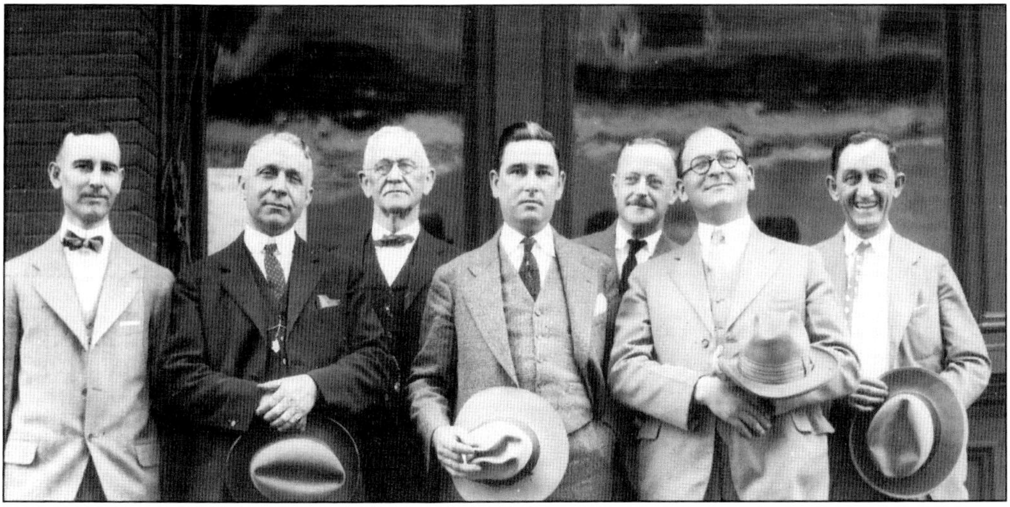

On June 19, 1927, a committee of West Point businessmen appeared before the State Highway Commission to appeal to the state to take over the West Point–area toll bridges. The committee members from left to right were M.T. Blassingham, E.D. Clopton, H.I. Lewis, C. Gouldman, G.H. Massey, W.J. Waring, and H. Brooks.

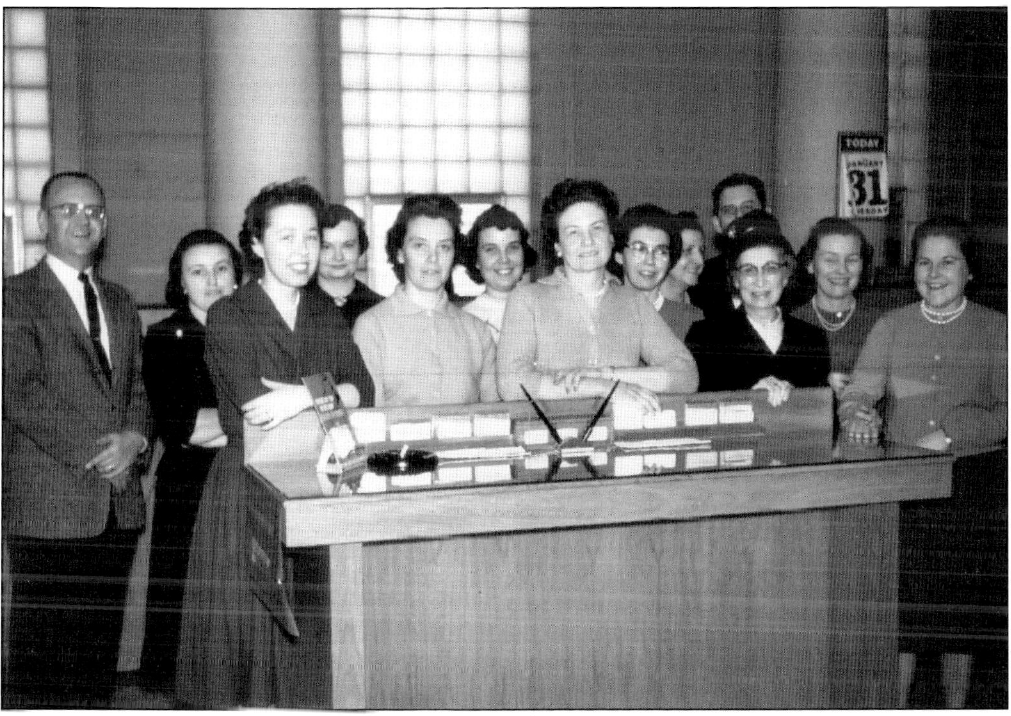

Staff of the Citizens and Farmers Bank pose in the lobby of its Main Street headquarters. William T. Robinson, who succeeded Lewis as president of bank in 1961, positioned it to become a regional bank with branches between Richmond and Norfolk. Robinson was succeeded in 1989 by Larry G. Dillon. In 2005, its operation center moved from West Point to Toano, though it retains its corporate headquarters in West Point. (Courtesy of C&F Bank.)

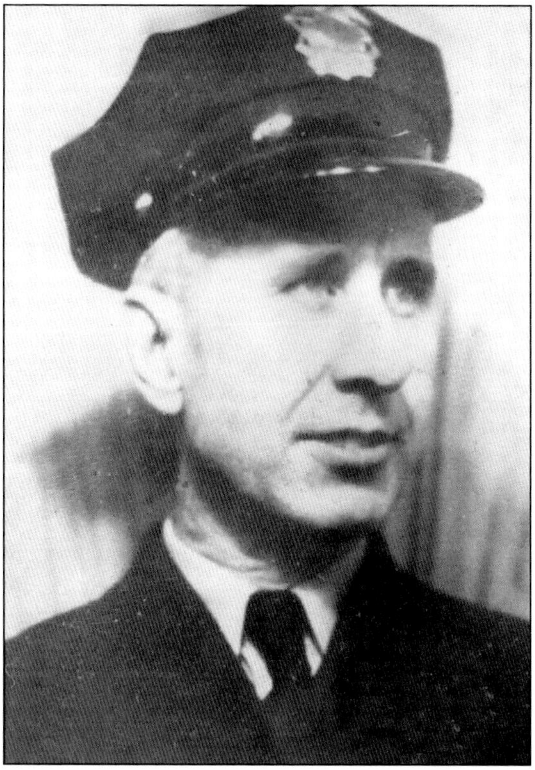

Irving L. Martin was head of the West Point police department from 1926 until 1973. He was not only chief of police and town sergeant, but he was also in charge of the general operation of the town. Everyone in West Point knew to "ask Mr. Martin" to solve almost every problem.

The West Point Town Council deliberates in the 1950s. For decades, the town hall on Sixth Street was also the firehouse, and the council chamber doubled as a courtroom. The town has had an independent government since 1870.

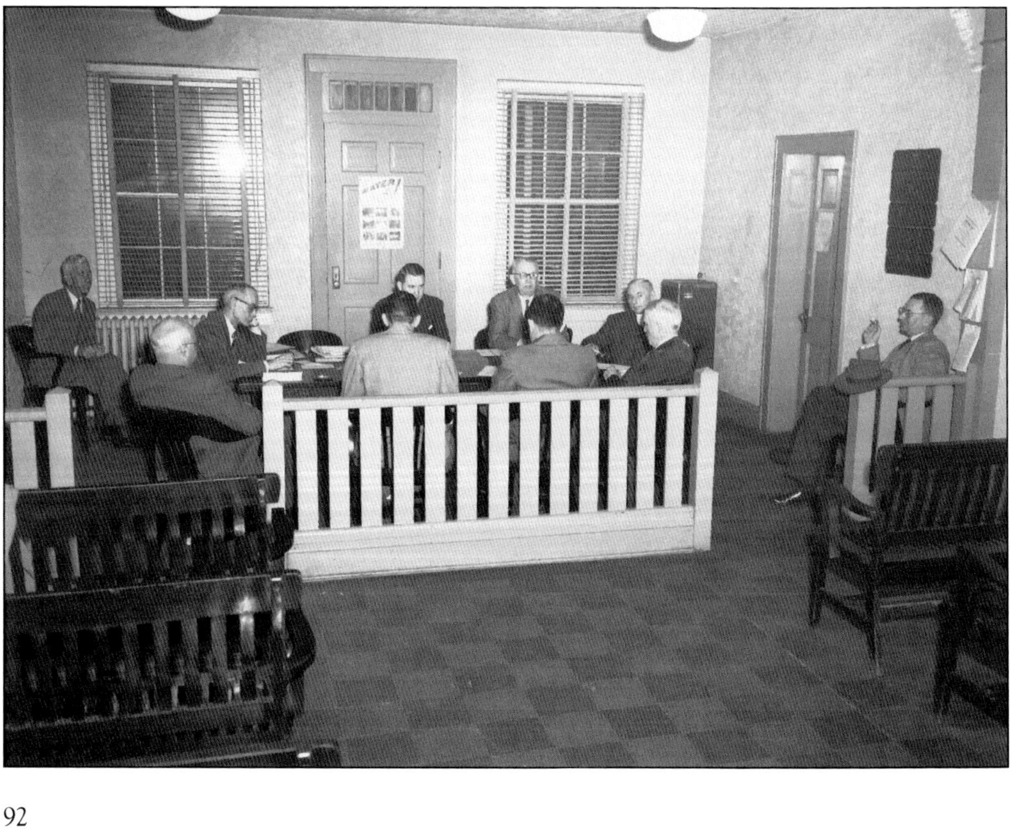

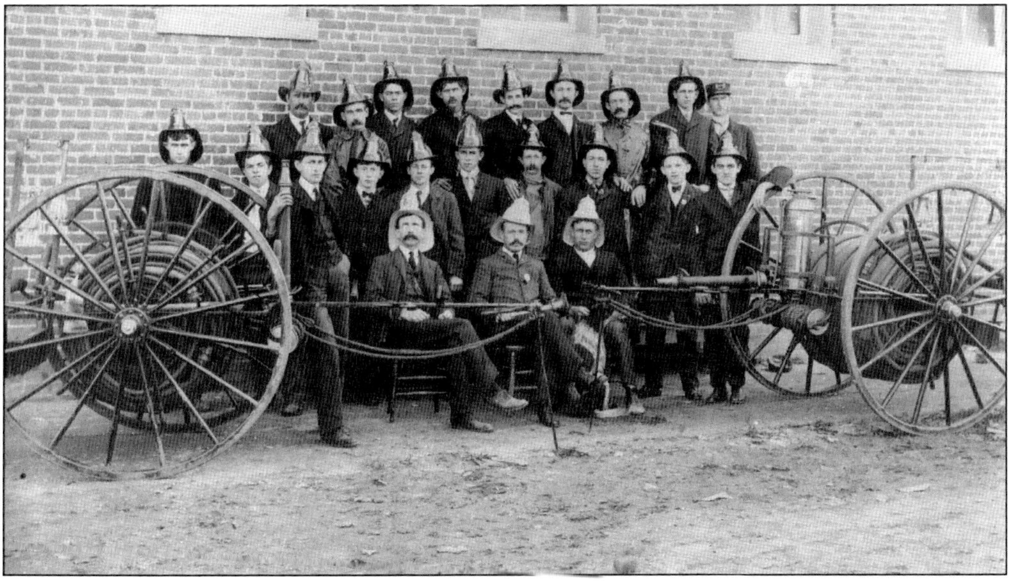

The West Point Volunteer Fire Company No. 1 poses between hose reels in 1905. This important civic group formed in response to the 1903 fire that consumed four blocks of shops and homes in the center of town. The town also installed a water and hydrant system after the fire. (Courtesy of West Point Volunteer Fire Department and Rescue Squad.)

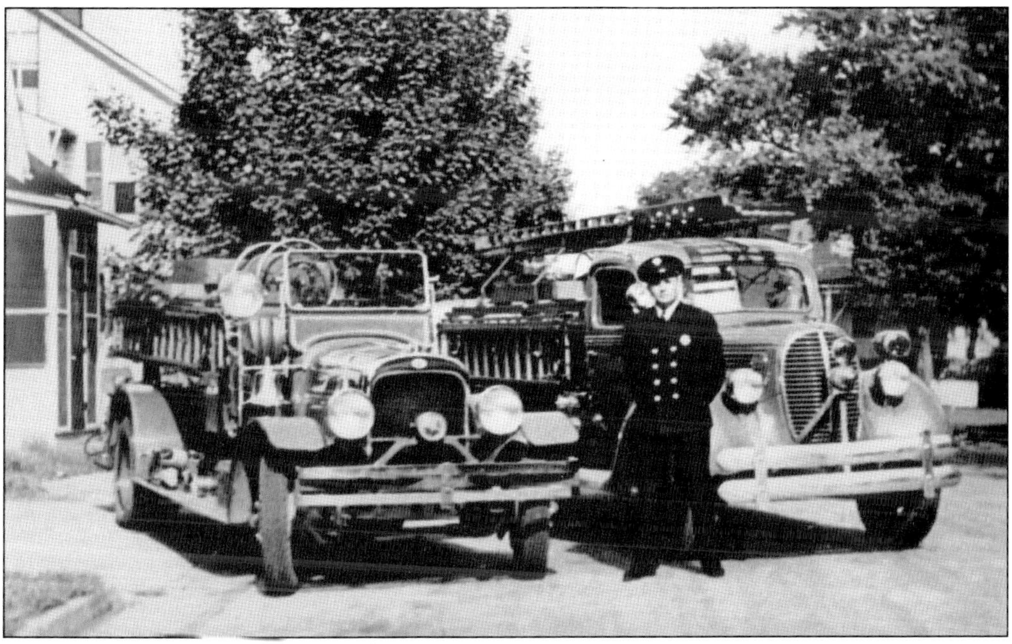

During the 1940s, West Point fire chief Charles Carlton proudly poses next to the town's two fire engines: a 1934 Seagrave Pump and a 1939 Ford. In the ensuing years, the 1934 Seagrave would be sold and resold. Just before it was to be scrapped, markings on the truck identifying it as belonging to the West Point Volunteer Fire Department prompted a kind soul to make a telephone call. The fire truck returned to its original home and was lovingly restored. It now proudly heads the annual Firemen's Parade and other celebrations in town. (Courtesy of West Point Volunteer Fire Department and Rescue Squad.)

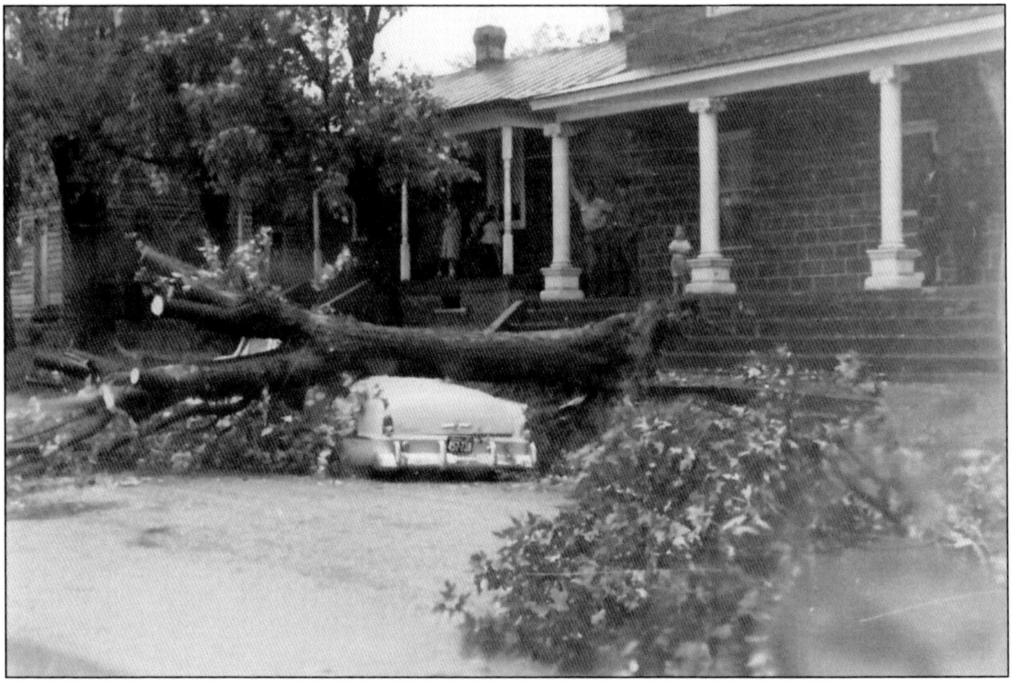

In 1954, Hurricane Hazel flooded low-lying areas of the town and region. Residents who enjoy close access to the rivers are ever aware that they must prepare for storms. The greatest hurricane-related damage to West Point resulted from Hurricane Isabel in 2003, which caused extensive flooding and wind damage.

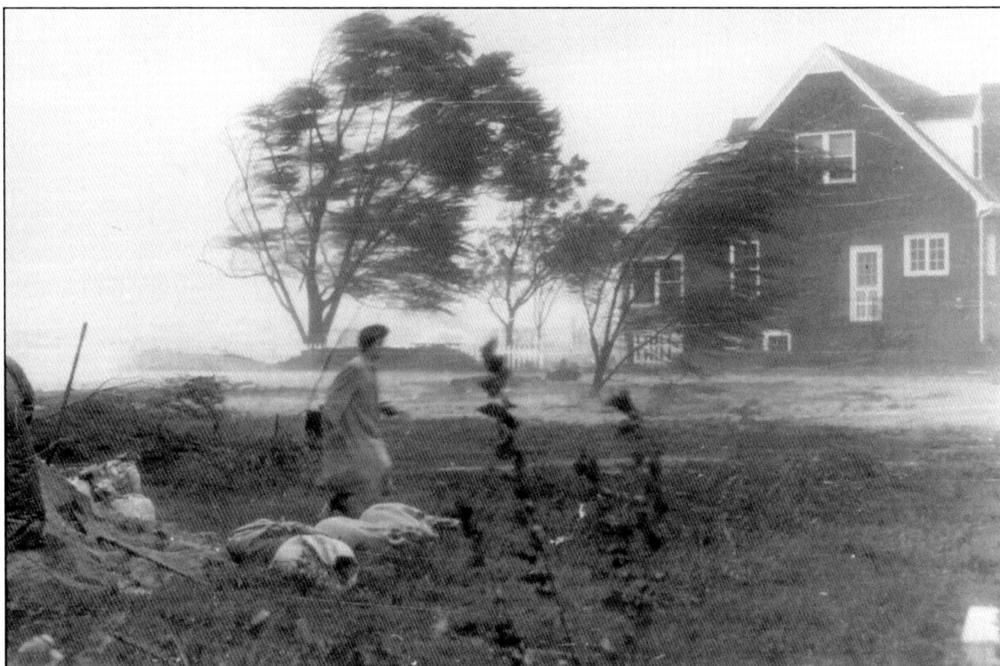

A resident braves the winds of Hurricane Hazel next to the swollen York River near Main and First Streets.

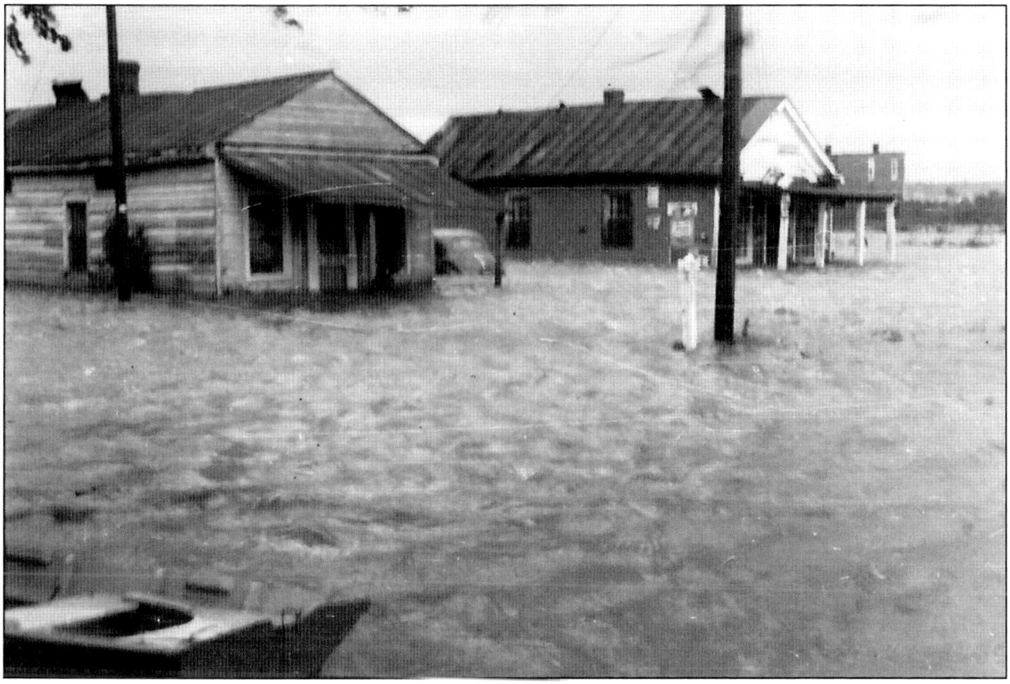

In this 1954 photograph, Hurricane Hazel floods businesses along Seventh Street. The business on the right was a seafood restaurant run by the Johnson family and known for its crab dishes.

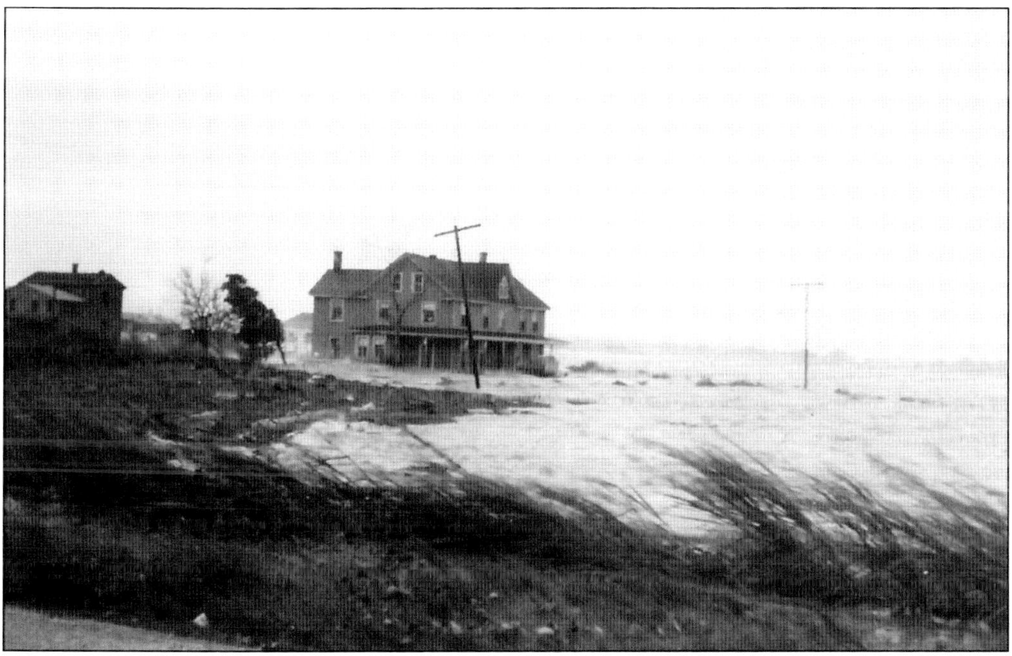

A home located on the Mattaponi River at the end of Fifth Street is engulfed in water during Hurricane Hazel.

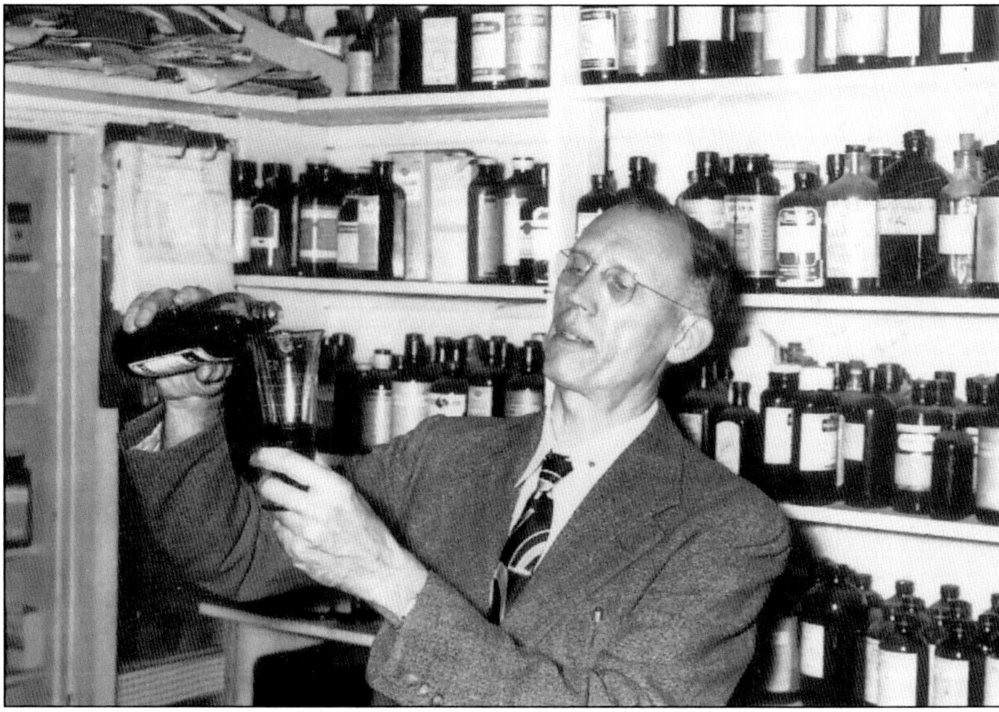

Dr. Leroy Riddle was a pharmacist and proprietor of a drugstore on Main Street for many years until his retirement in the 1950s. (Courtesy of Teresa S. Bohannon.)

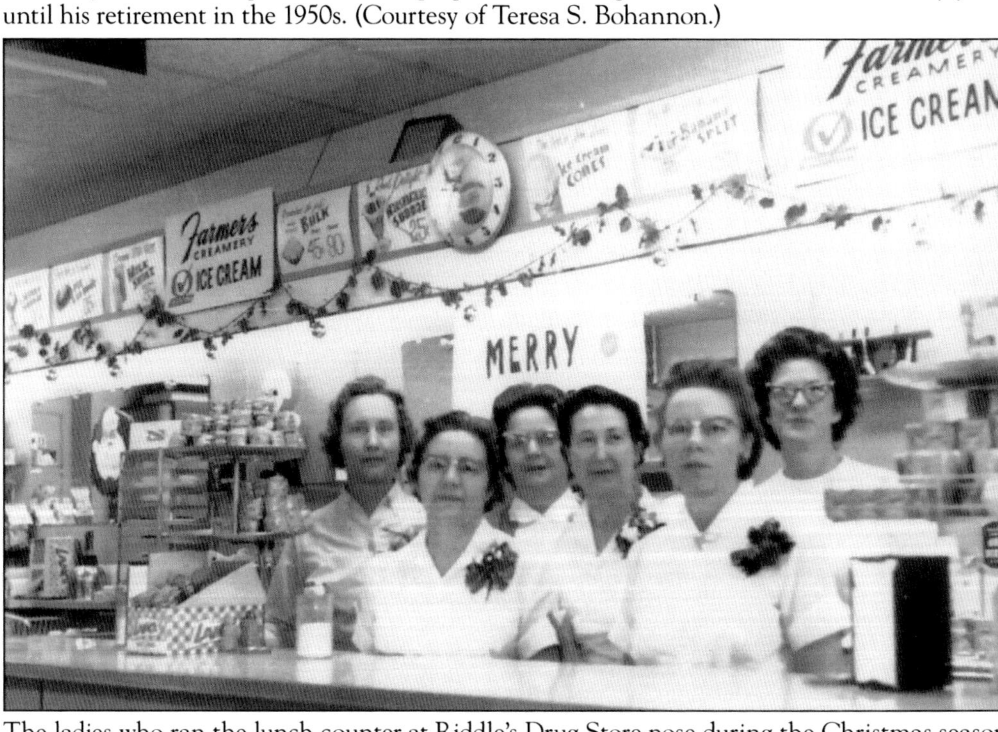

The ladies who ran the lunch counter at Riddle's Drug Store pose during the Christmas season in the 1950s. They are, from left to right, Frances Massey, Ellen Brown, May Downey, Arlett Rossom, Catherine Cox, and Flora Gordon. (Courtesy of Teresa S. Bohannon.)

A figure much loved by the citizens of West Point was Bernard Quarles, the mechanic at the Wyatt Esso station, pictured here in the 1950s. (Courtesy of Tyler Brand III.)

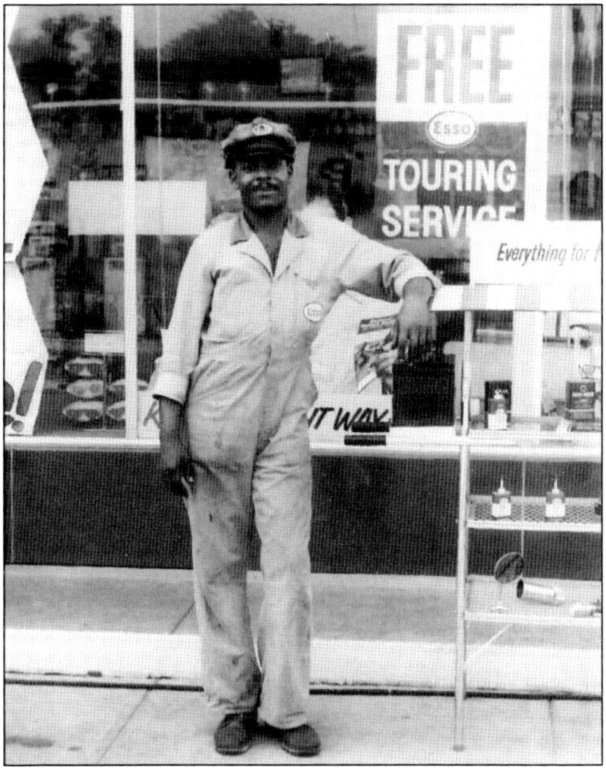

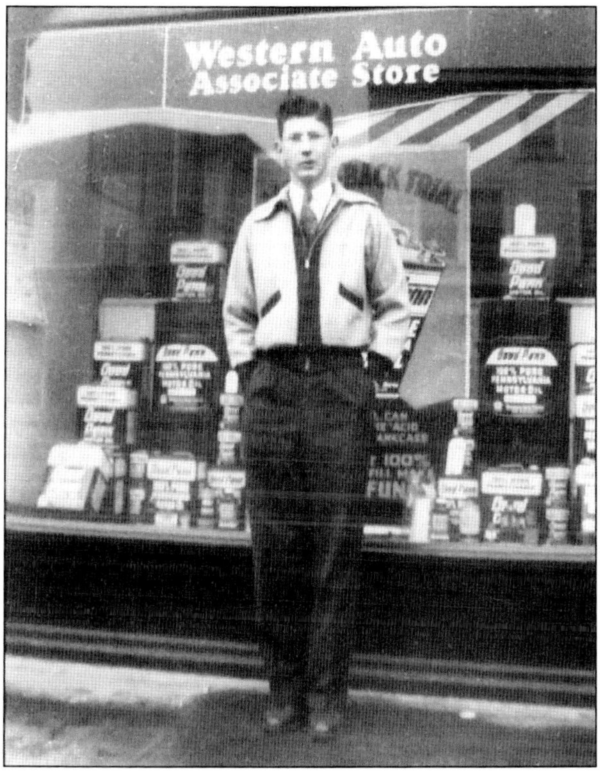

Another favorite personality of West Point was Frank P. Wyatt, whose working years were spent at the Western Auto store and Port Richmond Hardware. At the latter store, a failed robbery resulted in his death, a crime that shook the community. (Courtesy of William J. Addison.)

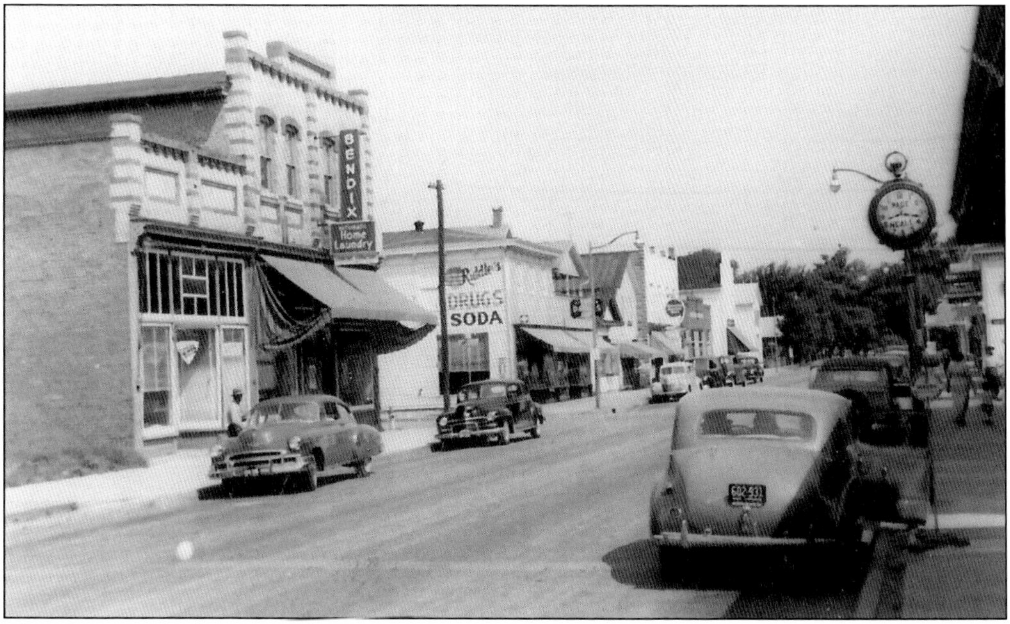

This photograph, facing northwest, shows downtown as it appeared in the late 1940s.

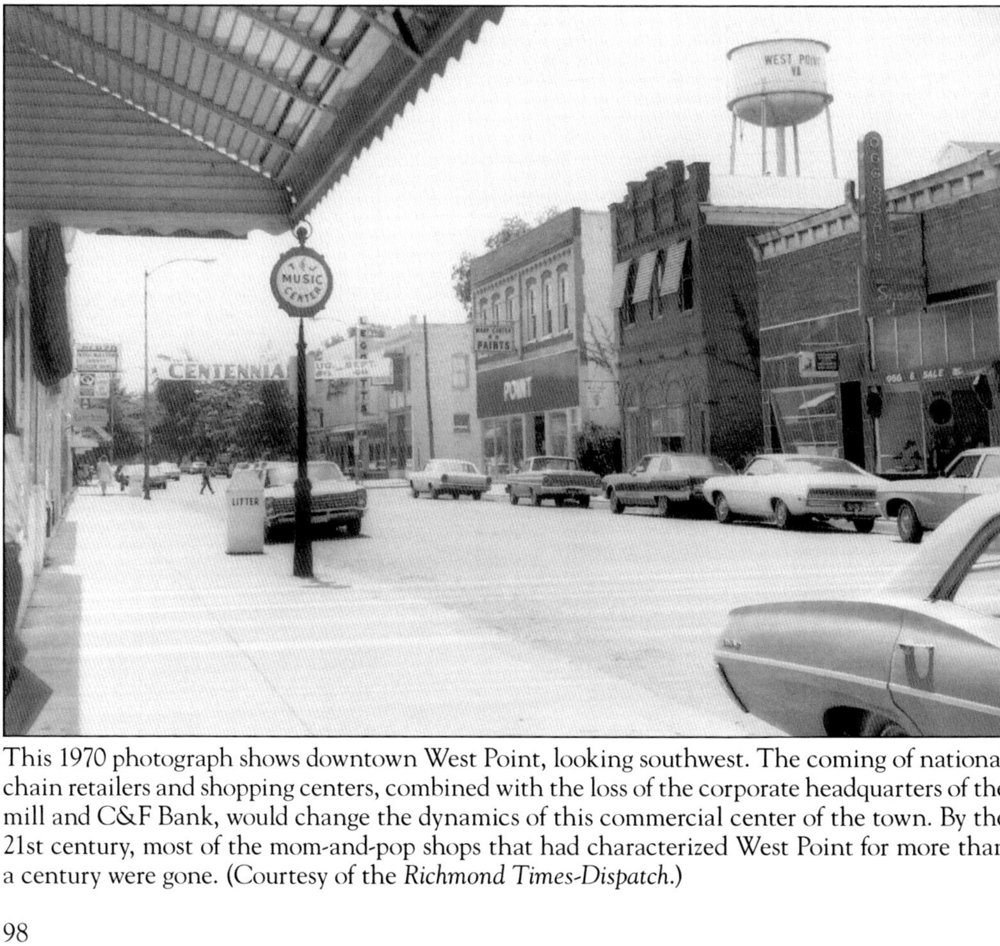

This 1970 photograph shows downtown West Point, looking southwest. The coming of national chain retailers and shopping centers, combined with the loss of the corporate headquarters of the mill and C&F Bank, would change the dynamics of this commercial center of the town. By the 21st century, most of the mom-and-pop shops that had characterized West Point for more than a century were gone. (Courtesy of the *Richmond Times-Dispatch*.)

Nine

Neighborhoods, Education, and Religion

While the native peoples had their paramount temple at Uttamassack, the early settlers of Tidewater Virginia generally were not as religious as, for example, the founders of the Massachusetts Bay Colony. So, while chapels dotted the region, they were not centers of activity. In 1680, the Anglican Church established St. John's Parish, by order of the Virginia Legislature, and erected a simple chapel in West Point. By the early 1700s, it had fallen into disrepair, and so, in 1734, a new church was completed seven miles away to replace the West Point chapel. Even that modest but handsome church would fall out of use after the Revolution because of its association with the Church of England.

Only when West Point became a true town after the Civil War did religious congregations start to form, beginning with one for former slaves—Mt. Nebo Baptist Church—that initially met in a railway toolshed. This group was soon followed by white Methodist, Episcopal, Disciples of Christ, and Baptist congregations. Catholics were only able to form a sizable congregation after the establishment of Port Richmond. The native reservations also built churches on their lands.

West Point area churches have historically worked together and shared facilities. Before there were church buildings, worship services were held at the Grove Hotel. Next, congregations shared an ecumenical chapel at the corner of Fifth and Main Streets near the site of the original Anglican chapel. Similarly, Trinity Chapel served a variety of congregations until it became the home of the Brett-Reid Presbyterian congregation.

Before the Civil War, wealthier families hired tutors or sent children to boarding schools due to the lack of public education in the area. The slave population in the region was primarily illiterate but eager to gain an education after they were freed. As West Point grew in the 1870s, private citizens began to offer educational instruction, first in homes and then through private academies. The first public school for white children was established in the 1880s at the corner of Main and Ninth Streets with four teachers. In 1890, a school building was completed for all grades. When a separate high school was finished on an adjoining lot, the original public school became an elementary school. African Americans, natives, and Catholics (if they wanted religious education) had to make other educational arrangements until 1953.

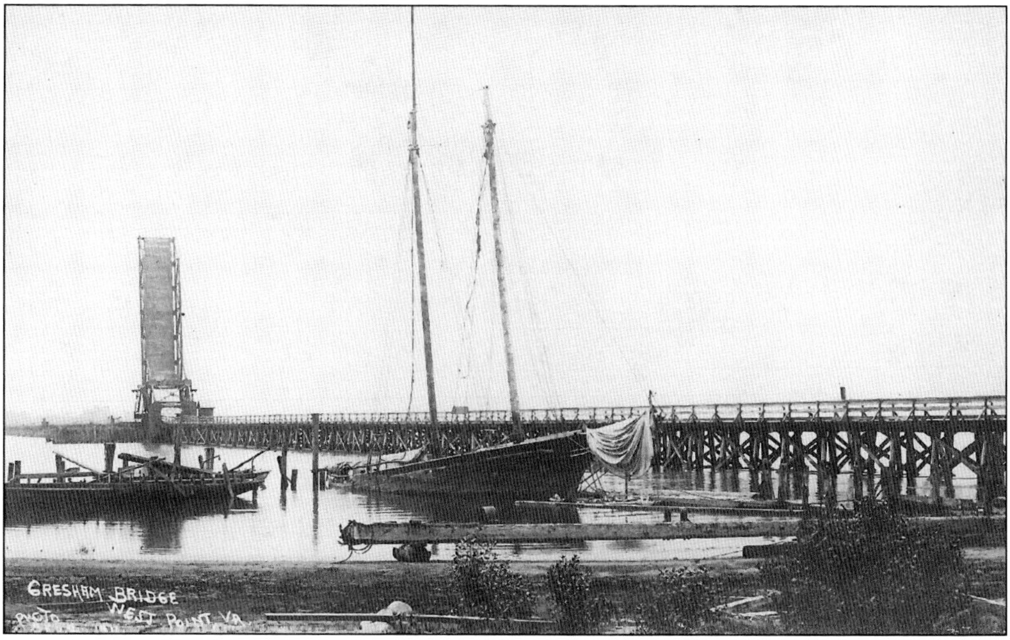

The 1914 completion of the Gresham Bridge spanning the Mattaponi at West Point gave the community easy access to other regions and new possibilities as the automobile overtook the train to become the primary mode of transportation. The bridge was so close to the water that it would become submerged during exceptionally high tides.

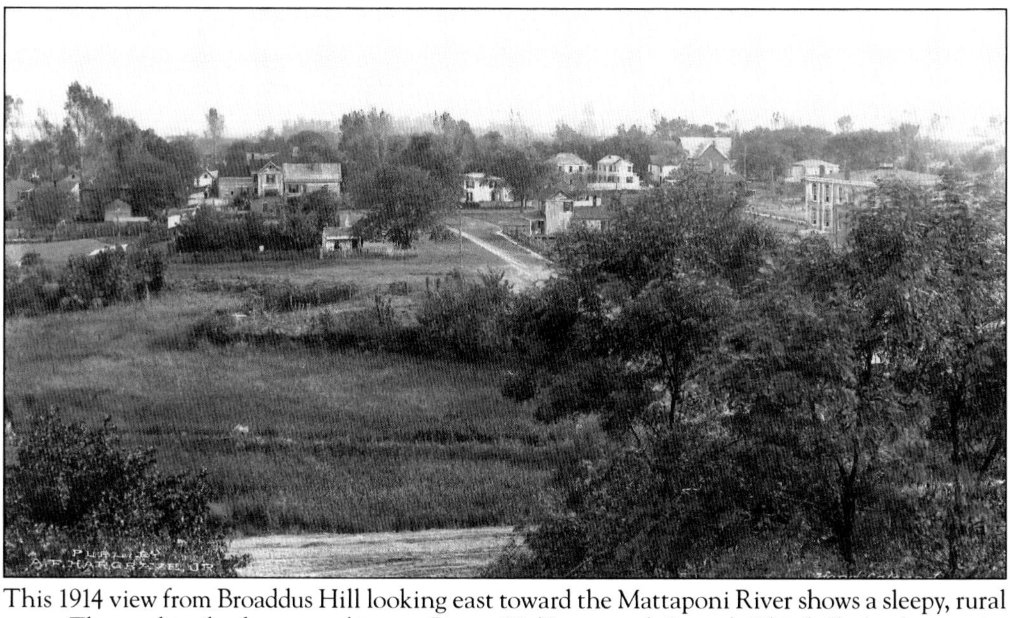

This 1914 view from Broaddus Hill looking east toward the Mattaponi River shows a sleepy, rural town. The road in the foreground is now Route 33 (Fourteenth Street). This hill, the former site of the native village of Cinqoteck, has been reduced in size by excavations for the highway and businesses. The town's first public school for white students, which was built in 1890 and served all grades, can be seen on the right.

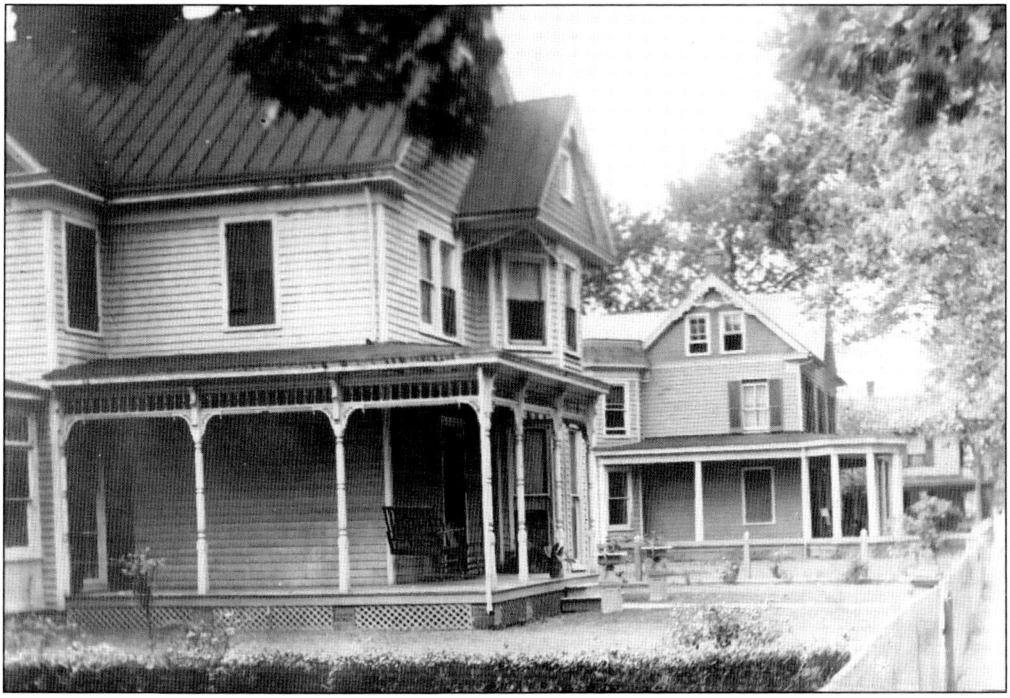

The residents of West Point have long loved their porches for sitting during milder weather to enjoy the breezes, the views of the rivers, and the opportunity to chat with passersby. This typical view of a residential section of West Point was taken in the early part of the 20th century.

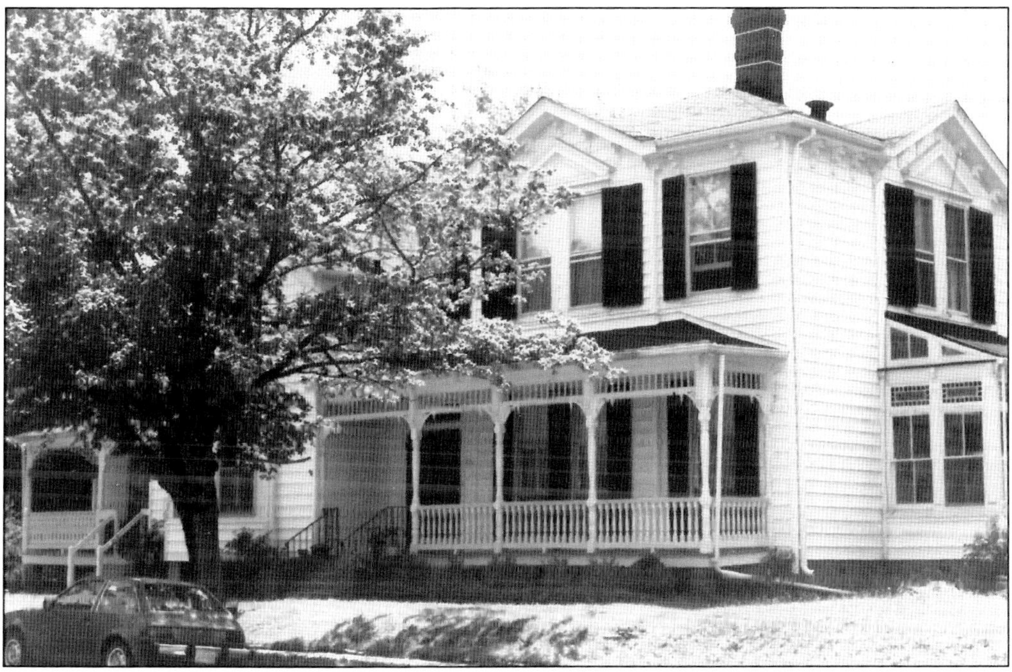

The wing on the left side of the Treat-Medlin home on Lee Street was used as the West Point post office from 1861 and as a general store in about 1870 before the larger home attached to it was built in 1898.

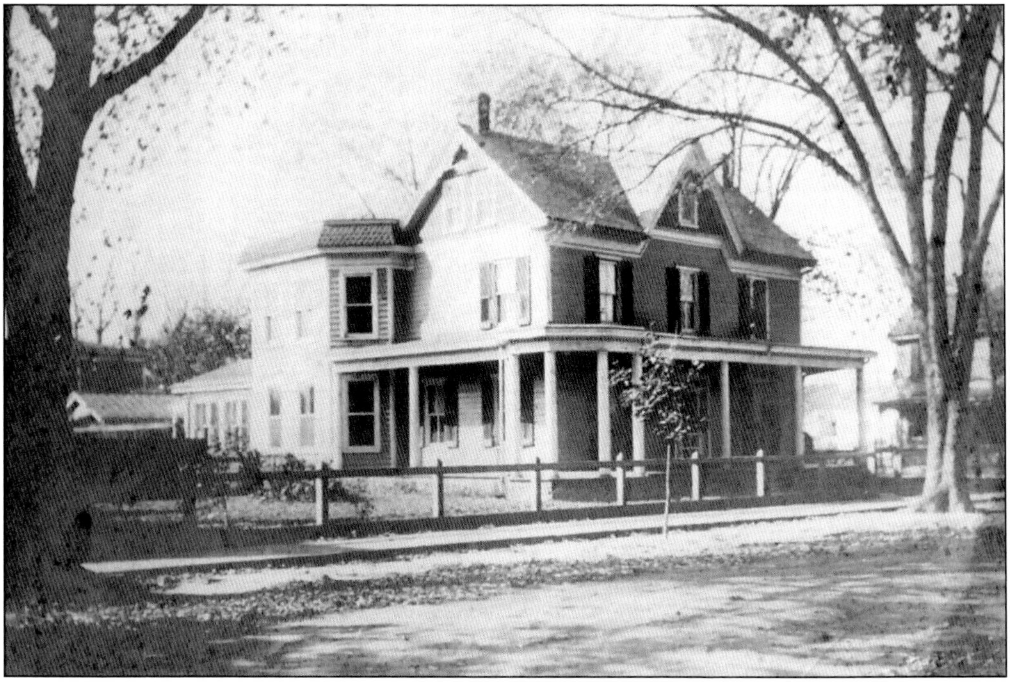

A fine example of the large homes constructed in West Point during the latter part of the 19th century is this one, built by Richmond Bland, who served as mayor. The house still stands on Main Street across from the Methodist church.

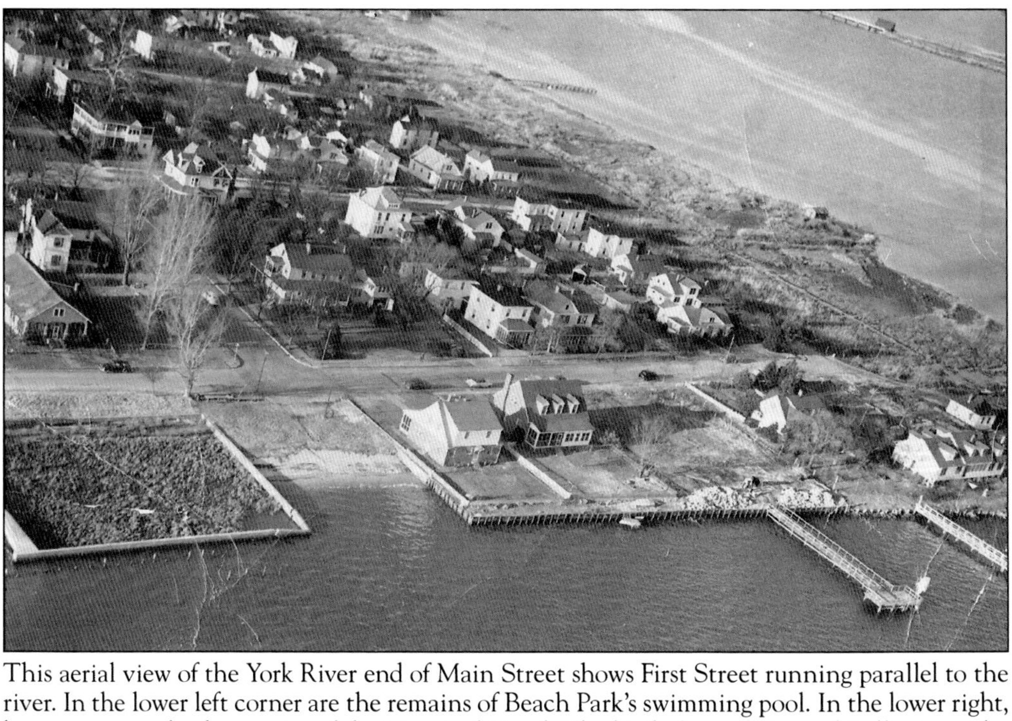

This aerial view of the York River end of Main Street shows First Street running parallel to the river. In the lower left corner are the remains of Beach Park's swimming pool. In the lower right, houses occupy the former site of the Terminal Hotel. The birthplace of General Puller is on the north side of First Street in the middle of the block.

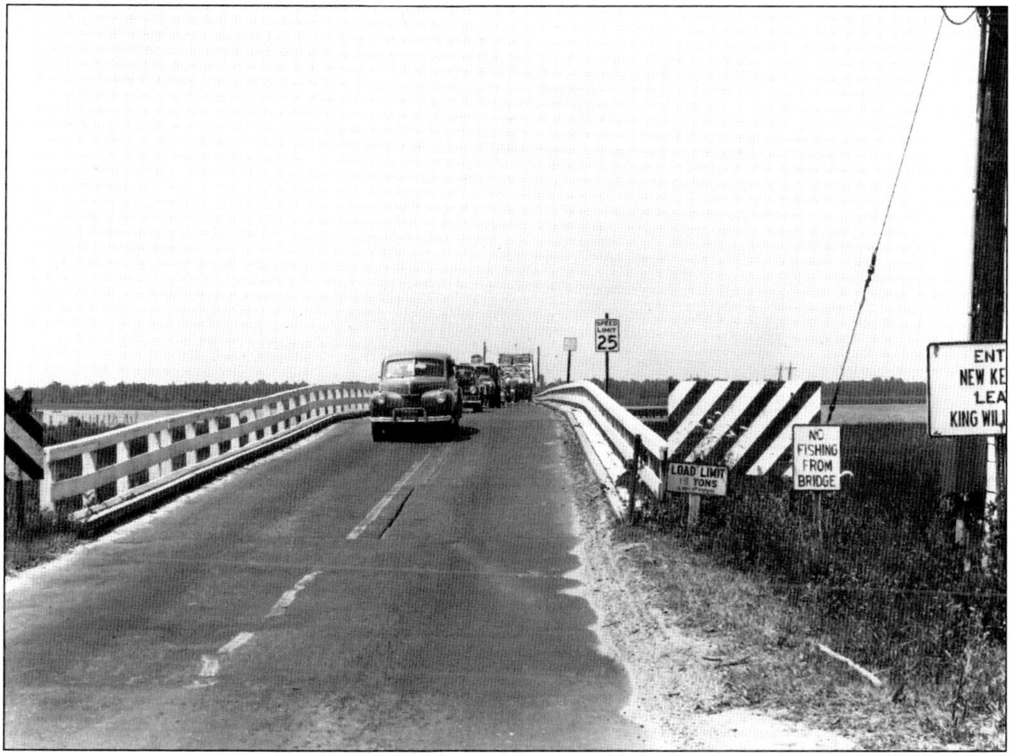

The Pamunkey River was first spanned with a bridge between Fourteenth Street and Eltham in New Kent County in 1927. Prior to that, crossings were made by ferry. This photograph was taken about 1950.

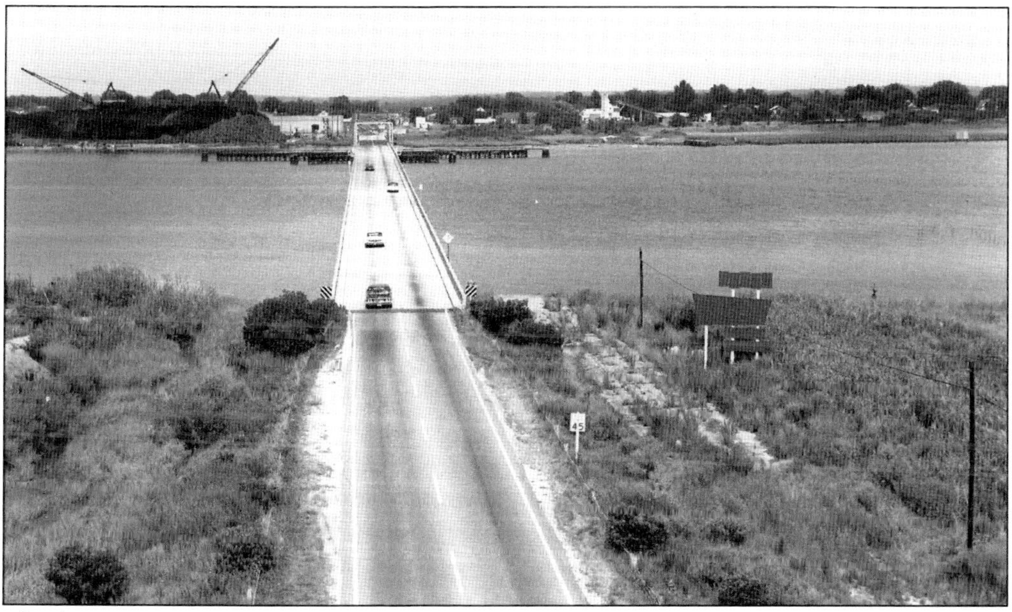

The first Pamunkey Bridge was replaced by a drawbridge in the 1950s and then by a higher drawbridge in 2010. In this 1967 photograph, note the piles of logs at the paper mill on the West Point side.

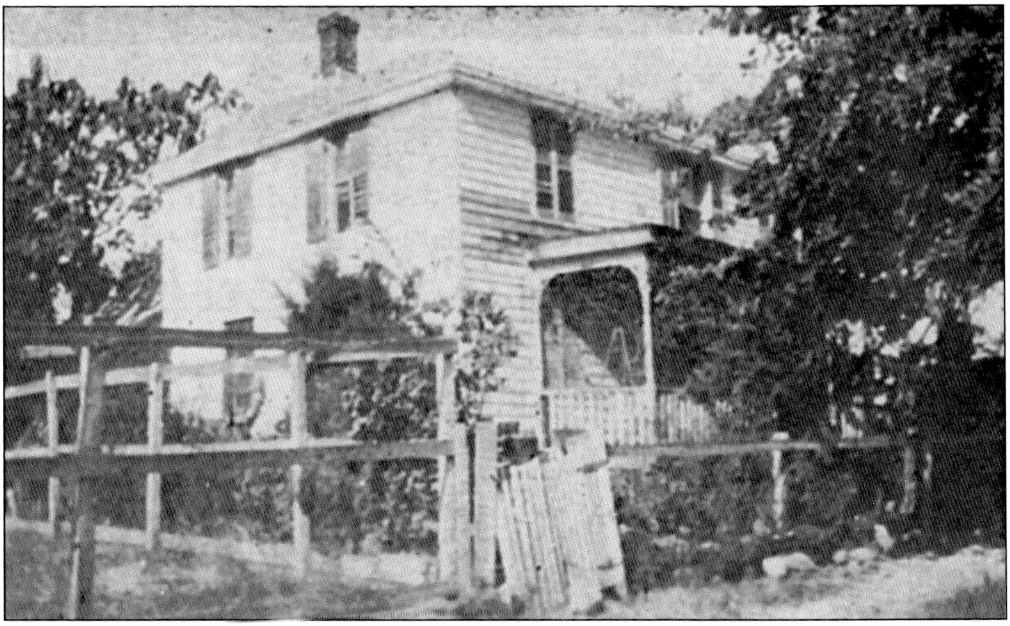

This home at the corner of Third and Lee Streets was built about 1870 by Beverly Allen, "a free man of color," civic leader, and member of the first West Point Town Council during the first decades after the Civil War. This man of great capacity was born into slavery. He was followed by his son, Beverly Allen Jr., who, along with his son's wife, Alice, devoted their lives to the education of African Americans. The Allens used a small building on this lot to conduct the first classes in West Point for African American students with the help of mission teachers from the Freedman's Bureau. Children were taught during the daytime and adults at night. (Courtesy of Mary Lipscomb and Frances Healy, *Recollections of Early West Point*.)

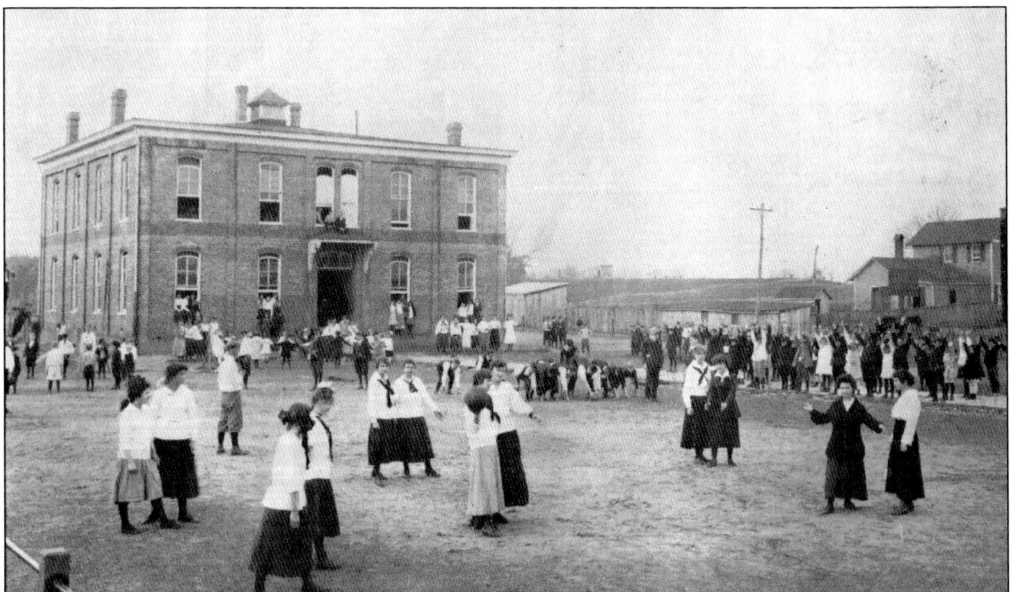

This page from the 1917 yearbook *Skeeter* shows pupils during recess at the West Point School, which accommodated all grades at that time.

Due in part to local African American leaders such as Beverly Allen and Beverly Allen Jr., who were able to receive a college education at Hampton Institute, the African American community of West Point valued education, despite the severely circumscribed opportunities to gain one. Educated women started kindergartens in their homes for that segment of the population and also taught at the Beverly Allen School. This is a 1903 portrait of Maude Allen Clark, one of the most beloved teachers at Beverly Allen School the only public school serving that segment of the population.

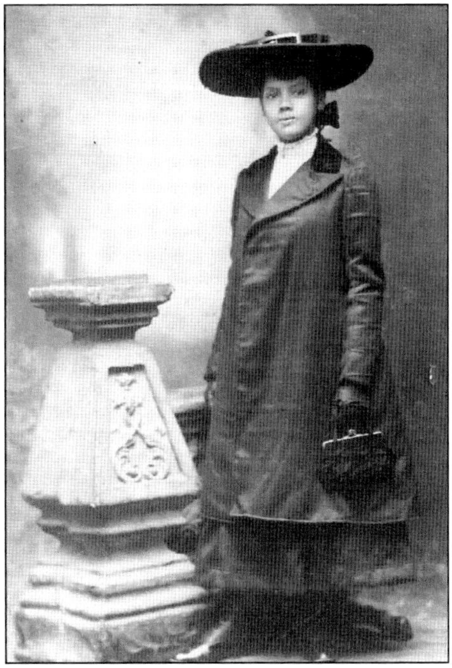

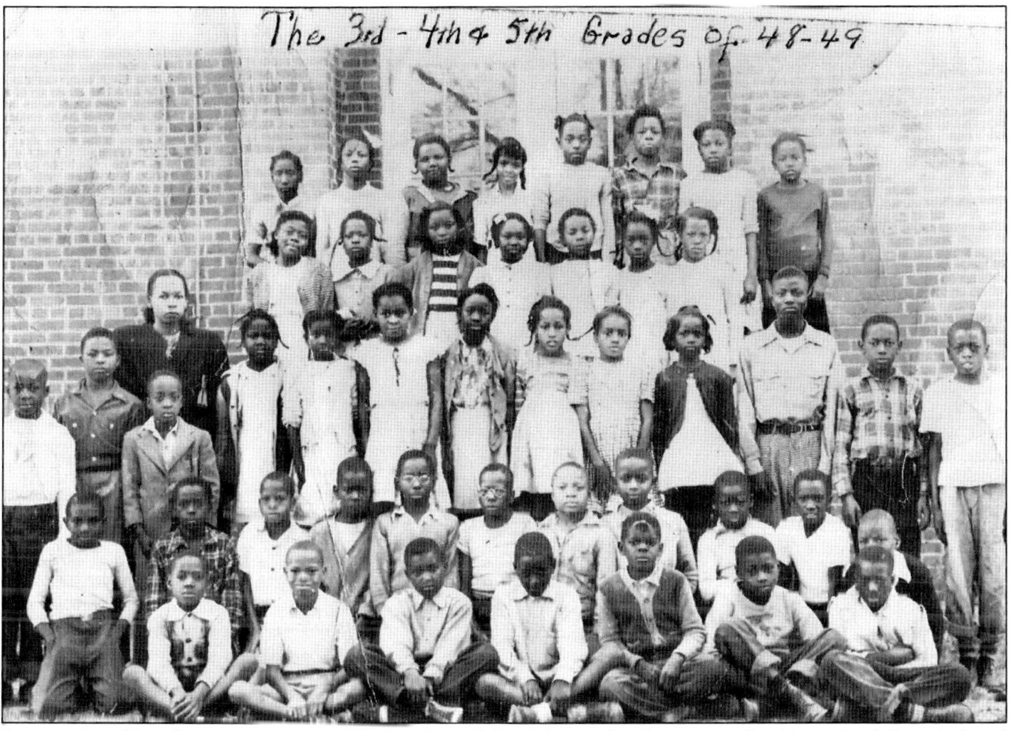

Posing for this photograph are the third- and fourth-grade classes at the Beverly Allen School for the school year 1948–1949. The school, built in part by the volunteer labor of parents, served the African American community when their children were denied access to the schools for white students. The building became an annex of the West Point Elementary School in 1966. (Courtesy of Rosetta Dobbins Jarvis.)

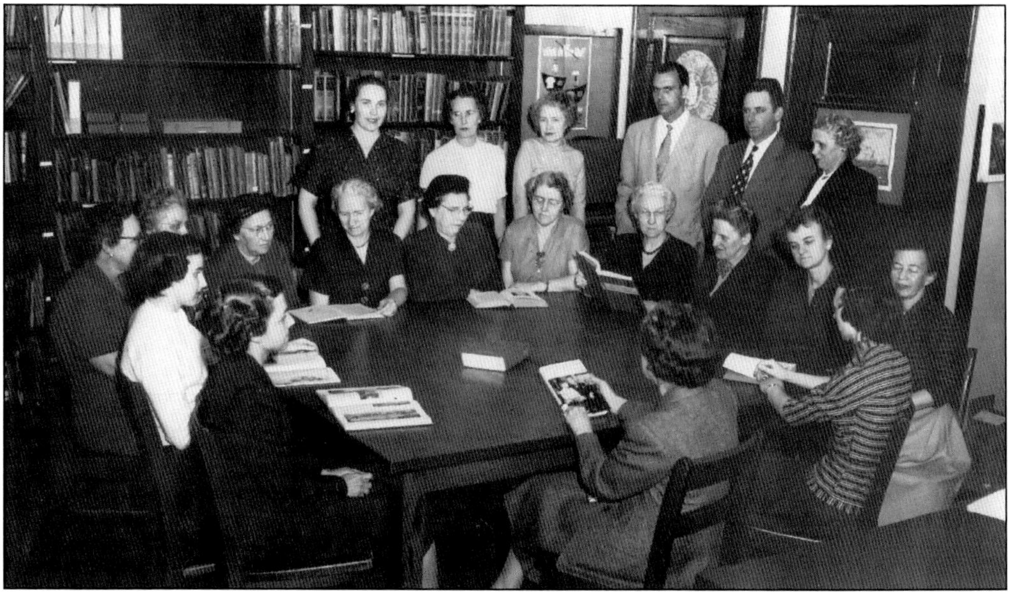

Faculty members of West Point High School gather in the school library during the early 1950s.

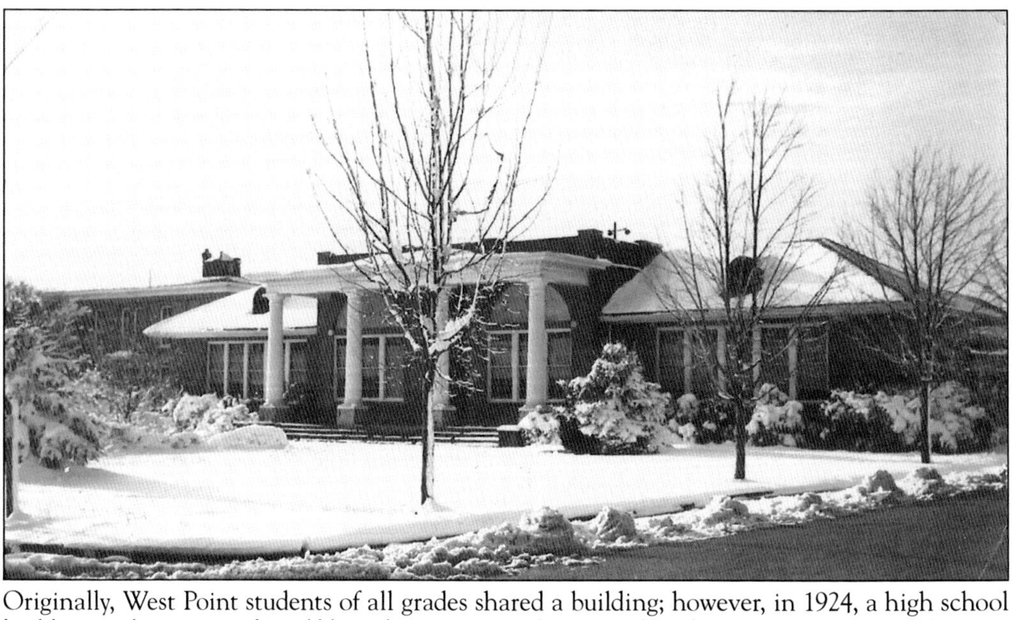

Originally, West Point students of all grades shared a building; however, in 1924, a high school building at the corner of Twelfth and Lee Streets, shown in this photograph, was erected. It was destroyed by fire after a new high school was completed.

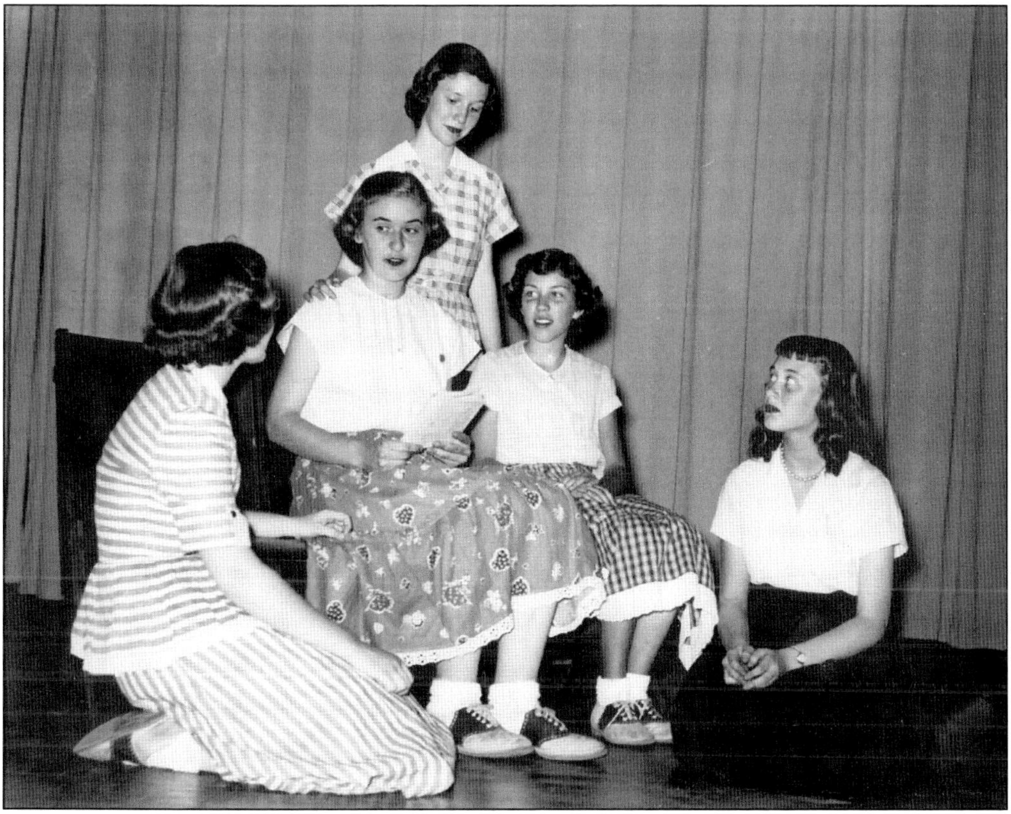

The 1950 production of *Little Women* at West Point High School drew a large audience. Pictured from left to right are budding actresses Jackie Johnson, Jane Topping, Barbara Traugott, and Nancy Godwin. Mary Langhorne Howell stands in the rear.

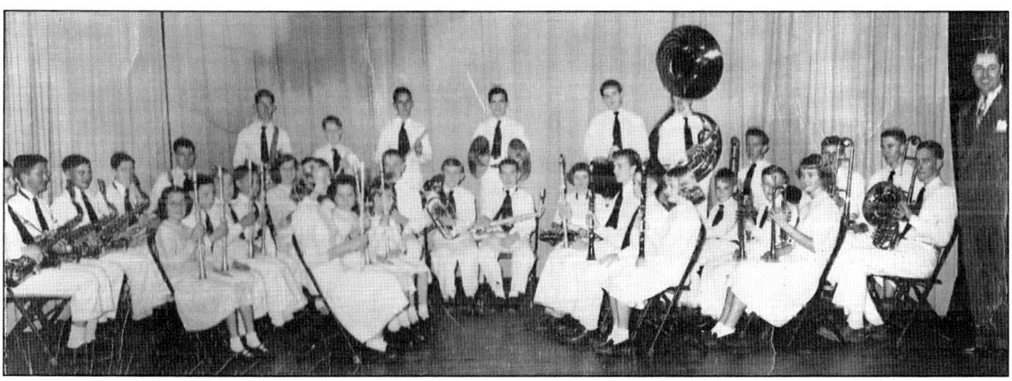

The West Point School band poses for this photograph in 1949. The band included members from both the elementary school and the high school.

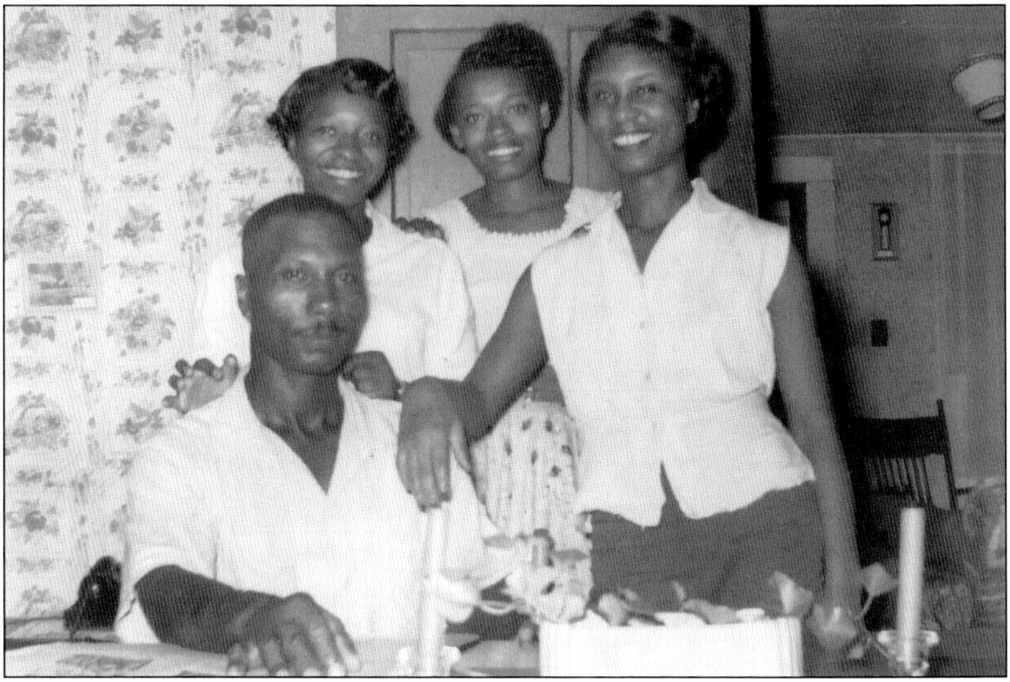

A group of parents defied the order to transfer their children to the King William County segregated high school, which was located many miles from their homes, and were criminally charged with truancy. Pictured here with his family, Charles James Dobbins was one of the eight parents ordered to pay a fine and given a suspended jail sentence. The parents demanded that their children be allowed to attend the schools in West Point within walking distance of their homes. (Courtesy of Rosetta Dobbins Jarvis.)

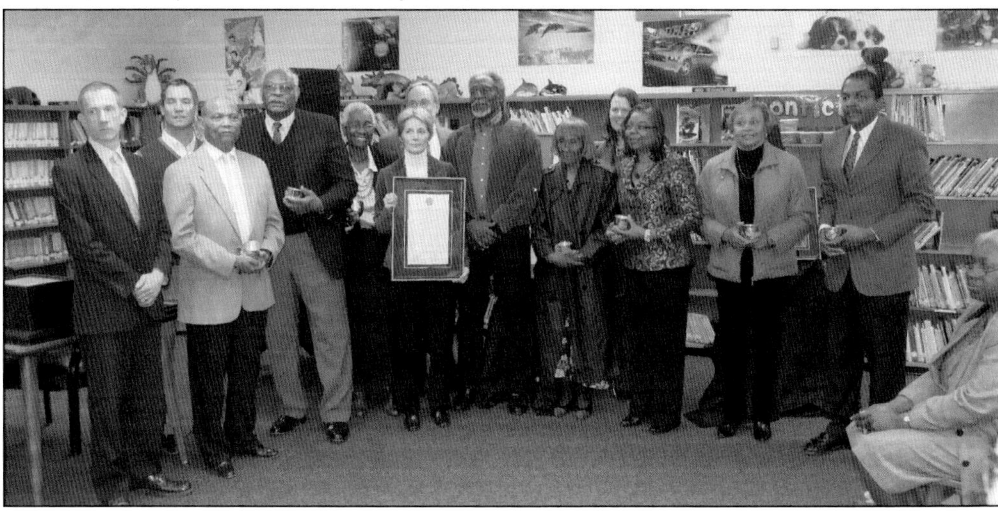

In 2011, the West Point School Board formally acknowledged the injustices of the past and honored the students who had courageously defied its order in 1952. The African American students missed a year of school during the litigation, though makeshift classes were arranged. Dudley Olsson, chairman of the West Point School Board, is holding a commemorative plaque. In 2009, Dr. Jeffrey O. Smith became the first African American superintendent of West Point Public Schools. (Courtesy of West Point Public Schools.)

The legal action against the West Point parents became the case *Dobbins v. Virginia.* The local court found in favor of the town, but the decision was reversed upon appeal to the Virginia Supreme Court. Here, two of the student litigants sit in court with their lawyers. This case received nationwide publicity. The *Tidewater Review* ran a feature article about the case in 2011; at that time, the West Point School Board honored the 29 students and their parents who stood up to the evils of segregation. (Courtesy of Rosetta Dobbins Jarvis and the *Tidewater Review.*)

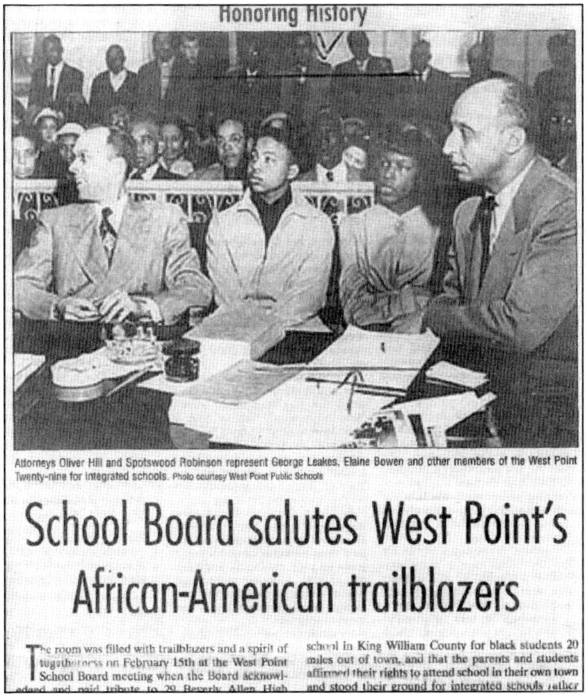
Honoring History

Attorneys Oliver Hill and Spotswood Robinson represent George Leakes, Elaine Bowen and other members of the West Point Twenty-nine for integrated schools. Photo courtesy West Point Public Schools

School Board salutes West Point's African-American trailblazers

The room was filled with trailblazers and a spirit of togetherness on February 15th at the West Point School Board meeting when the Board acknowl-

school in King William County for black students 20 miles out of town, and that the parents and students affirmed their rights to attend school in their own town and stood their ground for integrated schools rather

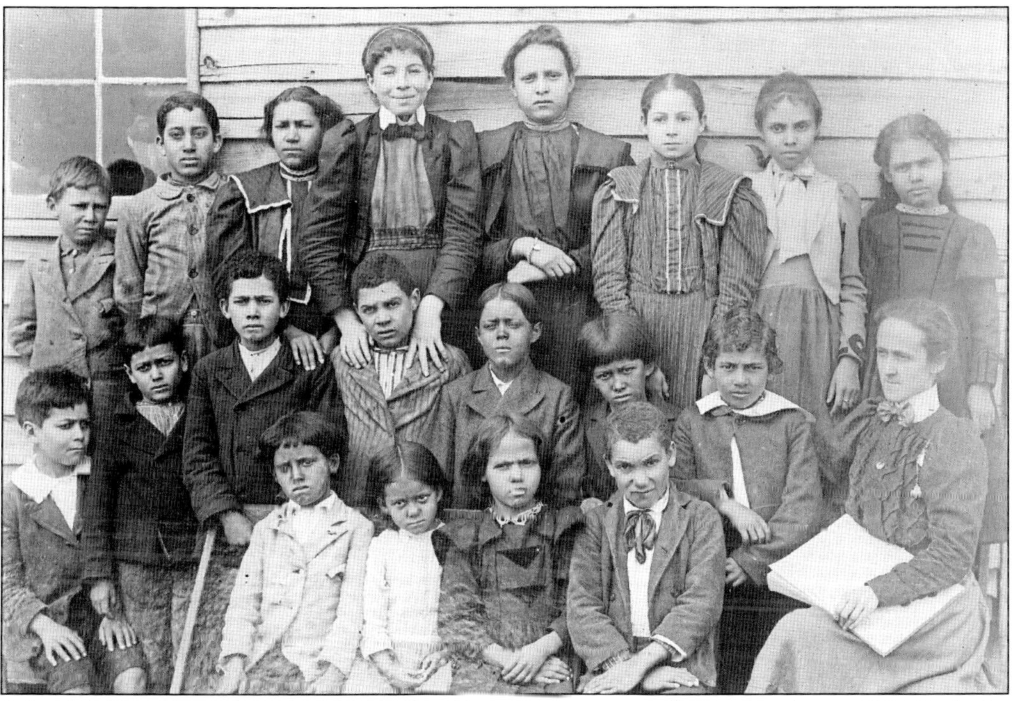

Schoolchildren from the Pamunkey Indian Reservation pose with their teacher in 1899. Both the Pamunkey and Mattaponi Reservations had their own schools until the 1950s, when the Native American students were finally integrated into the King William County school system as a by-product of the civil rights won by African Americans. (Courtesy of the National Anthropological Archives, Smithsonian Institution.)

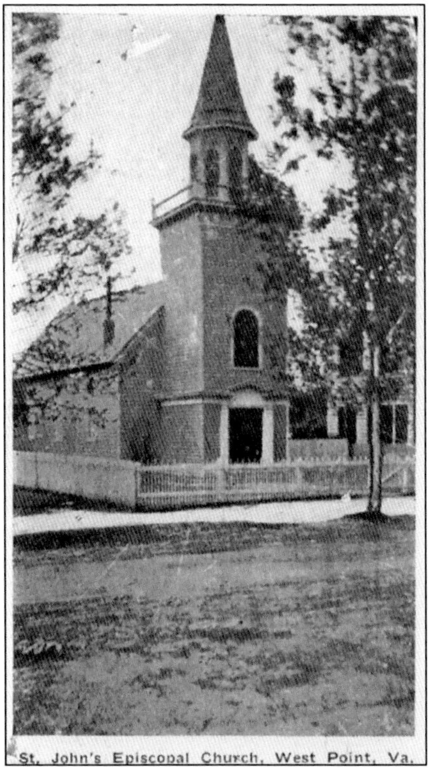

When the town began to grow at a rapid pace following the Civil War, church buildings began to spring up as well. The Anglican chapel was no more, and St. John's was miles away, so a new Episcopal church, also called St. John's, was constructed in the center of downtown along Main Street. This view is probably from the 1880s.

Rev. Charles Holt (seated in the center wearing a clerical collar) was rector of St. John's Episcopal Church for only 18 months before dying suddenly of a heart attack at age 56 in 1906. He left his mark on the congregation by expanding and modernizing the church building. The Holt family is shown here just before moving to West Point in 1904. Charles Holt Jr., seen on the far left, became a silent and sound film actor under the stage name Jack Holt, appearing in more than 70 films well into the 1940s. He (and later his actor children) is primarily remembered for his work in Westerns.

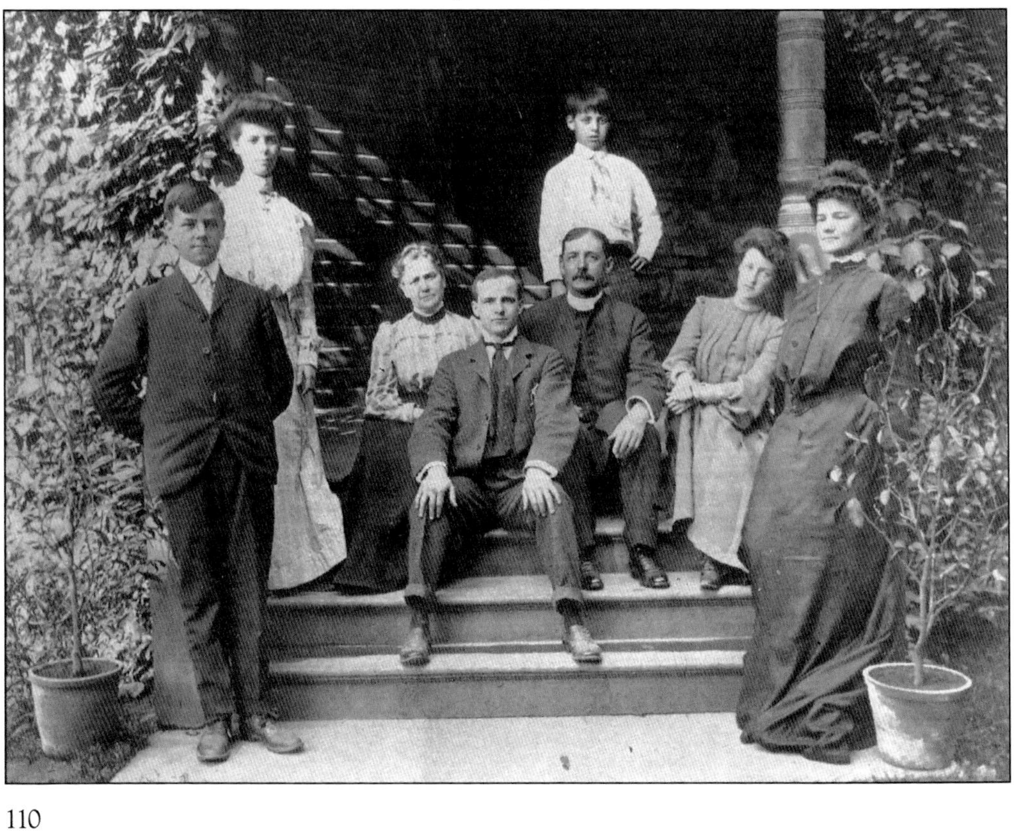

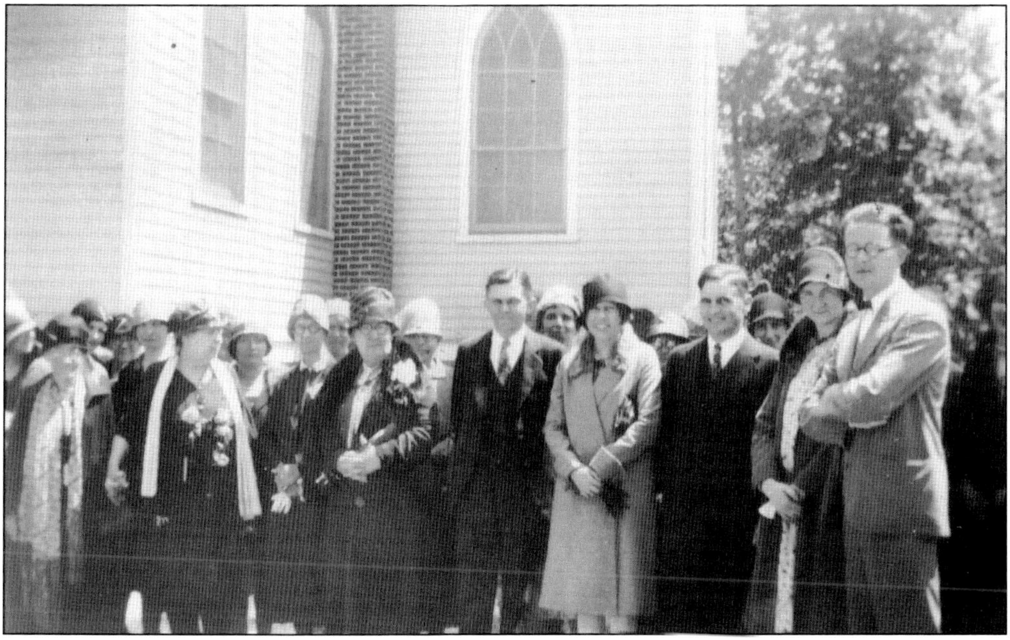

Trinity Union Chapel, built in 1908 near Sweet Hall, was a modest church in the woods that served a diverse interfaith congregation. In the early 1920s, it became a Presbyterian church and took the name Brett-Reed. Members of the congregation are shown at the 1925 dedication of the new sanctuary, erected at a different location along Route 30, in a photograph taken by nine-year-old Dorothy Martin. (Courtesy of Dorothy Martin Walker Krewatch.)

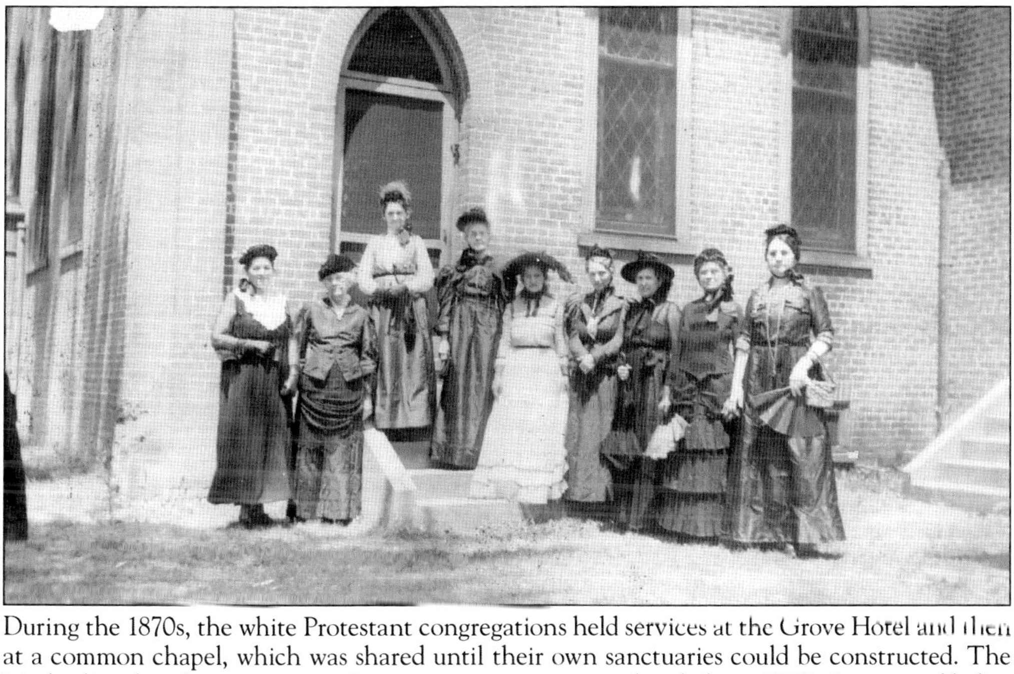

During the 1870s, the white Protestant congregations held services at the Grove Hotel and then at a common chapel, which was shared until their own sanctuaries could be constructed. The Methodist church sanctuary and its parsonage were completed about 1889. A group of ladies dressed in old-fashioned clothing pose in front of the original entrance to the church in the 1930s, probably as part of an anniversary celebration.

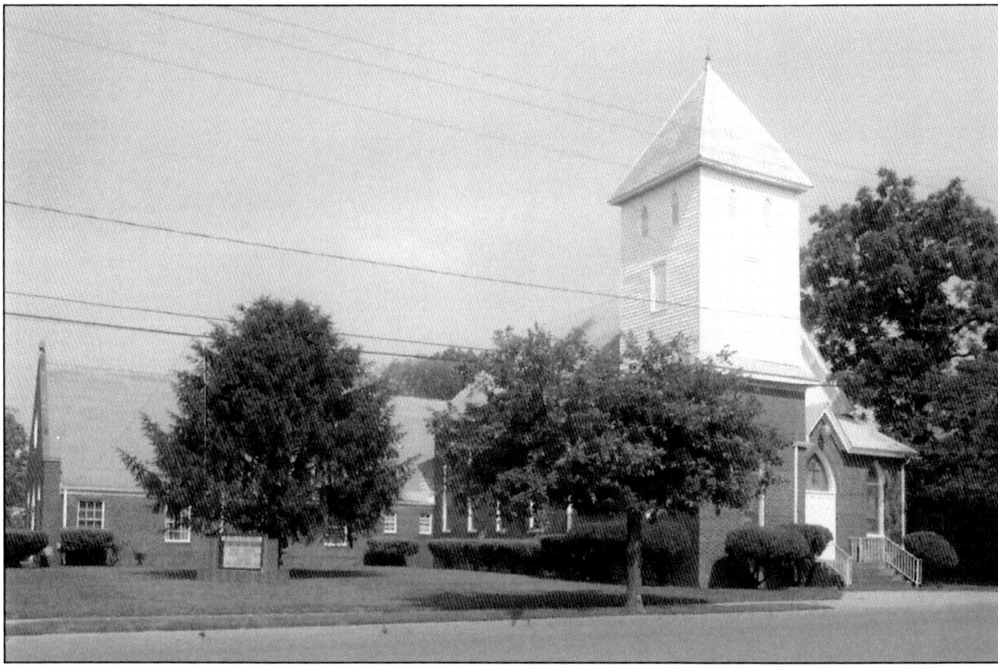

After the Civil War, a group of newly freed slaves began to worship together in a railway toolshed at West Point. In 1866, Rev. Jessie Dungee formed them into the embryo of Mt. Nebo Baptist Church, shown here in the 1980s. The church sanctuary was constructed in 1887.

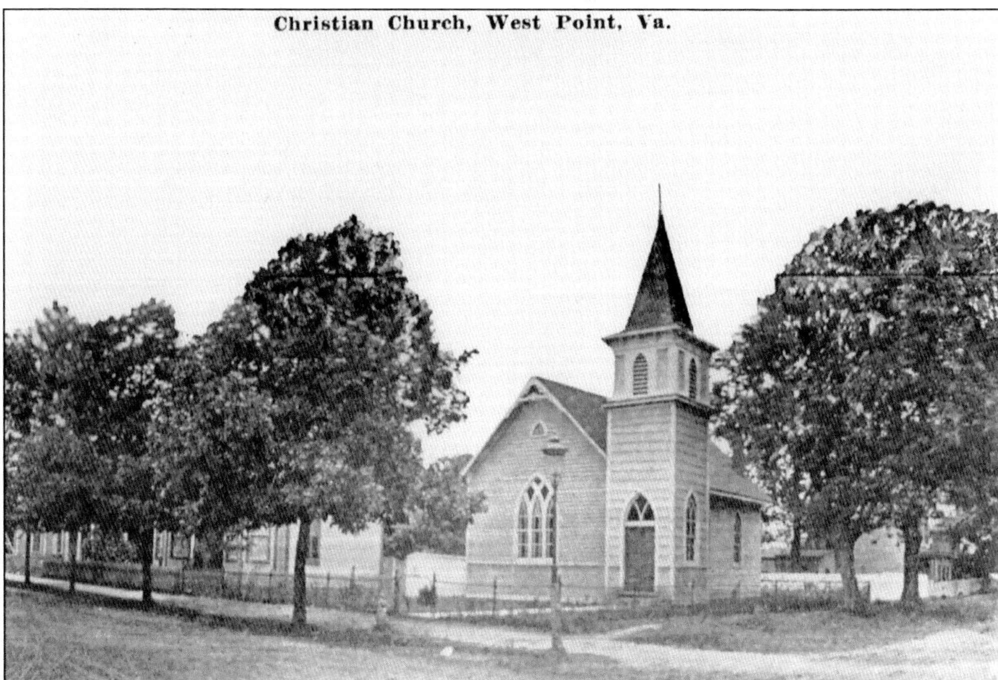

The Church of Christ, Disciples was built in 1906 at the corner of Fifth and Main Streets. The congregation has since moved to a new church building on Euclid Avenue. The earlier building now serves the West Point Church of God congregation.

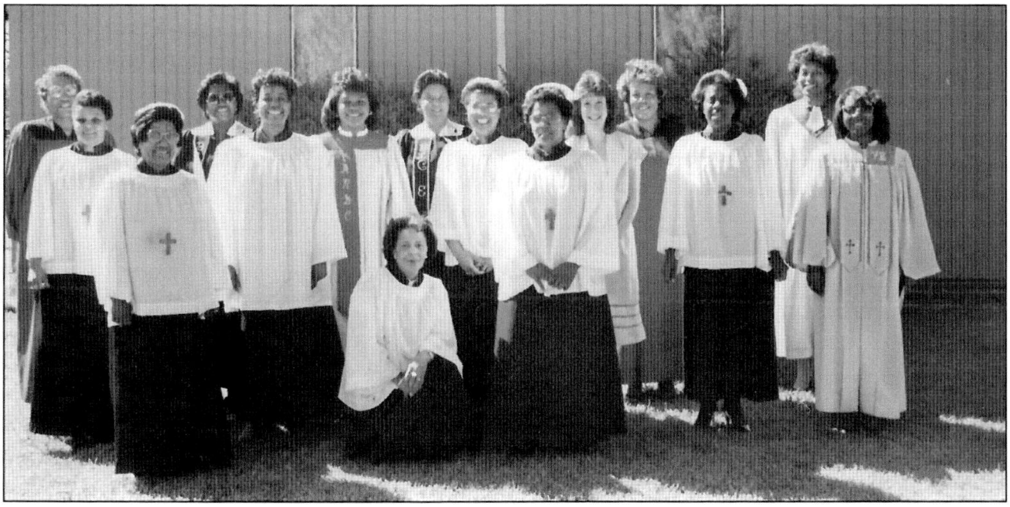

An ecumenical choir poses in front of St. Paul's Episcopal Church on Broaddus Hill in the 1980s. Congregations represented by the singers include St. Paul's Episcopal, Mount Nebo Baptist, and Ephesus Baptist. St. Paul's was formed through the efforts of Rev. John H. Scott, who came to West Point in 1924 with the mission to establish an Episcopal Church to serve the African American community. (Courtesy of Vincent S. Hodge.)

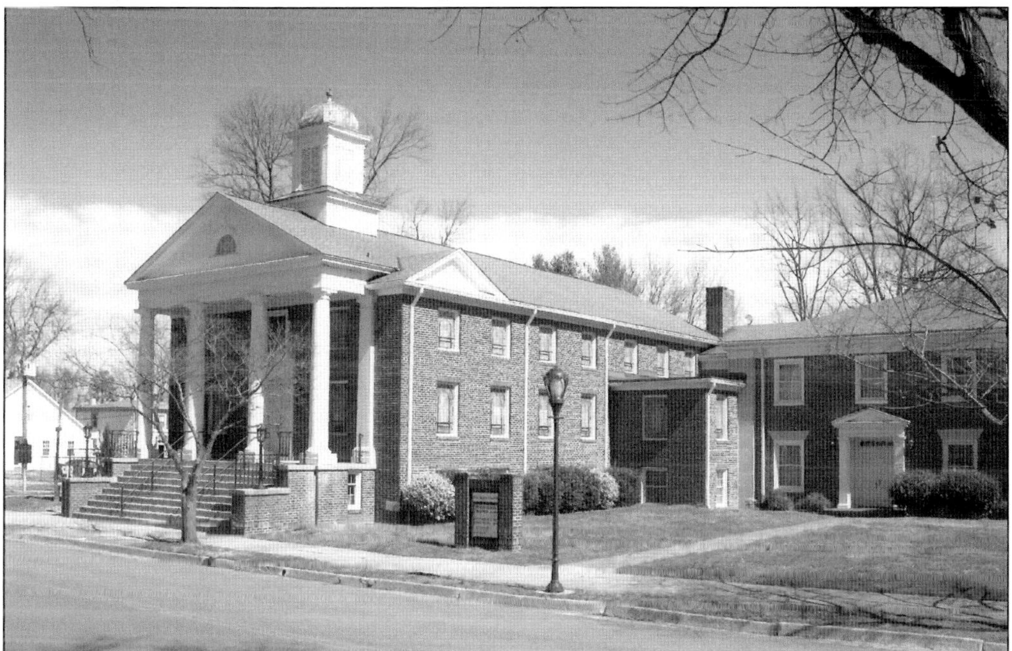

First Baptist Church, situated on Main Street between Fourth and Fifth Streets, is on the site of the first Anglican chapel and the Colonial cemetery of West Point. A few graves from the early 1700s are still visible at the north side of the building. A number of Union soldiers were interred on the site during the Civil War. Because of the entreaties of Susan Davis, Baptist meetings were started in West Point in 1870, and a congregation was officially established in 1873. The first Baptist church on the present site was completed in 1876 and replaced by the one shown here in 1927. (Courtesy of Carol Fetterolf.)

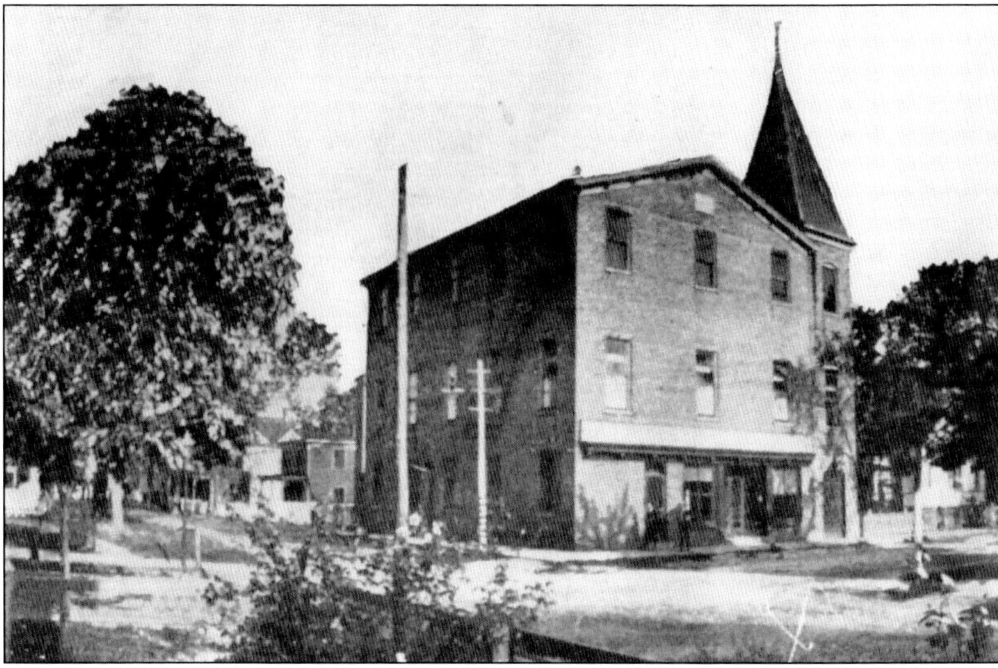

The West Point Masonic Hall, which held the offices of the *Tidewater Review* newspaper at one time, was constructed in 1884 and demolished in the early 1980s.

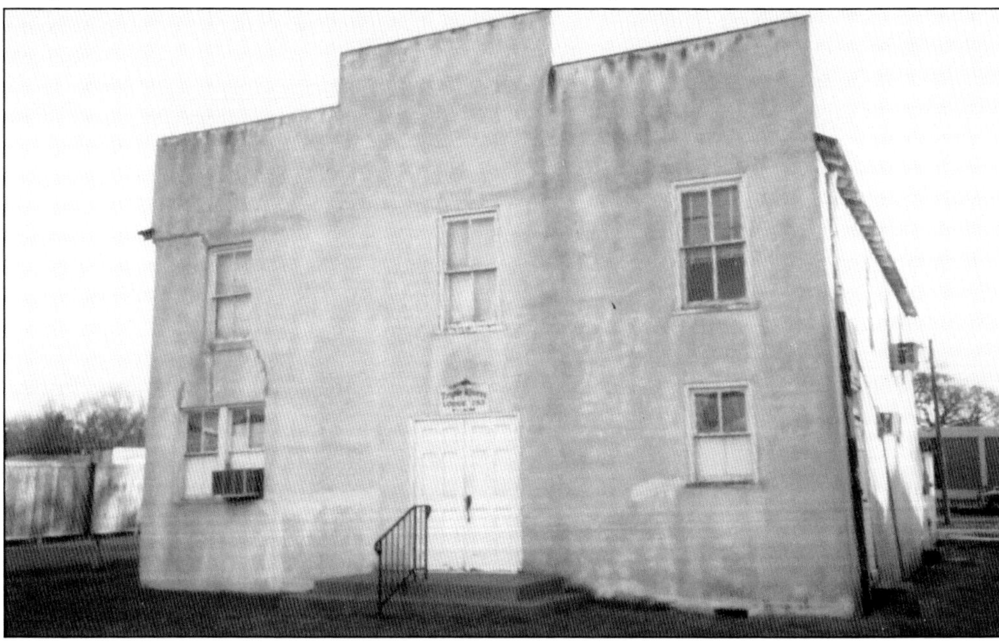

The Masonic lodge at Sixteenth and Kirby Streets served as a community center for the African American populace, where they could escape the indignities of Jim Crow laws. For example, movies were shown there so that the audience did not have to sit in the balcony of the downtown movie theater. It was also a popular location for dances. In 1952, it was used for makeshift classes for high school students boycotting the segregated school for African Americans. (Courtesy of John Lee.)

Ten

West Point at Play

Even though the days of West Point as a destination resort have passed, the town has never forgotten how to have fun. It has a vibrant civic life with a variety of community organizations, such as Kiwanis, Rotary, Ruritan, Women's Clubs, Boy and Girl Scouts, Knights of Columbus, the Masons, veterans' organizations, and sports groups. For years, the community hosted a fair on the remnants of Crosby Thompson's airfield and later on the grounds of the Middle Peninsula Airport. Farmers displayed their prize animals and produce while young and old enjoyed carnival rides. The success of the 1970 centennial celebration spawned the Crab Carnival, sponsored in recent years by the West Point Chamber of Commerce. The chamber also sponsors an annual Christmas on the Town celebration, with the arrival of Santa Claus, a house tour, and opportunities to mingle with friends amid booths full of potential Christmas presents. In the summer, bands perform for dancers and those out for a summer evening stroll under the new covered stage, evoking memories of the Saturday night dances held at a number of locations throughout the years.

Water sports have always been popular. The area is a magnet for fishermen. With the advent of motorized small craft, water skiers discovered the Mattaponi and Pamunkey Rivers. More recently, the town has added a boardwalk over creeks and developed a launching site for kayaks. Glass Island, the former site a shipyard during the 19th century, is the launching facility for small craft.

If there was one sport that captured the town, it was baseball. In the 1930s, the Chesapeake Corporation built a baseball stadium, and for years, the town had its own team. After the first National Guard Armory was built with a basketball court in the 1950s, the high school basketball program began to produce competitive teams, winning the state championships in 1961 and 1973. In recent years, the town also sponsored an annual 10-kilometer running competition in memory of Chesty Puller.

Arts Alive was established to promote arts in the community after a civic auditorium was constructed in 2000 on the high school campus. The organization has sponsored art exhibits featuring local artists, a concert series, arts and craft lessons, and an arts summer camp for children.

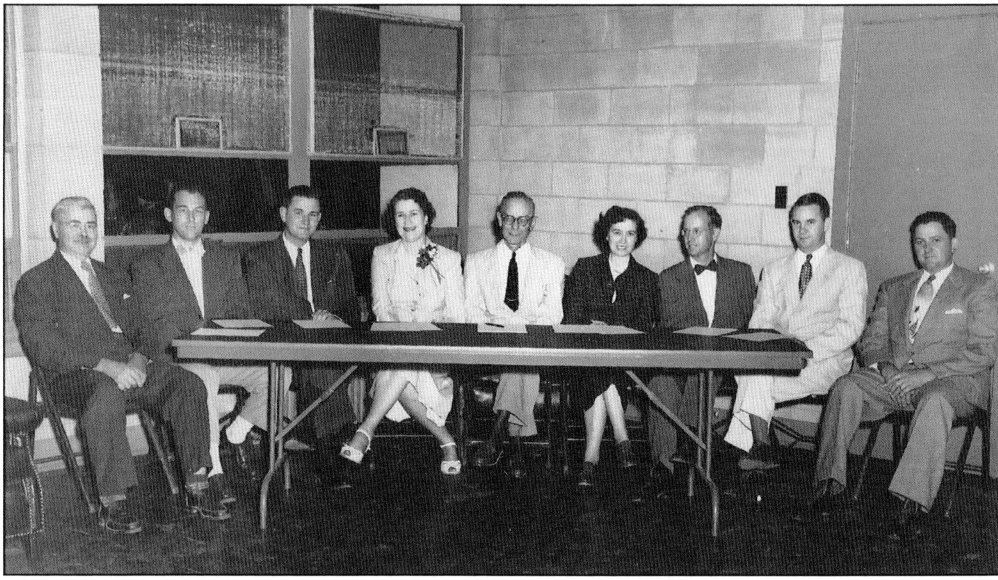

The Armory at West Point was used as a community center where townsfolk could play basketball, roller-skate, or dance. The Tommy Dorsey Band played for one such occasion in the early 1950s. Pictured from left to right are the trustees of that facility: J.T. Tokarz, R. Tyler Bland Jr., Sture Olsson, Mrs. Leroy Riddle, J.G. McClellan, Mrs. Rennie Marvin, C.D. Dennis, W.T. Robinson, and Harry Bland Jr.

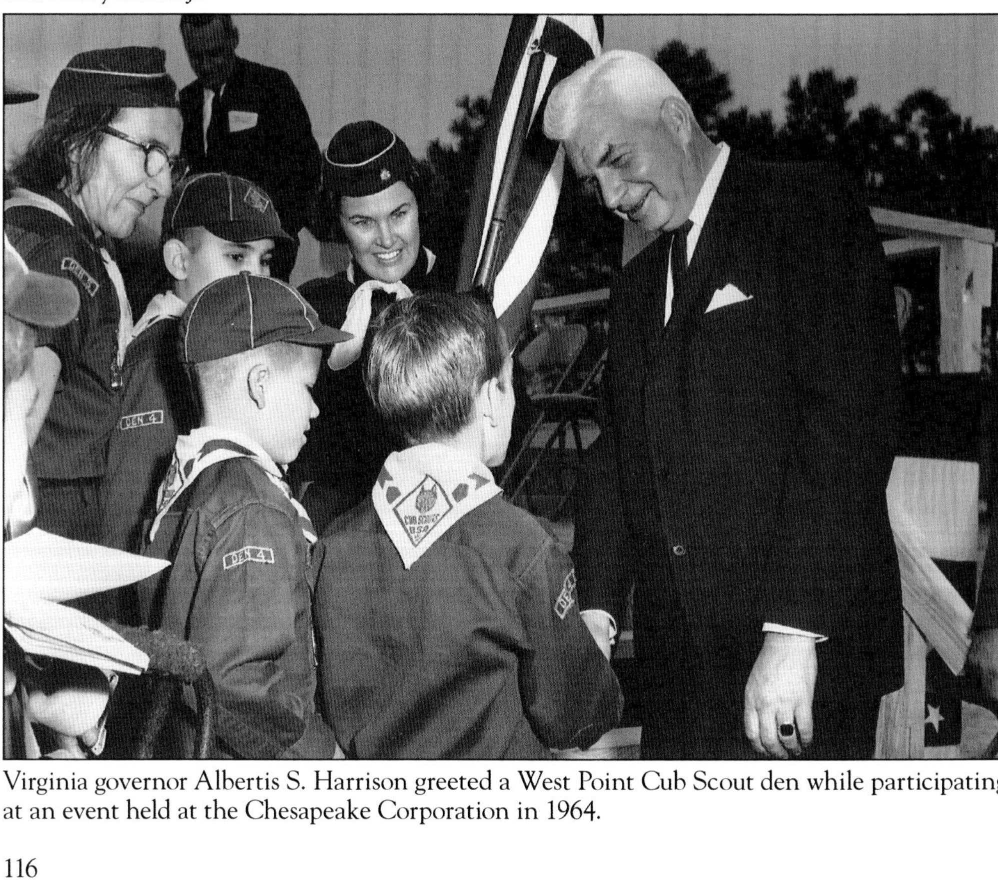

Virginia governor Albertis S. Harrison greeted a West Point Cub Scout den while participating at an event held at the Chesapeake Corporation in 1964.

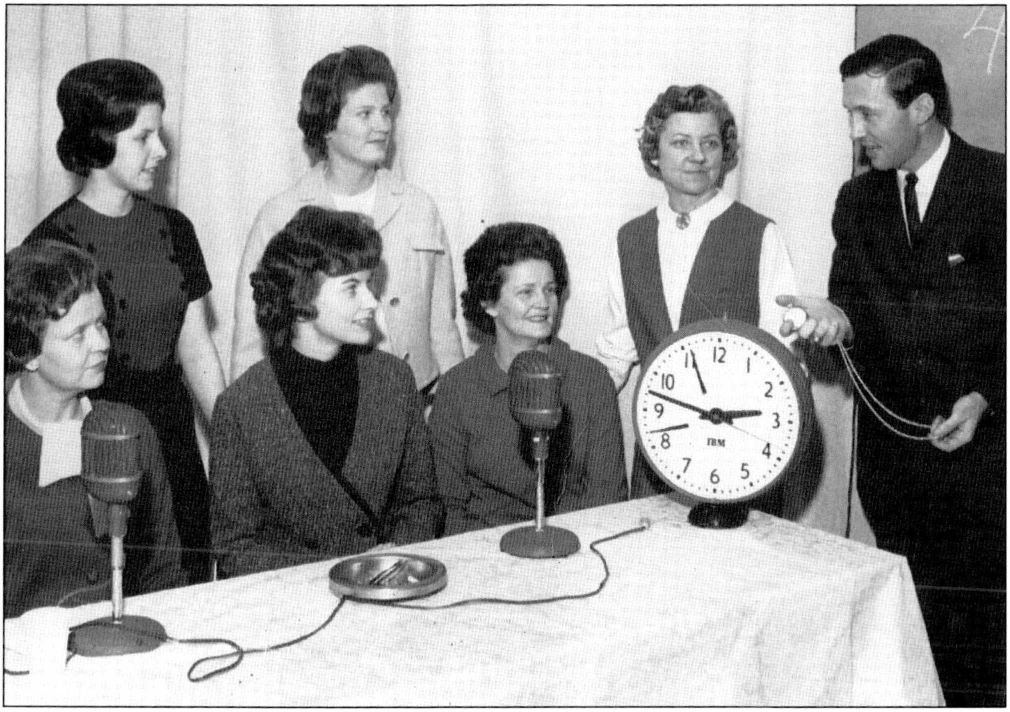

The Monday Club, West Point women's organization, participates in an on-air game show at WRVA Radio in Richmond during the 1960s.

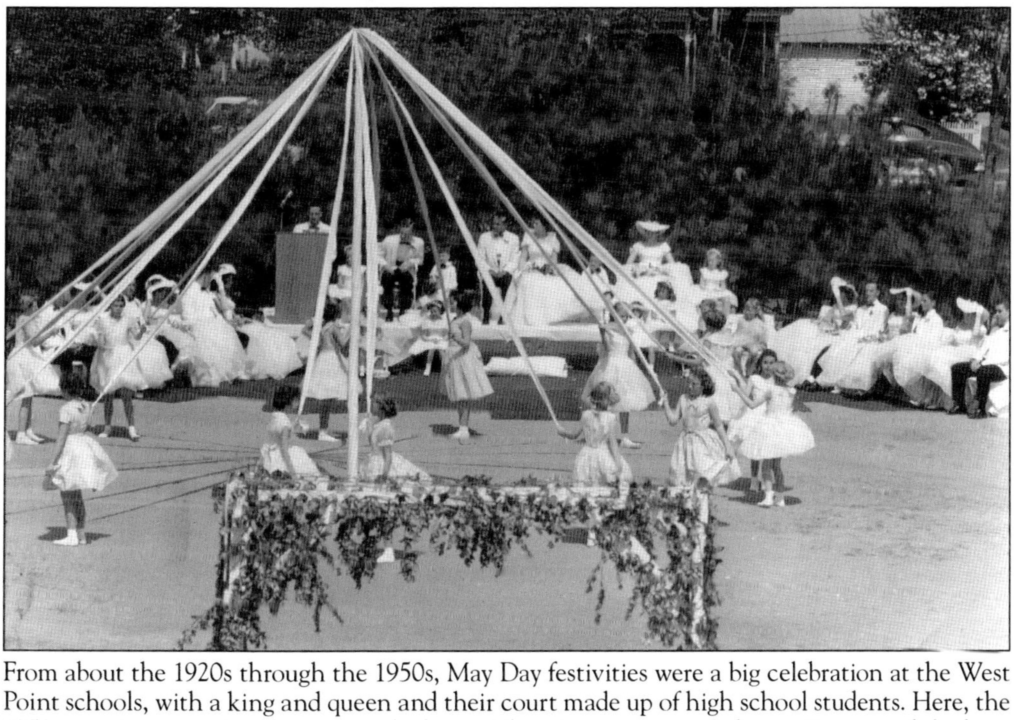

From about the 1920s through the 1950s, May Day festivities were a big celebration at the West Point schools, with a king and queen and their court made up of high school students. Here, the 1950 court is entertained by a maypole dance. The May queen was Rebecca Wyatt, and the king was Henry Vranian.

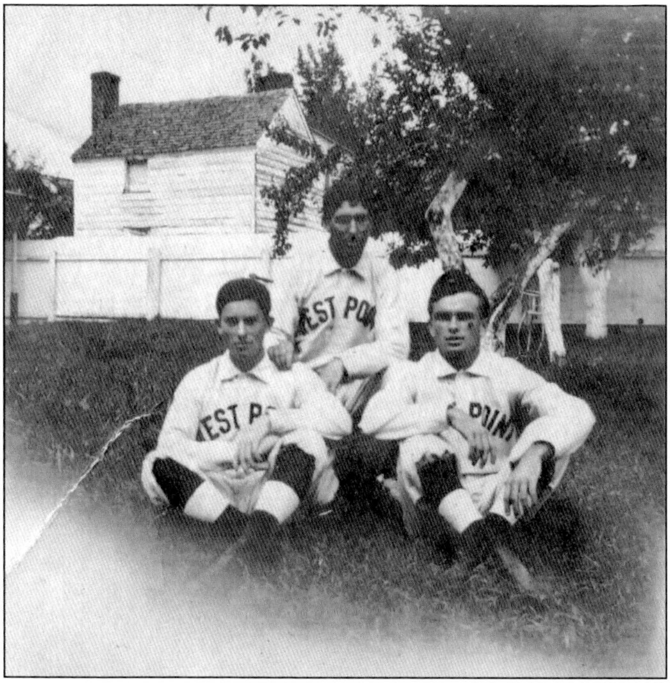

Three members of the West Point baseball team pose in the yard of the O'Connor Hotel. They are, from left to right, John McCanna, Harry Ginhart, and Jim O'Connor. The only known West Point native to play a sport professionally at the national level was Louis Louden, who played baseball as catcher for the Negro League's New York Cubans between 1942 and 1951. When the team bus passed through West Point, Louis's aunt would feed the entire team, as most restaurants were off-limits to African Americans. (Courtesy of Bill O'Connor.)

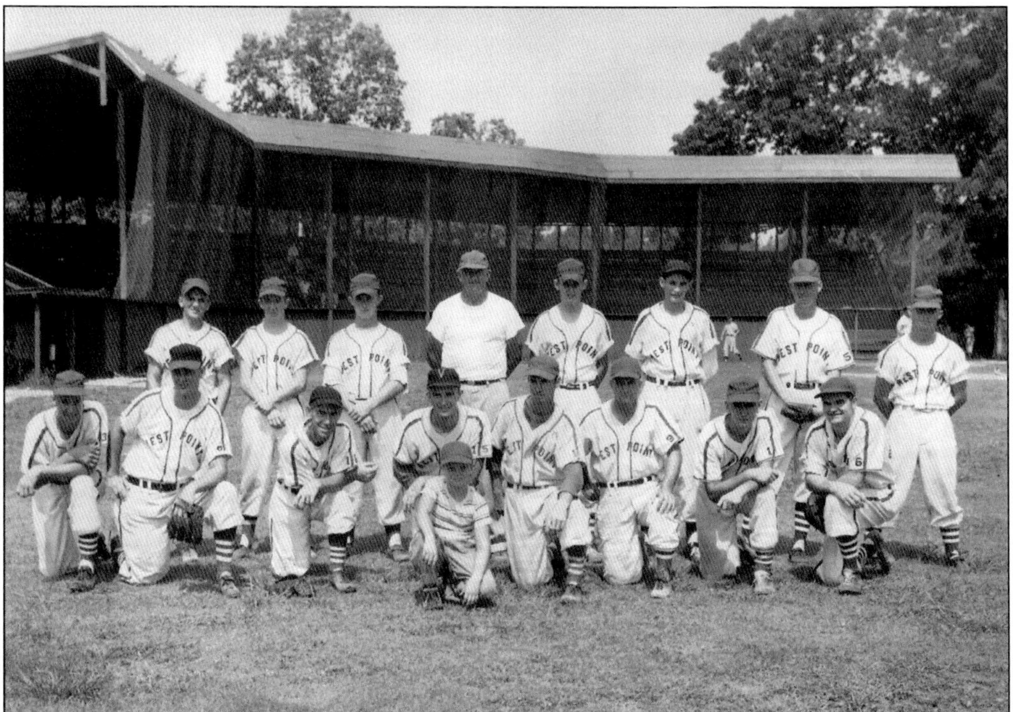

The town had a professional baseball team, primarily sponsored by the Chesapeake Corporation. The corporation also paid for the construction of a proper ballpark that served the town for many decades. It was located on Route 30 where the present National Guard Armory stands. (Courtesy of Richard Hosfield.)

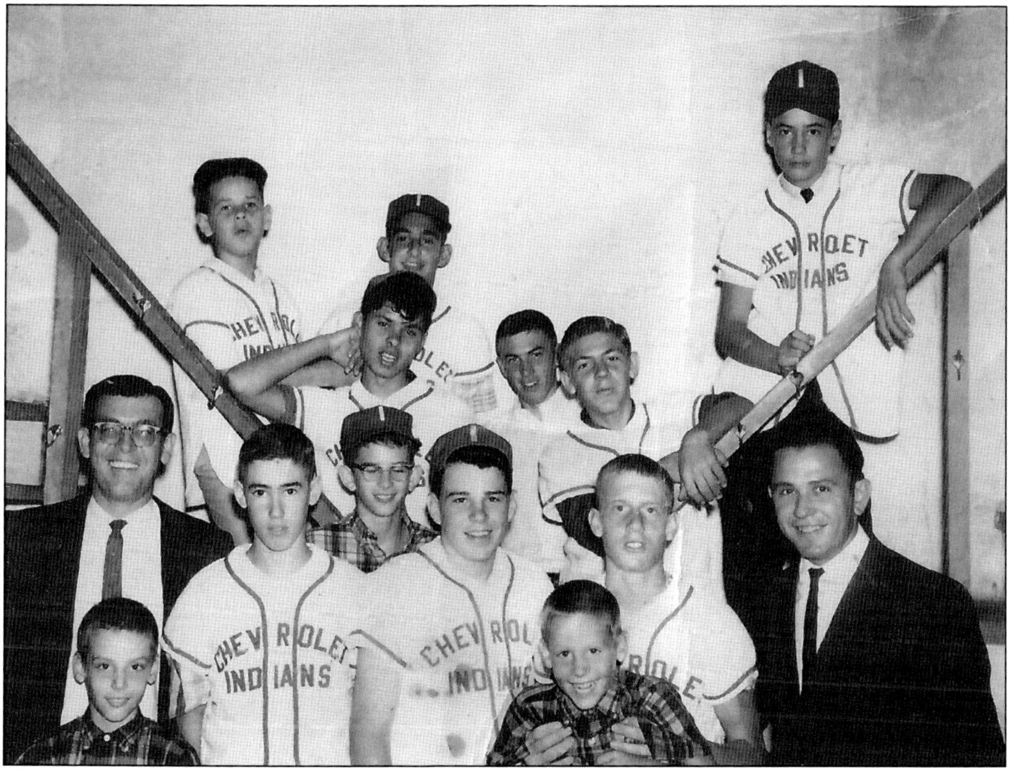

Little league team the Indians poses in the 1950s. The father and coach on the left is Harvey Bristow, a barber and baseball enthusiast. (Courtesy of Maureen Bristow Medlin.)

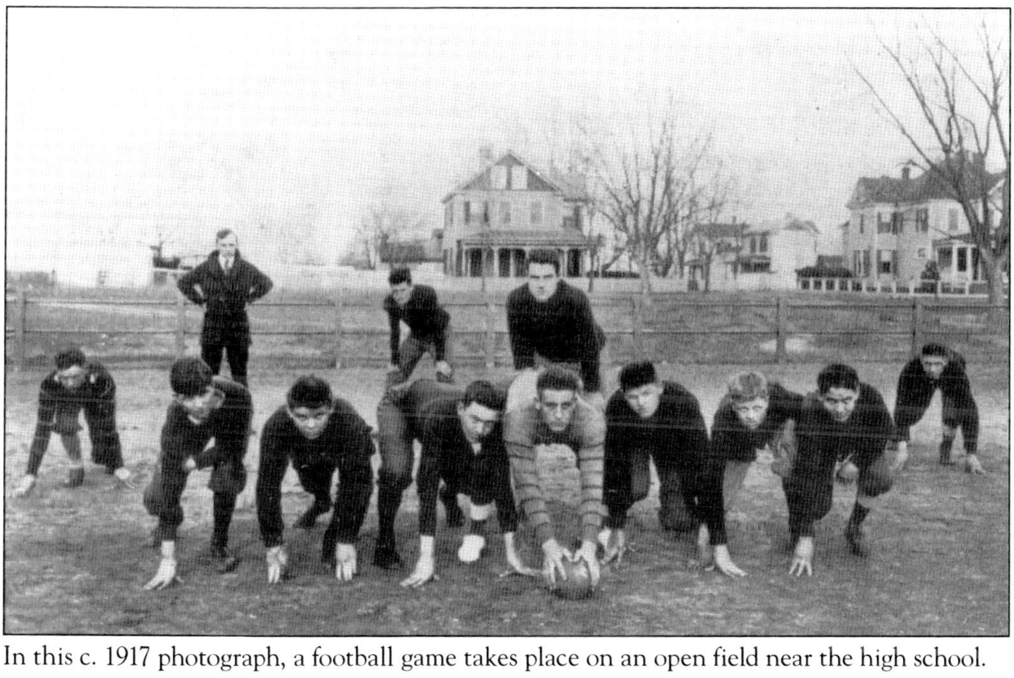

In this c. 1917 photograph, a football game takes place on an open field near the high school.

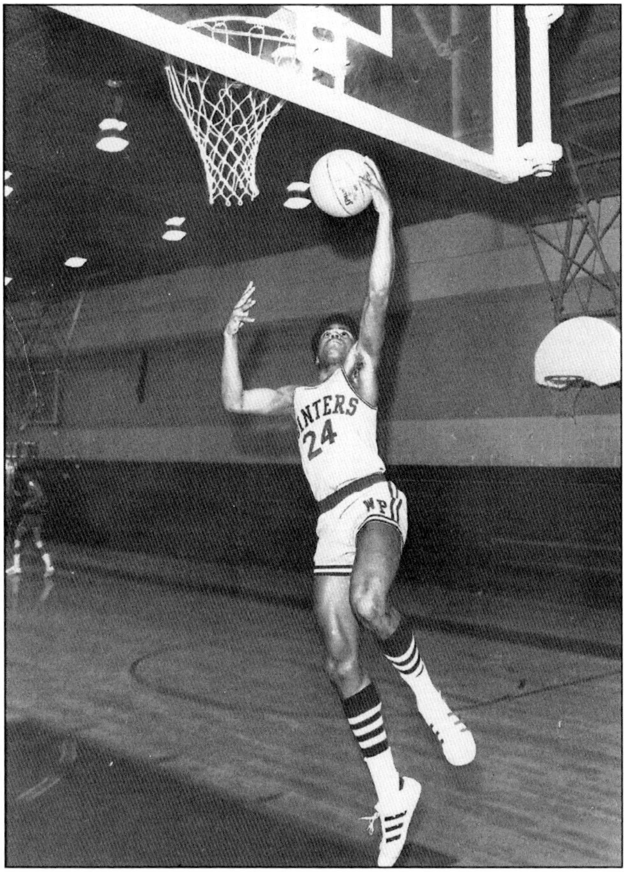

Clarence Epps is pictured playing basketball. During this time period, Duke Thorpe, one of the town's basketball legends, was part of the West Point High School team that won the Virginia High School League state championship on March 10, 1973. (Courtesy of Clarence Epps.)

The 1951 West Point High School junior varsity basketball team poses for this photograph. (Courtesy of Marianne Chestnutt.)

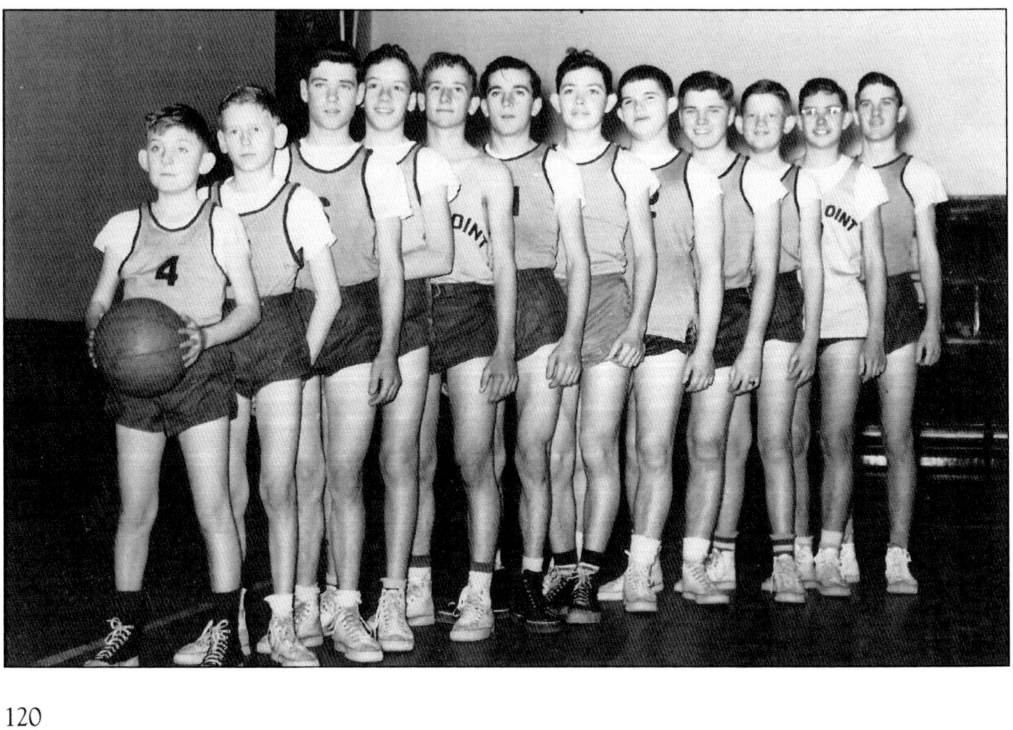

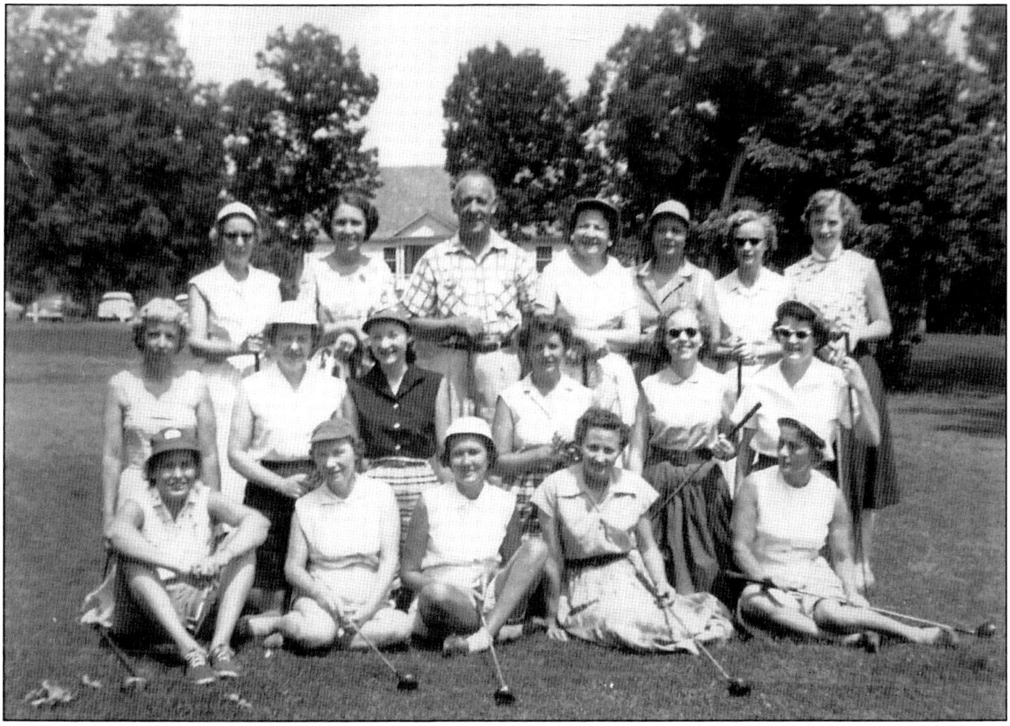

Women golfers at the West Point Country Club smile for the camera in May 1955. Instructor John Grove (standing third from the left in the third row) was the golf pro at the country club for many years. (Courtesy of Avril Williams.)

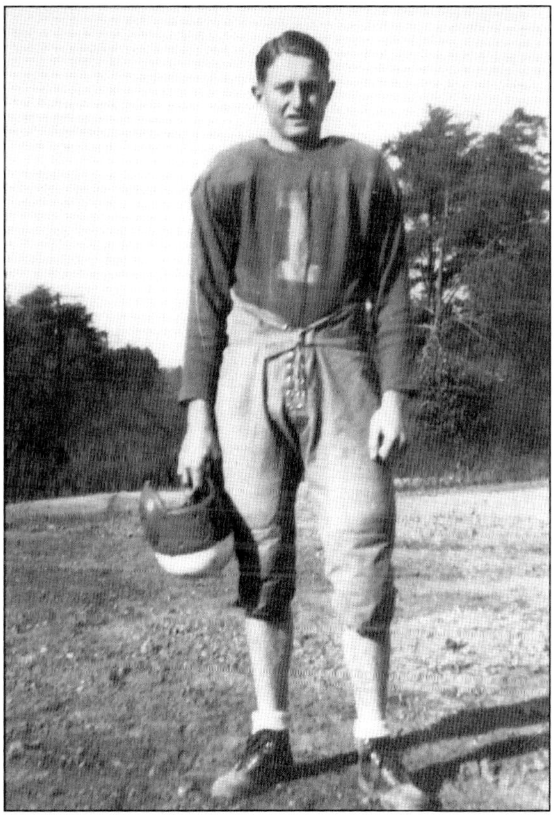

Jimmy Sears, team captain for the West Point High School football team, is pictured here in 1941. (Courtesy of Marianne Chestnutt.)

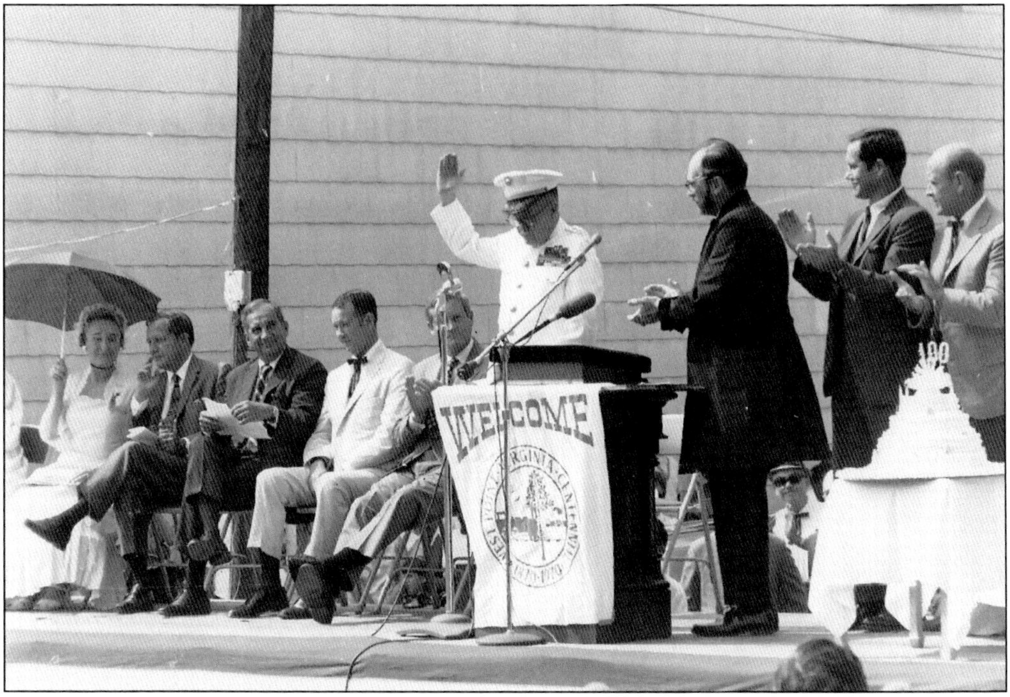

In 1970, the town held a big celebration of the 100th anniversary of its incorporation. The guest of honor was General Puller, born and raised in West Point, seen above in his dress uniform. To the left of General Puller is Virginia governor Linwood Holton, and on the left of the governor is Mayor William Robinson. The woman in a Colonial costume on the far left is Elizabeth Gray, a local historian and groundbreaking business woman.

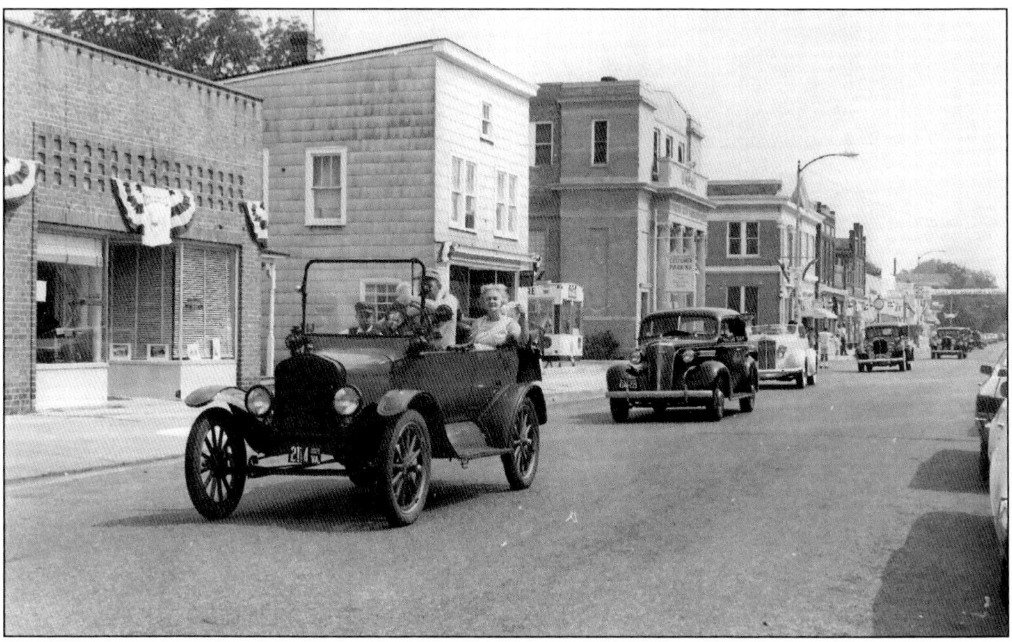

The Point of Destiny centennial celebration included a parade. Shown here is a line of antique cars that participated. (Courtesy of Tyler Bland III.)

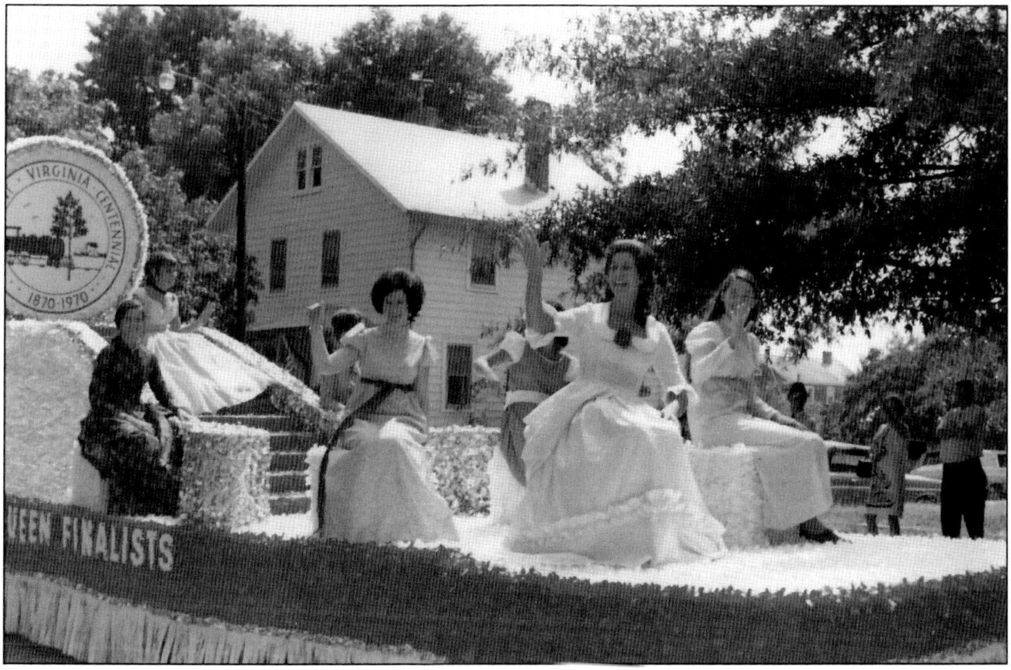

No big celebration would be complete without a queen and her court. Pictured here, the town royalty wave to the crowd from a float in the centennial parade. (Courtesy of Marianne Chestnutt.)

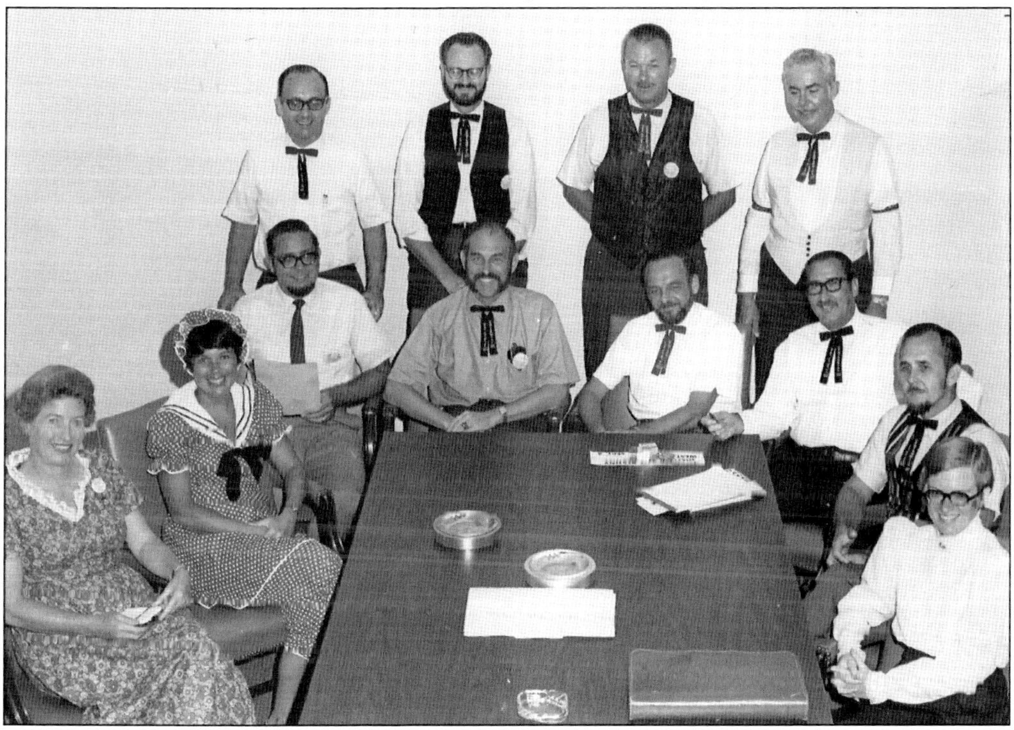

The organizing committee of the centennial celebration pose in their period costumes. This event was so successful, it spawned annual street festivals that evolved into the Crab Carnival, sponsored annually by the chamber of commerce. (Courtesy of Tyler Bland III.)

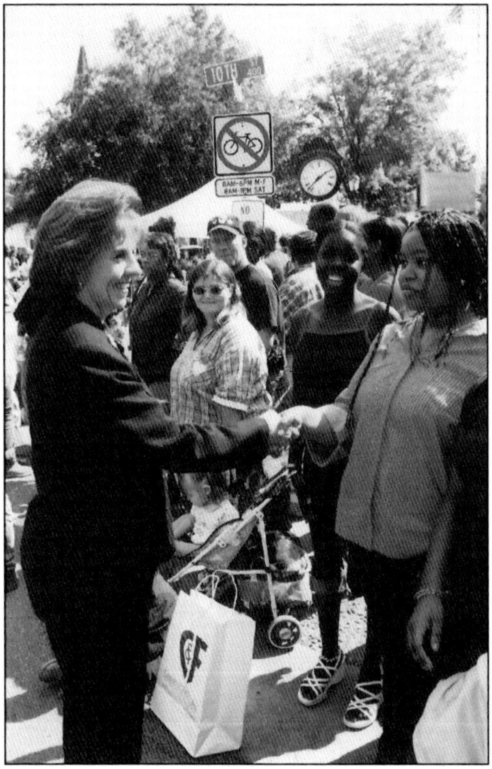

The late congresswoman Joanne Davis greets revelers at the Crab Carnival. Congresswoman Davis represented the area until her death in 2007. (Courtesy of Janice McGowan.)

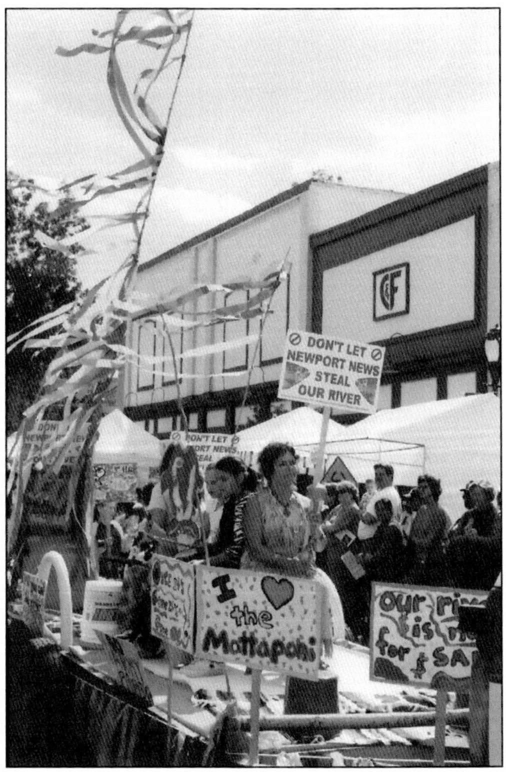

Shirley "Little Dove" Custalow McGowan sits in the front of a float during the Crab Carnival, wearing her traditional Mattaponi dress. This float aimed to raise public awareness of the fight of the Mattaponi Indians to prevent the City of Newport News from creating a reservoir with water from the Mattaponi River. The Custalow family has long been dedicated to educating the people of America about the heritage of native peoples and make frequent presentations throughout the United States. (Courtesy of Janice McGowan.)

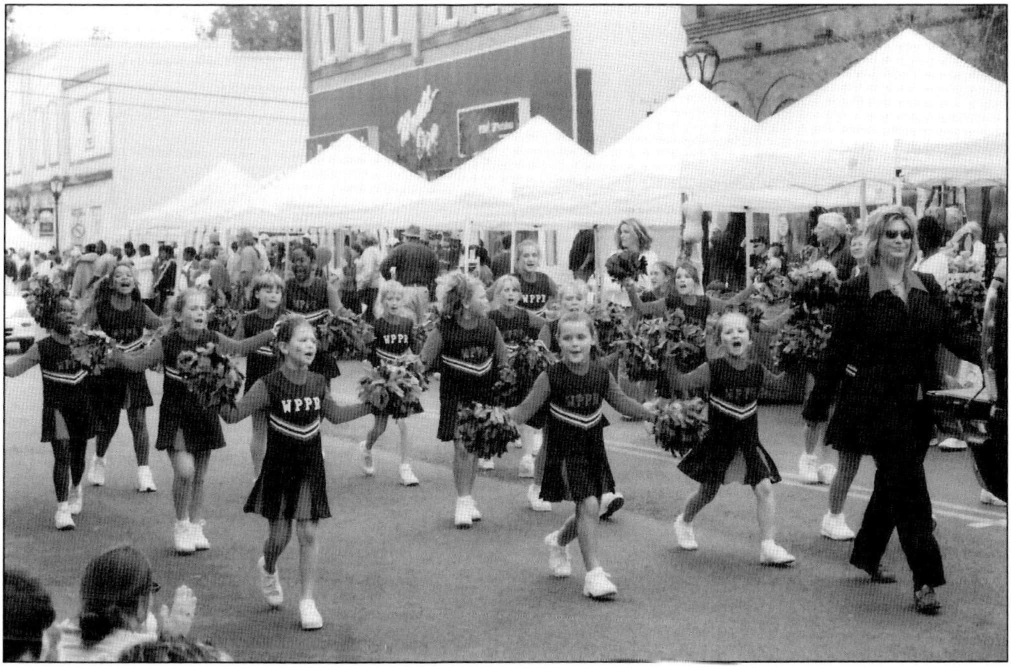

West Point cheerleaders march in the annual Crab Carnival parade. (Courtesy of Janice McGowan.)

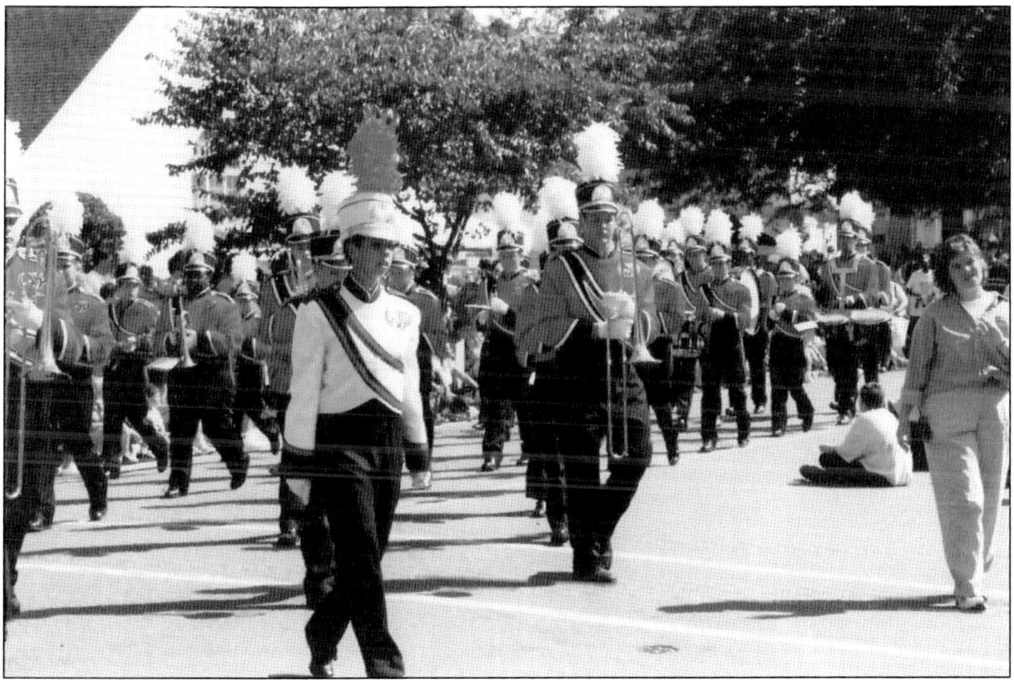

The West Point High School Band participates in the annual Crab Carnival parade. (Courtesy of Janice McGowan.)

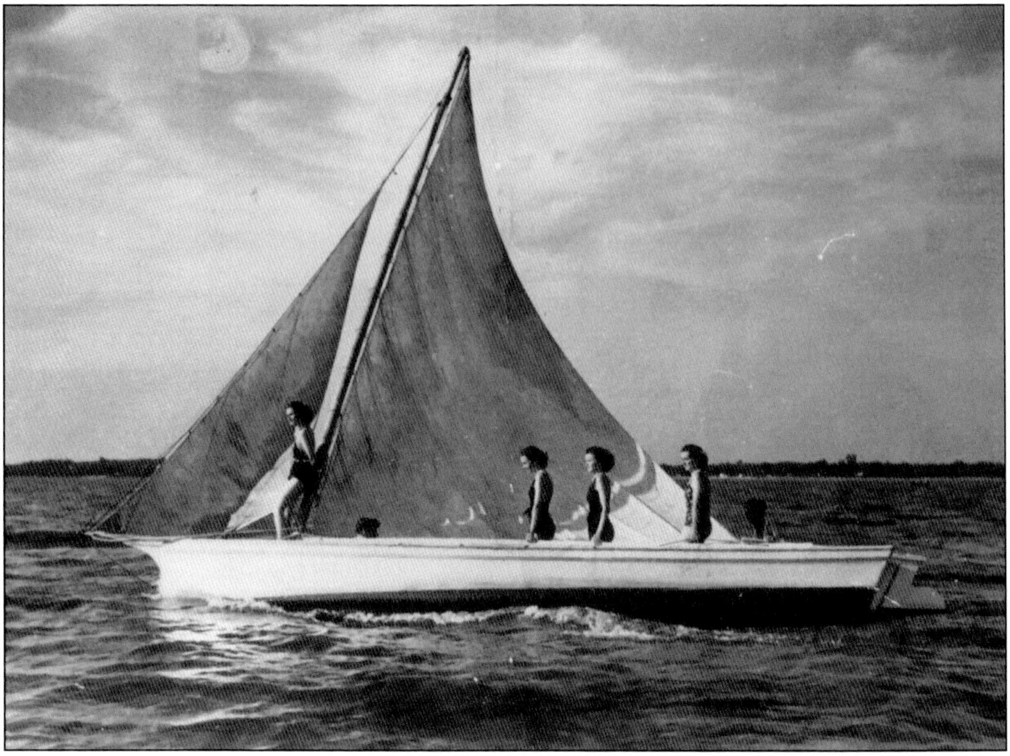

Boating on the York River in the 1930s sometimes included races and at least one regatta. In the late 1950s and early 1960s, there was a West Point Boat Club with a clubhouse over the boathouse at the Seventh Street marina on the Mattaponi River. This picture was taken in 1939 or 1940.

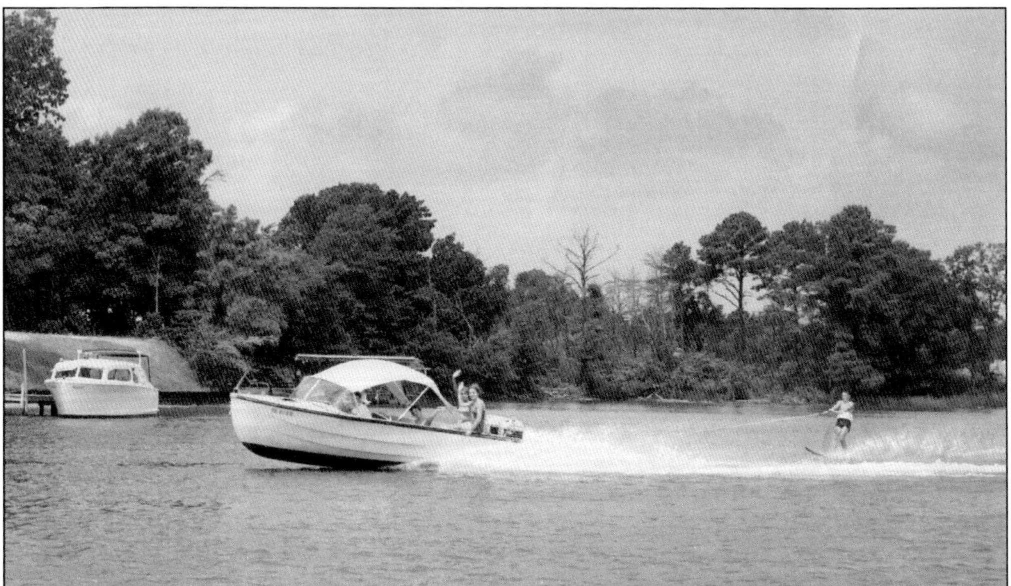

Waterskiing demonstrations were part of the centenary celebrations in 1970. The first waterskiing in the area started in 1950, and by the 1960s, ski jumps were erected at the mouth of the Mattaponi River. This image was captured in the late 1950s or early 1960s.

Bibliography

Custalow, Dr. Linwood "Little Bear," and Angela L. Daniel "Little Star." *The True Story of Pocahontas: The Other Side of History*. Golden, CO: Fulcrum Publishing, 2007.

Dickon, Chris. *Chesapeake Bay Steamers*. Charleston, SC: Arcadia Publishing, 2006.

Dill, Alonzo Thomas. *York River Yesterdays: A Pictorial History*. Norfolk, VA: The Donning Company, 1984.

Gray, Elizabeth Stuart. "West Point's History Begins Almost with the Founding of Nation." *Program: 250th Anniversary of the Founding of King William County, Virginia*. April 1952.

Harris, Malcom Hart, MD. *Old New Kent County Some Account of The Planters, Plantations, and Places: New Kent County, King and Queen County*, vol. I. Baltimore, MD: Clearfield Company, Inc., 1977.

———. *Old New Kent County Some Account of The Planters, Plantations, and Places in King William County St. John's Parish, West Point Va*, vol. II. Berryville, VA: Virginia Book Company, 1977.

Heritage Foundation. *Mattaponi Atlas: We Are the People of the River: Endurance in Tidewater Virginia*. Mattaponi Indian Reservation, King William County, VA: prepublication manuscript, 2012.

Kirby, Jack Temple. *Mocking-bird Song: Ecological Landscapes of the South*. Chapel Hill: The University of North Carolina Press, 2006.

———. *Poquosin: A Study of Rural Landscape and Society*. Chapel Hill and London: The University of North Carolina Press, 1995.

Rountree, Helen C., Wayne E. Clark, and Kent Mountford. *John Smith's Chesapeake Voyages, 1607–1609*. Charlottesville and London: University of Virginia Press, 2007.

———. *Pocahontas's People: The Powhatan Indians of Virginia Through Four Centuries*. Norman and London: University of Oklahoma Press, 1990.

———. *Pocahonas, Powhatan, Opechancanough: Three Indian Lives Changed by Jamestown*. Charlottesville and London: University of Virginia Press, 2005.